Violence against Women in Families and Relationships

Violence against Women in Families and Relationships

Volume I
Victimization and the Community Response

Edited by
EVAN STARK AND EVE S. BUZAWA

Praeger Perspectives

PRAEGER
An Imprint of ABC-CLIO, LLC

A B C CLIO

Santa Barbara, California • Denver, Colorado • Oxford, England

Library of Congress Cataloging-in-Publication Data
Violence against women in families and relationships /
edited by Evan Stark and Eve S. Buzawa.
    v. ; cm.
  Includes index.
  Contents: vol. 1. Victimization and the community response —
vol. 2. The family context — vol. 3. Criminal justice and the law —
vol. 4. The media and cultural attitudes.
    ISBN 978-0-275-99846-2 (set : alk. paper) — ISBN 978-0-275-99848-6
(vol. 1) — ISBN 978-0-275-99850-9 (vol. 2) — ISBN 978-0-275-99852-3
(vol. 3) — ISBN 978-0-275-99854-7 (vol. 4) — ISBN 978-0-275-99847-9 (ebook)
    1. Abused women. 2. Family violence. I. Stark, Evan.
II. Buzawa, Eva Schlesinger.
  HV6626.V56   2009
  362.82'92—dc22   2009006262

13   12   11   10   9   1   2   3   4   5

This book is also available on the World Wide Web as an eBook.
Visit www.abc-clio.com for details.

ABC-CLIO, LLC
130 Cremona Drive, P.O. Box 1911
Santa Barbara, California 93116-1911

This book is printed on acid-free paper ∞

Manufactured in the United States of America

Contents

Set Introduction
Evan Stark and Eve S. Buzawa   vii

Introduction to Volume 1
Evan Stark   xix

Chapter 1: The Story of the Shelter, "Women's Advocates"
             Sharon Rice Vaughan   1

Chapter 2: The Evolution of the Shelter Movement
             Deborah DeBare   15

Chapter 3: Changing from Victim to Survivor
             Hilary Abrahams   33

Chapter 4: Evaluating Community-Based Services
             Cris M. Sullivan and Tameka L. Gillum   55

Chapter 5: Intimate Partner Violence and Economic Disadvantage
             Claire M. Renzetti   73

Chapter 6: The Trapping Effects of Poverty and Violence
             Jody Raphael   93

Chapter 7: Domestic Violence and the Postindustrial Household
             Deborah M. Weissman   111

Chapter 8: Understanding Violence in Lesbian Relationships
             Janice Ristock   129

Chapter 9: Domestic Violence and the African
             American Community
             Katherine E. Morrison   151

Contents

Chapter 10: The Health System Response to Domestic Violence
Emma Williamson   163

Chapter 11: A Betrayal Trauma Perspective on Domestic Violence
Melissa Platt, Jocelyn Barton, and Jennifer J. Freyd   185

Index   209

About the Editors and Contributors   217

Set Introduction

Evan Stark and Eve S. Buzawa

The first call for shelter in the United States was made to Women's Advocates in St. Paul, Minnesota one afternoon in May 1972. The story of this group of courageous women opens *Violence against Women in Families and Relationships*. As recalled by Sharon Vaughan, a founder of the program and a pioneer in the battered-women's movement:

> The call was ... from Emergency Social Services. A worker said a woman was at the St. Paul Greyhound bus station with a two-year-old child. To get a job, she had traveled 150 miles from Superior, Wisconsin, with two dollars in her pocket. What were we expected to do? Where would they stay after two days at the Grand Hotel? One of the advocates borrowed a high chair and stroller and we took them to the apartment that was our office. These were the first residents we sheltered. The two-year-old destroyed the office in one night because all the papers were stacked on low shelves held up by bricks. His mother didn't talk about being battered; she said she wanted to go to secretarial school to make a life for her and her son. She tried to get a place to live, but no one would rent to her without a deposit, which she didn't have.... After a couple of weeks, she went back to Superior, and every Christmas for several years sent a card thanking Women's Advocates for being there and enclosed $2.00, the amount she had when she came to town.

This recollection captures several major themes highlighted in volume 1: the importance of women reaching out to other women, the reinforcing effects of poverty and domestic violence, and the extent to which those who escape abuse are intent on reconnecting with their hopes and dreams for a better life.

The shelter started in St. Paul was one stimulus for a domestic violence revolution that quickly circled the globe, stirring women from all walks of life, of all races, religions, and ages, and in thousands of neighborhoods, to challenge men's age-old prerogative to do with them as they willed. Even as these grassroots movements offered victims options for safety and empowerment that were never before available, they called on their governments to do the same. Importantly, these calls elicited an unprecedented response, almost certainly because women had become a formidable political and economic force. In its scope and significance, the domestic violence revolution is a watershed event in our lifetime.

On the ground, the domestic violence revolution consists of four critical components: the proliferation of community-based services for battered women; a growing sensitivity to how domestic violence affects families and particularly the children who are exposed to this violence; the criminalization of domestic violence and the corresponding mobilization of a range of state resources to protect abused women and their children and to arrest, sanction, or counsel perpetrators; and challenges to the normative values that have allowed men to exercise illegitimate forms of power and control in relationships and families. Although huge obstacles remain to changing cultural mores, these challenges now extend to the popular media, which shape how tens of millions of children and adults interpret the world around them.

Violence against Women in Families and Relationships takes stock of the seismic changes instigated by the domestic violence revolution, devoting separate volumes to its major components: community-based services (Volume 1), the family (Volume 2), the criminal justice response (Volume 3), and popular culture and the media (Volume 4). In addition to describing what happened, two overriding questions link these volumes. How is our world different today than when the domestic violence revolution began? Are abused women and their children better off because of these changes? We also identify the remaining obstacles to eliminating sexual injustice in relationships and families, ask what can be done to remove these obstacles, and identify a host of innovative programs designed to do this. The major conceptual contribution of these volumes is to provide an understanding of abuse that extends far beyond physical violence to the broad range of tactics actually used to coerce and control women and children in relationships.

THE DOMESTIC VIOLENCE REVOLUTION

Our goal is to provide a map of the scope and significance of the domestic violence revolution.

Since the opening and diffusion of shelters, the policies and the legal landscape affecting victims of partner abuse have changed dramatically. Reforms include billions of dollars in federal support for intervention, removing discretion in deciding whether to arrest those who assault their partners, a range of new protections for victims, the burgeoning of a vast network of researchers, specialized and integrated domestic violence courts and prosecutorial approaches (called "dedi-cated" or "evidence based"), one-stop justice centers, and putting part-ner abuse center stage in decisions about custody and visitation. In the past, battered women who retaliated against abusive partners hid their abuse, fearing it would provide a motive for their crimes. Today, women accused of crimes against abusive partners can use a "battered woman's defense" and call on a new class of experts to support their claims of victimization. The constitutional rationale for these reforms in the United States is straightforward: under the Equal Protection Clause of the Fourteenth Amendment, women assaulted by present or former partners are entitled to the same rights and protections as those who are assaulted by strangers. In other countries, domestic violence has been identified as violation of basic human rights.

The helping professions have also undergone radical changes in response to the domestic violence revolution. Medicine, nursing, public health, psychology, psychiatry, social work, and child welfare have intro-duced a range of innovative programs to identify and respond more appropriately to the adult and child victims of abuse. Forty years ago, when Anne Flitcraft asked the director of the emergency medical services at Yale–New Haven Hospital if she could study "battered women" for her medical school thesis, he was puzzled. "What's a battered woman?" he asked. Today, in part as a result of pioneering research by Dr. Flitcraft and hundreds of other scholars, training in the health, mental health, legal, and social service professions would be remiss if it did not include specialized units on domestic violence. Every major health care organization has made domestic violence a priority. Hundreds of hospitals in the United States have protocols requiring that medical personnel identify and refer victims of abuse. In hundreds of communities, once perpetrators are arrested, they are offered counseling as an alternative to jail through "batterer interven-tion programs." Moreover, several thousand localities now host collabora-tive efforts to reduce or prevent abuse in which community-based services such as shelters join with courts, law enforcement, local businesses, child protection agencies, and a range of health, education, and service organi-zations. In dozens of communities, small and large businesses alike have taken initiatives to extend protections from abusive partners to employees or supported broader community-based initiatives.

Never before has such an array of resources and interventions been brought to bear on abuse or oppression in relationships and families. By any conventional standard, the domestic violence revolution has been an incredible success. Politicians across a broad spectrum have embraced its core imagery of male violence and female victimization. As telling is an increasing sensitivity to the portrayal of abused women by the mass media and a growing awareness of how mainstream mes-sages conveyed by sports, popular music, and other cultural media con-tribute to abusive behavior by males.

Hundreds of thousands of men, women, and children owe the fact that they are alive to the availability of shelters, to criminal justice and legal reforms, and to equally important shifts in research, health services, and popular culture. Just recently, historically speaking, a man's use of coercion to chastise or discipline his female partner or his children was widely considered a right inherited with his sex. This is no longer so.

In 1977, during one of the many incidents when Mickey Hughes assaulted his wife Francine, their 12-year-old daughter Christy called police. He threatened to kill Francine with police present. This seemed like "idle talk," an officer testified at Francine's trial for murder. "He hadn't killed her before; he wouldn't do so now." A few hours after they left, Francine set fire to the bed in which her husband was sleeping and he was fatally burned.

Things have changed dramatically since 1977. Mickey was never arrested, though he had raped Francine on several occasions and assaulted her dozens of times. Not until 1979, as the result of lawsuits in Oakland, California, and New York, were police required to replace their "arrest-avoidance" strategy, respond quickly to domestic violence calls, and presumptively arrest whenever they had probable cause to believe a felonious assault had occurred or when a misdemeanor assault was committed in their presence. Marital rape was still not a crime in 1977, and in New York and a number of other states was not even considered grounds for divorce. In several states, Francine could have gotten an injunction, though police had no role in enforcing these orders, and only if she was married, and only pursuant to a divorce.

Farrah Fawcett portrayed Francine in a TV film version of this story, *The Burning Bed*. In the mid-1990s, when her boyfriend slammed Fawcett to the ground and choked her after an argument at a restaurant, he was arrested, tried, and convicted. By this time, the marriage-rape exemption was largely abolished, police in most areas were mandated to arrest perpetrators whom they believed had committed a domestic violence crime, and courts in most countries were routinely providing a range of protections for abuse victims. On the two occasions that Francine left Mickey to return to her parents, he stalked and harassed her without consequence. Today, stalking is a crime and harassment is widely recognized as a facet of abuse. Aside from her family, Francine had no recourse, no shelter to enter, and no support services. A woman faced with a burning-bed situation today would mount a "battered woman's defense" rather than plead "temporary insanity," as Francine did. The forces of law and order that protected a man's right to "physically correct" his wife in 1977 now target this bastion of male authority for destruction.

Perhaps the most significant change that resulted from the domestic violence revolution involves the portrayal of male violence against women in the media, particularly in film and on TV, the ultimate family medium. As women made unprecedented gains in economic, political, and cultural status after 1960, the hazards that men pose to their wives and girlfriends became a moral compass for the integrity of relationships generally. From Johannesburg to Caracas, from Jerusalem to Dayton, Ohio, young girls understand that no male has the right to lay his hands on them if they do not want him to do so. Well into the 1980s, violence continued to be glamorized as the penultimate test of manhood (the ultimate test remains sexual conquest), as illustrated by the popularity of gangsta rap and *James Bond* and *Rambo* films. But male violence has increasingly been forced to share the stage with images of women as equally capable of using force and of abusive men as purposeful, obsessive, and cruel rather than romantic. Julia Roberts' portrayal of a housewife who kills an abusive husband who is stalking her in *Sleeping with the Enemy* (1991) contrasts sharply with Eleanor Parker's role in the 1955 film *The Man with the Golden Arm* as a wife who sets out to heal her husband (played by Frank Sinatra) while enduring his physical abuse, betrayal, heroin addiction, and mental torment.

Partner violence against women is no longer "just life." And yet, anyone with reasonable sympathies and a passing acquaintance with abuse or current interventions will have a range of questions about the impact of even the most dramatic reforms.

VICTIMIZATION AND THE COMMUNITY RESPONSE

Volume 1 reviews the development, operations, and effectiveness of battered women's programs; the progress of intervention in health; and the interplay of domestic violence with race, poverty, sexual identity, and the changing economic landscape of communities caused by globalization. The core questions addressed in this volume are as follows: what do battered women's programs actually do? Has the "success" of the shelter movement led it to compromise its original ideals? Is the support that advocates provide sufficient to help victims regain their footing? To what extent does help "help"? Or does it actually make things worse by blaming victims for their abuse? Does the medical system need to look beyond physical violence to improve its response? What special problems face lesbian victims of abuse? What unique dynamics are put into play in the experience of abuse by the disadvantages associated with poverty, racism, or deindustrialization? How must intervention change to accommodate these dynamics? Where do we go from here?

THE FAMILY CONTEXT

Volume 2 looks at the ways in which domestic violence shapes family dynamics in general and affects children in particular and at the two major systems responsible for managing these effects: the child welfare system and the family court. How are children threatened by domestic violence and coercive control? Domestic violence is the most common background factor for child abuse and neglect, and it is typically the same man who is abusing the mother who is the source of harm to children. After much prodding, the child welfare system began to address domestic violence. But its first steps were missteps. Instead of protecting mothers and their children, the child welfare system punished them for being beaten. Why did this happen, and what can be done to correct this problem? Family courts have also been pressured to consider domestic violence in custody and divorce cases. But are they doing so? How can the family court reconcile concerns for the safety of women and their children in abusive relationships with the widespread belief that children must have access to both parents after divorce? To what extent are each of the systems confronted by victims of battering and their children sending contradictory messages that do as much to confuse and further entrap them as to provide for their safety? What reforms are needed to set child welfare and family court systems on the right track? And what about the offending fathers? How do they extend their abusive strategies during custody disputes? And what about the movement for "father's rights"? Is it a positive or negative force in this process? Can offending men learn to father more appropriately? How does working with them on fathering affect how they understand and treat the women in their lives? What is at the root of the problems with these systems? Are we dealing primarily with individual bias or something more systemic? How would broadening our understanding of abuse to include the multiple ways in which men subjugate their partners enhance the child welfare or family court response?

CRIMINAL JUSTICE AND THE LAW

From the start, the domestic violence revolution in the United States called on the state to mobilize its justice resources to protect victims and hold offenders accountable for their acts, usually through some combination of arrest, incarceration, and/or reeducation. Volume 3 reviews the revolutionary changes in policy, criminal law, and policing affected by the domestic violence revolution. Severe violence against wives had been against the law for centuries. But it was only in the 1980s, as states passed domestic violence laws and made arrest mandatory in abuse cases, that police, prosecutors, and the criminal courts treated it as a crime. How are these reforms working? Has the domestic violence revolution relied too heavily on criminal justice? Have the changes in policing, prosecution, and criminal law gone too far or not far enough? Are abusive men changed by arrest? Does counseling for batterers work, and, if so, with what kinds of men? How should we understand and respond to partner violence by women or to families in which both partners are abusive?

THE MEDIA AND CULTURAL ATTITUDES

However much the domestic violence revolution may have reformed the helping and justice professions, these changes are unlikely to endure unless the underlying cultural supports for domestic violence are displaced. Prevailing cultural norms reproduce the sex stereotypes that underlie sexual inequality even as women win formal legal equality and make unprecedented gains in education, income, and political participation. Volume 4 maps how these stereotypes are represented and challenged in a range of cultural media, including newspapers, film, women's magazines, video games, and rap. After explaining how the core narratives in a culture shape experience, the chapters in this volume consider what the stories told about sexual violence in these media suggest about how and why violence against women happens; who or what causes it; whether it is the by-product of specific social factors, malevolence, or just "bad luck" for instance; and how it can be ended. How these stories are constructed is as important as what they say. This volume considers the transformative potential of the media, including theater, as well as the role they play in reinforcing the status quo. The closing chapter considers whether community values have, in fact, changed over the course of the domestic violence revolution.

WHAT YOU'LL FIND HERE

An estimated 13,000 books and monographs about domestic violence have appeared since the early 1970s. Digesting and translating this published material are obviously beyond our capacity. Nevertheless, we started this project by scouring this literature for the major trends and cutting-edge ideas about abuse. Next, we reached out to both established scholars as well as to younger researchers doing cutting-edge work. We asked these writers to do three things: tell us *what* has changed; tell us *how* these changes have affected families, particularly the women, children, and men most immediately involved; and speculate about *what is next*. Where are we likely to go, and where *should* we go from here? We welcomed criticism of existing approaches. We are not pushing a particular cause. But if there are new approaches, innovative practices, or changes in policy that would help set things right, we wanted readers to know about them. And we insisted they write for educated readers who have little or no prior knowledge of the subject, not always an easy thing for scholars whose main audiences tend to consist of academics like themselves. The model we suggested was a feature article for the Sunday newspaper. Think of yourself as the expert you are, we told them. This meant limiting notes to direct quotations and controversial statistics. We gave the contributors the option of directing readers to further information likely to be available on the Web or at a public library. Frankly, this charge posed an editorial challenge we had not anticipated.

One might think that summarizing the wealth of research on violence in families would be sufficient. Not so. One of the most insidious characteristics of the type of oppression we address in personal life is that it typically occurs "behind closed doors" and proceeds in ways that are often hidden from outsiders, often including close friends, neighbors, coworkers, and helping professionals. Researchers too have little direct access to victims or offenders and typically meet them or hear their stories only after they call police, come to court, or enter a shelter. Since whether victims report what is happening to them is largely a function of the opportunity to do so as well as the fear of possible consequences, millions of battered women and their children have no contact with police, shelters, courts, hospitals, or child welfare and so never appear in the public spaces where data are collected. Telephone surveys pick up some of this hidden abuse. But the questions asked on surveys are too broad to capture its meaning, contexts, dynamics, or far-reaching consequences. We were less interested in generalities about abuse than in the nuances, the particulars. We are not after sensationalism. But we wanted readers to know battered women as people, to walk in their shoes to some extent, as well as read *about* them. Another problem is that researchers can ask questions only about things they already know are present. A key theme in these volumes is that the images of violence and physical injury that have dominated our understanding of abuse miss an underlying reality of coercion and control in these relationships that can be as devastating as assault and is almost always more salient for victims. The harms caused by these coercive and controlling tactics are rarely recognized, let alone documented, even among those who are able to get help. The fact that so many of those affected are poor or from disadvantaged groups also contributes to their invisibility.

To unlock the knowledge contained in what Yale University political scientist James Scott calls the "hidden transcripts" of these lives, it is necessary to listen directly to the voices of women and children who experience battering as well as to their abusive partners. This means allowing them to tell their stories as they were lived rather than as filtered through the preconceptions we all bring to the field, ourselves included. In addition to chapters that summarize what is known about particular aspects of interpersonal violence, therefore, we have called on practitioners who work or have worked directly with victims, perpetrators, and their children in a variety of settings. A number of the practitioners herein have helped to design or implement imaginative programs. We include authors who have started or worked in shelters, facilitated batterer intervention programs, trained child welfare workers, and directed a state coalition for battered women. We have several chapters by lawyers who have represented battered women and their children in family and criminal courts and other chapters by forensic psychologists and social workers. Several of our authors have translated their research into practice. In a chapter in volume 4, anthropology professor Elaine J. Lawless describes a theater project she started with a colleague and some students at the University of Missouri. Professor Lawless had conducted fieldwork for a book at a battered women's shelter in her community. Feeling dissatisfied with a purely academic presentation of her "findings," she helped students perform the stories she had collected as monologues to stimulate a broad, community-wide discussion about abuse. The presentations not only gave audiences a picture of the abuse going on around them but also opened up a space in which student actors and audience members could tell their own stories about abuse, some of which became part of subsequent "performances," creating a community of witnesses that enhanced the overall safety of women and children in that neighborhood.

A basic premise of the shelter movement is that those who are battered by their partners are the only real "experts" on their experience and that their expertise is the centerpiece of any real knowledge about how abuse unfolds. We have tried to respect this view by interspersing the informational chapters with chapters that rely heavily on women's stories or explain why "storying" domestic violence is so important. If we have succeeded, the topical chapters should dovetail with lived experiences of abuse. Like the Missouri theater project, we hope these volumes help stimulate a broad-ranging conversation and new ways of seeing, listening to, and interpreting what is happening in our midst.

These volumes also have an international dimension, though it is unfortunately limited to English-speaking countries. We include writers from England, Canada, Scotland, and Australia. The authors of these chapters have done groundbreaking work in their particular areas for which there was often no parallel in the United States. For example, the report on child homicides prepared by Hilary Saunders on behalf of Women's Aid Federation England (WAFE) is a stunning model of advocacy that has elicited family court reforms that are long overdue in the United States. But the international focus also reflects the fact that both the grassroots women's movements in these countries and the systemic changes they elicited have grown from a continuing interchange between researchers and practitioners in these nations.

In each of the respects outlined above, this set of volumes is unique—in its breadth, its mix of researchers and practitioners, the emphasis on victim voices, the attempt to weigh changes in popular culture, its international scope, and its focus on what lies ahead.

But our approach will not satisfy everyone.

Most of us initially got involved in the domestic violence field because we hoped to call attention to and ameliorate the injustices suffered by millions of women and children who were being subjugated in their relationships, mainly (but not only) by male partners, and because we found the response to this suffering by the courts, police, hospitals, and other institutions woefully inadequate. From this vantage, behavior is seen as abusive and as meriting public concern if it involves coercive and/or controlling behavior whose primary intent and/or consequence is to hurt, threaten, frighten, or control a partner. Notice the broad understanding of abuse.

From the day we welcomed the first victims to our shelters, our strongest feelings of sympathy and anger were elicited by the physical scars caused by their partner's violence. Even though many women insisted that the "violence wasn't the worst part," hinting at a yet-to-be-identified range of tactics used by their partners that they found even more hurtful than physical abuse, it was the woman's bruised face or broken bones that held our attention as well as the media's.

We now know that abuse is limited to physical and psychological abuse in only a minority of cases, somewhere between 20 and 40 percent. In the rest, the vast majority, forms of coercion such as violence, threats, or stalking are combined with a pattern of control that can include tactics to isolate victims; restrict their access to money, food, transportation, medical care, or other basic necessities; and microregulate their everyday activities, such as how they dress, cook, clean, talk on the phone or relate to their children. This pattern, known as coercive control, is referred to repeatedly throughout the volumes and is the major focus of chapters by Stark (volume 2), Lischick (volume 2), and Turkheimer (volume 3). Because the aim of coercive control is to limit a victim's resources as well as their opportunities to escape, it greatly heightens women's risk of being seriously injured or killed as well as of developing a range of medical, behavioral, and mental health problems. But the major consequence of being subjected to this strategy over time is that victims become entrapped. Their autonomy is compromised, and their basic liberties protected by the U.S. Constitution are abrogated, such as the right to free speech, their freedom of movement, and their right to make decisions about their bodies. Many of the rights that are violated by coercive control are so tightly woven into the fabric of everyday life that they are rarely protected explicitly (such as the right to cook, clean, dress, or toilet as they wish) and have to be inferred as rights by our general right to pursue our lives as we please. While women frequently assault male and female partners, coercive control appears to be largely committed by men against female partners. Of the estimated 15 million U.S. women who are battered, somewhere between 8 and 12 million are victims of coercive control.

If our major focus is on the use of violence in these relationships despite our broad definition and on the provision of safety, this is because of the appalling consequence of violence for the women who seek help and because most research and almost all interventions are designed in response to domestic violence, not coercive control. But even here, it is not violence per se that concerns us, but coercion used in the context of inequality, coercion that exploits and strengthens existing disadvantages.

Our framework will make at least two groups unhappy. A significant minority of researchers in the domestic violence field morally opposes the use of violence in any form in families or relationships and believe that trying to distinguish the use of force by its motive, context, or consequence or by the relative standing of its victims expresses a personal bias. To this group, couples who use force during fights among relative equals are as wrong to do so as is the man whose violence is unilaterally designed to quash his partner's autonomy. So committed are many in this group to a vision of families and intimate relationships as nonviolent spaces of cooperation that they oppose a vigorous police response in any but the most extreme cases, favoring couples counseling and other forms of conflict resolution instead. This group also holds that women's use of force with their partners is as significant a matter of public concern as men's use of force, even though the probability of injury is far greater to victimized women in these situations; women are far more likely to report being threatened or controlled by abuse than men and they are far more likely to seek or require outside help. Another group will also be unhappy with us. This group opposes vigorous state intervention in abuse less because of its devotion to the family than because they worry that inviting the state into people's personal lives will ultimately do more harm than good, no matter the rationale. This group is willing to accept a wide range of controlling and physically hurtful behavior in relationships to preserve privacy.

We are concerned with preserving and protecting physical integrity at all levels of relationships. But we hope this set helps shift attention from the sheer physical violations caused by abuse to the ways in which coercion and control are used to deny persons their rights and liberties in personal life. However imperfectly they may do so, we believe that governments have an obligation to address these harms and with the same commitment they bring to stemming harms in public life.

Many of those who pick up these volumes will undoubtedly do so because they have experienced abuse in their own lives or known someone who has. As several of the authors eloquently report, the forms of violence, intimidation, isolation, humiliation, and "control" that excite much of the help sought by women who have been battered by partners are closer in their dynamic to hostage taking than to what we normally think of as assault. Except, of course, these victims are "hostages at home"; they have been prisoners in their personal lives. It is easy to be depressed by the statistics and descriptions presented in these pages or to become cynical about the willingness of humans to inflict cruelty even on those they supposedly care for.

But we ask readers to also consider this: that the women who populate these pages have survived to tell their own stories. And many women and children subjected to abuse have done more than merely survive, as Hilary Abrahams illustrates in volume 1 in her record of women who have left shelter: "I sometimes feel like a spring flower." Some elements of women's stories may elicit pity; other details we provide about abuse may provoke anger, even outrage, as they should. Clearly, no community can be truly whole or free so long as one group is allowed to use the means of coercion and control to subjugate others, whether sex or some other factor is the basis for this practice. Once we know such crimes are occurring in our midst, we cannot turn away. But in addition to our protection and concern, the women in these volumes deserve our respect and admiration because of the courage, strength of character, and resolve required to survive the forms of oppression they faced.

We have recently completed a presidential race in which one of the candidates was justly celebrated for his ordeal as a POW (prisoner of war) during the Vietnam War. To those of us who have worked in this field, it is absolutely clear that resisting, standing up to, or even just surviving coercive control is often comparable to the heroism exhibited by returning POWs. If only as a token, we offer these volumes in lieu of a public monument to those who have survived the horrors of personal life. And there is a larger lesson too. Once we appreciate what the women here have accomplished, we see that each of us may be capable of remaking the world we are given, even against what may seem at first impossible odds.

The final justification for this set is that our society has invested billions of dollars and hundreds of millions of human service hours in managing the domestic violence in our midst. Apart from the unprecedented commitment of resources to protect women and children and hold perpetrators accountable are the enormous costs of not effectively addressing abuse in families and relationships. We have made a huge investment in ending an age-old form of injustice. Readers deserve an accounting.

Introduction to Volume 1

Evan Stark

The chapters in volume 1 track the background of the domestic violence revolution, identify the dynamics in abusive relationships—particularly how abuse is shaped by race, poverty, sexual identity,
globalization, and psychological trauma—and assess the response by
shelters and health services.

THE DOMESTIC VIOLENCE REVOLUTION

We begin volume 1 where the domestic violence revolution began,
with the founding of battered women's shelters in the early 1970s, the
development of the shelter movement into a formidable political force,
and the challenges it faced as it attempted to sustain its ideals in the
face of "success."

Sharon Vaughan's chapter about Women's Advocates details the steps
and missteps and the conflicts and hopes that preoccupied the little band
of sisters who opened the nation's first shelter for battered women. During the next three decades, similar scenes were enacted in thousands of
communities throughout the United States, England, Canada, and dozens of other countries, as private homes or apartments opened as safe
houses for women in trouble evolved into free-standing safety zones or
refuges. Reflecting back on her experience, Vaughan echoes three themes
that would distinguish the battered women's movement from other
social movements in the last century: the centrality of women's stories in
shaping how we understand abuse; the extent to which the women who
sought emergency housing became key decision makers about their fate;
and the degree to which shelters were designed to challenge the hierarchical, paternalistic, and victim-blaming form in which traditional
services were delivered, as well to close the gender gap that led to the
denial or misidentification of domestic violence at points of service.

Shelters and other community-based services for abuse victims would not have been needed had hospitals, courts, or police been providing adequate protections for women and children in personal life. To this extent, the emergence of shelters resembled food co-ops, parent-run day care, reproductive health services, and other community-based alternative institutions invented in the 1960s and 1970s to satisfy unmet needs. But they also differed from other service agencies in their heavy reliance on volunteers, many of them formerly battered women with little or no professional training in service delivery, and on activists who believed that feminist organizations should empower women individually by giving them a key role in running the facilities and, collectively, by mobilizing their creative energies to elicit changes in the systems that caused and perpetuated sexual inequality. Another difference between shelters and other organizations designed to redress social problems arose from the danger engaging male violence posed to those who stepped into the breach to provide assistance.

Adding to the power of Vaughan's account is her willingness to confront the dilemmas created as the ideals of the early shelter movement clashed with the realities of having to secure funding and services from traditional agencies. Deborah DeBare, the executive director of the Rhode Island Coalition Against Domestic Violence, picks up the story where Sharon Vaughan leaves off, drawing parallels between the spread of shelters nationwide, the growth of the movement's access to government funding and professional sophistication, and the broadening of organizational capacity to encompass far more than emergency housing. Over time, shelter funding became more stable, paid staff became the rule and volunteer labor the exception, and shelters took their place at the table with the very services they began by challenging. A National Coalition Against Domestic Violence was organized at a dramatic meeting of domestic violence advocates, researchers, and health and social service professionals convened by the U.S. Civil Rights Commission in 1978, and state coalitions were developed shortly afterward.

Passage of the Violence Against Women Act in 1994, its reauthorization in 2000 and 2005, and passage of the Domestic Violence, Crime and Victims Act of 2004 in the United Kingdom were other watersheds in the legitimation of the movement, and not merely because of the financial largess involved. Critics charge that their very success has led shelters to downsize their original vision and to mimic the hierarchical, apolitical style of the agencies they started out to change. DeBare confronts this issue head on, remaining hopeful despite acknowledging the potential pitfalls when a grassroots movement comes to rely so heavily on the very state system that helped to perpetuate sexual inequality at the root of domestic violence in the first place.

An important signal that the battered women's movement has come of age is the extent to which it has allowed service professionals and academic researchers access to its work. In chapter 3, British psychologist Hilary Abrahams reports on findings from a study sponsored by the Women's Aid Federation of England (WAFE) of women's emotional and support needs while at the refuge and during the postshelter recovery from the condition that psychiatrist Judith Hermann compares to "being taken prisoner by courtship." Abrahams highlights a recurrent theme in the stories of survivorship: that recovery from the isolation, fear, and control imposed by abuse is often far more gradual than is recovery from physical injury. As she tracks women's journeys from victim to survivor through stages of recovery, as women gradually learn to look beyond the next day and regain the hopes and life projects they once tried to share with their partners, we appreciate the significance of the ongoing psychological support and material resources advocates provide as well as ongoing material resources. Abrahams gives us a poignant glimpse of the long-standing scars left by abuse. In the end, however, it is the courage of day-to-day survivorship that comes across most vividly from the stories she recounts of women returning to school, finding an apartment, reconnecting with old friends, and regaining confidence in their child rearing.

By the 1980s, most community-based domestic violence services provided a range of resources to victims and their children in addition to emergency housing. The chapter about shelters, by community psychologists Cris Sullivan and Tameka Gillum, focuses on a question implicit in the other three: what do these services actually do, and are they effective? The chapter describes how shelters operate from day to day and critically reviews the rules that govern behavior during the shelter stay and the services available. Although rules may be justified as a way to keep order and protect safety, some rules, such as mandating that women get out of bed by a certain time, complete certain chores, or participate in specific services, can have the unintended effect of reinforcing feelings of being controlled rather than empowered. Women generally rank shelters as one of the most effective and supportive resources available, and the few evaluations of their services have been extremely positive. Nevertheless, the authors identify a range of persistent barriers in the shelter movement to women with complex medical or mental health needs, younger women, older women, lesbians, women of color, and immigrant women. They conclude by describing a host of innovative programs to remove these barriers as well as to extend support after a shelter stay and to provide community-based services for women who may not want or need emergency protection.

What is remarkable in the end is not that shelters are less than perfect or continue to face many of the same difficult choices between empowerment and "help" debated by Sharon Vaughan and her sisters in the early 1970s. What is remarkable is that an institution born out of community struggle, staffed largely by nonprofessionals, and designed almost literally on the fly in response to the needs of those who came, has prospered.

POVERTY, EMPLOYMENT, SEXUAL IDENTITY, AND RACE

Readers are undoubtedly aware that abuse is commonplace in middle-class and affluent families as well as among the poor. But as the women to whom Abrahams talked made clear, the effects of abuse can be far more devastating for women who live on the edge of the economy to start, particularly when these effects are aggravated by racial discrimination, a sexual identity that has been socially marginalized, or by the dislocations in employment occasioned by globalization, issues taken up in Chapters 5, 6, 7, 8, and 9 and particularly salient at the moment.

Early in the domestic violence revolution, magazines such as *Redbook* and *Vogue* publicized the stories of Tina Turner, Oprah, and other successful women who had suffered domestic violence, largely to send the message, "It can happen to *you*." Advocates often endorsed this imagery as well, fearing that societal interest in abuse would wane if it was shown to affect poor or minority women primarily. Moreover, if abusive behavior derived solely or primarily from men's sense of sexual entitlement as men, as some feminists claimed, then the roles of poverty, employment, and social class were clearly secondary, as was the incidence of violence by women with same-sex partners. An unintended consequence of this focus was that domestic violence was painted with a single brush and interventions proceeded as if the predicaments victims and their children faced were identical regardless of their race, sexual identity, or socioeconomic status. The contribution of socioeconomic inequality, race, and sexual identity was lost.

The chapters by Claire Renzetti, Jody Raphael, Deborah Weisman, Janice Ristock, and Katherine Morrison offer a sobering antidote to this short-sighted approach, showing how poverty, economic dislocation, race, and a marginalized sexual identity can dramatically increase women's vulnerability to abuse and how domestic violence, in turn, can lock women into grinding poverty and isolation.

Claire Renzetti provides a comprehensive summary of how social class shapes sexual violence and the particular consequences of abuse for poor victims. As a sociologist who edits *Violence against Women*, the leading academic journal on abuse, Renzetti is uniquely qualified to consider exactly which dimensions of economic disadvantage contribute to an elevated risk of victimization among poor women and how they do so. These dimensions include physical and mental health problems as well as substance abuse; community and neighborhood violence; employment issues; racial discrimination; and weaknesses in social support networks and social services systems such as Temporary Assistance to Needy Families (TANF), commonly known as welfare.

Jody Raphael puts flesh and bones on the research evidence summarized by Renzetti. She sketches the stories of three women whom she got to know well in the course of her legal advocacy work in Chicago. Bernice's experience of violence is compounded by a regressive welfare system that repeatedly frustrates her need for protection and for job training. In her attempt to avoid dependence on men, Olivia becomes a street worker and heroin addict. Escaping from a middle-class childhood of sexual abuse, Tammy also struggles against addiction and imprisonment as well as abuse. Despite important differences in their experience, the institutions to which these women turned for help aggravated their predicament, adding to the entrapment they experienced because of poverty and violence by stigmatizing their behavior, increasing their felt sense of shame, and reinforcing their propensity to escape from self-loathing into drugs or alcohol and abusive relationships. The alternative, argues Raphael, is to recognize the extent to which each of these women does her best to survive in a constrained universe of choices and to broaden her options rather than blame them for making poor choices.

Raphael helps us hear the voices of the women she got to know. A unique facet of Renzetti's argument concerns what might be termed the "ecology of violence," the extent to which the high levels of violence and social disorder characteristic of the neighborhoods in which poor people live breed what sociologist Kai Erickson has termed "community traumatization," increasing the generic risk of all residents. In chapter 7, law professor Deborah Weissman links the local concerns that propel Raphael and Renzetti to changes in the global economy. She shows how unemployment, deindustrialization, and convergent economic currents threaten personal security and community identification in ways that undermine social, family, and gender roles. One result is an increase in domestic violence. For Weissman, however, the answer is not an even greater reliance on criminal justice intervention—the first temptation when we confront social disorder—but rather a broadened alliance between those suffering the scourge of abuse and those experiencing the brunt of economic dislocation.

A common theme in these chapters is the relative invisibility of victimized women, particularly if they are poor. Invisibility plays a key role in Janice Ristock's analysis of violence in lesbian relationships. For one thing, many of the lesbian women Ristock interviewed were abused in their first lesbian relationship, while they were still "in the closet" (and so could not access the few services available to lesbians). This allowed lesbian partners to exploit homophobia in the larger society, threatening to "out" partners who refused to yield to their demands and so subject them to ostracism from family members or employers. Fear of reprisal because of their sexual identity also isolated these victims. For another thing, heterosexism—the assumption that all relationships be judged by the standard of a heterosexual relationship—also dominated the advocacy movement to which these victims would normally have turned for help. Many advocates share homophobic attitudes, while others fear that acknowledging violence in same-sex relationships will compromise their focus on male violence against women. Ristock also discusses other themes that shaped the experiences of the women she interviewed, including dislocation, the overlap of racial and sexual stigma, the dilemmas created by "fighting back," and the ambivalence about turning to police, courts, or other institutions that have histori-cally discriminated against gays or transgendered persons.

In chapter 9, Katherine Morrison offers a critical overview of the expe-rience of abuse in the African American community. She summarizes evidence that African American women are not only more likely to be abused by their partners than are white or Hispanic women but also are more likely to suffer devastating physical and psychological effects. Mor-rison summarizes various theories of why this is so, highlighting how many black men may react to the dehumanizing legacy of slavery and institutionalized racism by adopting a "tough guy" profile, acting out sexually, and becoming "playas" who believe they must prove their manhood by dominating and controlling "their" women. Conversely, some black women also internalize sex stereotypes, presenting them-selves as "strong" rather than vulnerable, a posture that makes them reluctant to seek help or to acknowledge their problem. Fortunately, the race-specific dynamics and effects of abuse are being addressed by cul-turally sensitive media campaigns and by new organizations whose sole focus is on domestic violence among African Americans. Morrison calls on the black church and other mainstream institutions in African Ameri-can communities to become more involved.

HEALTH AND MENTAL HEALTH

By the mid-1980s, two things were clear: battered women turned to a range of community services and institutions for problems related to abuse, and there were few personnel at these sites who could either identify the problem or treat its victims appropriately. As we've seen, the grassroots movement became a springboard for protest against the failure of the mainstream service response. Health care was a major target of reform. In part, this reflected the significance of domestic vio-lence as a cause of women's injuries and a host of related medical, psy-chological, and behavioral problems. In part, too, though, it reflected the systematic failure of medical personnel to screen for domestic vio-lence and the lack of appropriate training for health professionals on how to respond. Even when health professionals did identify abuse, they responded in ways that often made a woman's predicament worse, by prescribing pain medication rather than interventions to enhance her safety, for instance, or by applying a pseudo-psychiatric label such as "woman with well-known complaints" that discouraged others from taking her problems seriously.

In her chapter on the health care response, Emma Williamson identifies the major health consequences of partner abuse, reviews what we know about the costs of these problems if left untreated, and links the response in England and the more aggressive response in the United States to the different ways in which health care is financed in the two countries. She pays particular attention to professional training in domestic violence and routine screening, issues about which there is considerable debate. But her main point is that, even at best, because the definition of domestic violence that health professionals bring to their work relies heavily on a criminal justice model of violence and injury, it virtually guarantees that practitioners will miss or seriously undervalue the range of common problems, and particularly of mental health problems, caused by nonviolent forms of coercion and control. Only by changing the definition to more closely approximate what women experience is this situation likely to change.

The emphasis on how abuse affects a victim's mental health is carried over in the chapter by psychologists Melissa Platt, Jocelyn Barton, and Jennifer J. Freyd. Like Williamson, they summarize the major medical and mental health consequences of domestic violence. But their main concern is to address a paradox that has confounded observers since the onset of the domestic violence revolution: why abused women appear to "stay" with their abusive partners and to deny, minimize, or blame themselves for the abuse. Their explanation lies in the profound feelings of betrayal women suffer in the context of abuse by an intimate and in the protective—and so adaptive—role of denial in this context. Children often dissociate from a traumatic experience to preserve a relationship to an abusive parent on whom they are dependent. In a similar way, the authors argue, abused adults may also adapt to the loss of trust by suppressing the details of a particular abusive event or even a sequence of events and clinging even more tightly to the abuser. In this case, dependence may be rooted in literal structural deprivations imposed by a partner who takes their money or denies them access to resources vital to their survival, such as a phone, car, or medication—common examples of coercive control. In addition, dissociation is prompted by the risks associated with withdrawal and confrontation, the logical response when a trust is betrayed. Unfortunately, betrayal trauma is often reinforced by the victim-blaming response of those to whom victims turn for help, their culture, or the larger normative messages communicated by the media, as well as by their immediate world of friends, family, neighbors, or coworkers. The authors conclude by describing how asking about abuse and a willingness to listen in a nonjudgmental way to women's stories can go a long way toward reversing the effects of betrayal trauma. These are skills any of us can master.

Chapter 1

The Story of the Shelter, "Women's Advocates"

Sharon Rice Vaughan

THE BEGINNING

In the early 1970s, battered women began to tell the truth about their lives. How this happened, story by story, is also the account of one of the first shelters for battered women in the United States. It was a time of social change and confronting authority. There was the struggle for women's rights and racial equality and protests in the streets against the Vietnam War. This climate of social reform was essential for the stories of battered women to emerge from their previous silence. But nobody fought for women to be safe in their own homes until the women themselves spoke out. This is the story of the Women's Advocates shelter.

The story begins with a consciousness-raising group in St. Paul, Minnesota. After meeting for about a year to talk about the inequality women experienced in their own lives, the group decided to "go public" and looked for a project. A lawyer in the Legal Assistance office told them that women frequently didn't get the information they needed to make difficult legal choices. St. Paul had a large Catholic population for whom legal separation was seen as an alternative to divorce, but women were sometimes unsure of the legal and financial difference between the two. And to get a divorce, two witnesses were required and fault had to be proved. The consciousness-raising group wrote a divorce rights booklet that generated a large number of responses from women wanting more information. The Legal Assistance office then obtained two positions through Volunteers in Service to America (VISTA), a national service program designed to fight poverty, to staff a telephone information service for women. They named the phone service Women's Advocates. Many of the women in the consciousness-raising group volunteered with the phone service. Another goal of the consciousness-raising group was to establish a space for classes, workshops, and weekend retreats to be called Woman House, discussed later in this chapter.

One discovery from answering the telephone was that women with legal questions had a lot of related problems. It seemed that many women had gone around the block, so to speak, asking for help and getting referred somewhere else until someone suggested they call the Legal Assistance office. This was surprising since we were the least qualified and experienced of any social service; only one of our volunteer members was a professional social worker.

Early on, some of us embraced the anti-establishment attitude of the 1960s toward traditional social services, viewing them as embodiments of the top-down hierarchical, imperialistic, war-mongering society we wanted to change somehow. Still, we saw that it was important for us to find out what was available in our community so we could help the women who were calling and so compiled a resource list of community services to keep next to the phone. Once we knew what was available, we also found out what was missing. And the extent of that amazed us. Our Women's Advocates phone service seemed to become a dumping ground for all kinds of problems. But we found there was one request we could not satisfy: it was a woman calling and needing a place for herself and her children to stay in an emergency. She could go to the misnamed Grand Hotel in downtown St. Paul for one night or over the weekend until the welfare office opened on Monday, but this meant she had to prove she was poor enough to qualify for welfare, she could only stay a day or two, and the place was not safe.

We felt so indignant that most women had nowhere to stay in an emergency that we decided to create a place. At that time, Minnesota was supposed to have one of the best social services systems in the country. How could such a basic need go unmet? As the need for emergency housing emerged through women's phone calls, we decided that Woman House—which was still a goal of the group—could serve this function as well as be a retreat center. I had been going to the Tuesday night meetings and volunteering on the telephone, invited by Susan Ryan, one of the VISTA workers. When the other VISTA worker quit, I got the job. At about this time, to raise money for Woman House, we went to the offices of the Ramsey County Mental Health Center one evening and telephoned about 200 people, friends and friends of friends, asking for monthly pledges. Pledges started coming in, the average being five dollars per month; the largest was twenty dollars. In addition, we started a newsletter to inform supporters about our progress.

As the calls increased, the Women's Advocates phone line moved from the Legal Assistance office to the apartment of one of the VISTA workers who had moved in with her partner. We became Women's Advocates Inc. with a board of directors. The VISTA workers and volunteers took turns answering the phones. Calls came from the police, the emergency room of the county hospital, the welfare office, as well as Legal Assistance and other agencies and individuals. Not surprisingly, many calls came at night when the social services were closed. For nights, we hired the least expensive answering service we could find, a burglar alarm company, which happened to be staffed by women.

The first call for shelter came one afternoon in May, 1972, from Emergency Social Services. A worker said a woman was at the St. Paul Greyhound bus station with a 2-year-old child. To get a job, she had traveled 150 miles from Superior, Wisconsin, with two dollars in her pocket. What were we expected to do? Where would they stay after two days at the Grand Hotel? One of the advocates borrowed a high chair and stroller, and we took them to the apartment that was our office. These were the first residents we sheltered. The two-year-old destroyed the office in one night because all the papers were stacked on low shelves held up by bricks. His mother didn't talk about being battered; she said she wanted to go to secretarial school to make a life for her and her son. She tried to get a place to live, but no one would rent to her without a deposit, which she didn't have. This was our first encounter with a standard problem faced by battered women, the "catch-22" of housing that had women running in circles between social services offices and their own desperation until they went back home. After a couple of weeks she went back to Superior, and every Christmas for several years sent a card thanking Women's Advocates for being there and enclosing two dollars, the amount she had when she came to town.

Three months and several women and children later, after being evicted from the adults-only apartment building that contained the office, the phone service moved to my house. I was a single parent with three young children. And the women started to come. When my family was away on vacation, my house filled up. One young woman from central Minnesota with an 18-month-old daughter had told her husband she wanted to leave, and his answer was to shoot a row of bullets into the wall above her head. She then called her local legal aid office and was given our phone number. Another woman came with her four-year-old daughter. A migrant worker in another part of the state called her local legal aid office for a peace bond, hitchhiked over a hundred miles, and left nine children behind. She stayed a day and went back. Later, when the shelter was open, she brought her six youngest children. A woman from Elkert, Indiana, came and went back a couple of times. As women who came shared the stories of their lives with us and one another, mutual support and self-reliance turned them into a collective tale. As the advocates became aware of battering, we felt that groups and programs like ours, small and self-sufficient, could start all over the country.

THE PHILOSOPHY

What were important were the relationships. But the point was we hadn't known that women were battered until they told us, one after another, again and again, as they sought our help. A critical moment came in 1972 at a weekend retreat for the phone line volunteers and VISTAs. An argument over how to answer the telephone led to a split in the group. One of the volunteers later described the two positions:

> *These women are in a crisis and they don't know what they want because they're in a crisis. We have to tell them what's good for them. We have to tell them what they should and can't do. And the other side was arguing, "We are not in her shoes. We cannot decide for her and insist on what she's going to do or not do because we don't know what's holding her back." (Interview 6-1)*

The debate ended with a vote, and the second view prevailed. What followed was new knowledge acquired from women's stories; we discovered what was in our midst by standing still and listening. Then, we could "walk with" that person to where she wanted to go. This decision framed advocacy, rather than advice, as the group's method of working.

We were already using advocacy, but this decision brought us closer to women's stories. From this point on, the caller was considered the expert on herself and her issues. As an advocate for the caller, the phone answerer's job was to find the information the caller sought and the assistance she requested and to make sure she could navigate social services systems that had been designed to help but did not do so. So, although we had yet to explicitly recognize their importance, we made women's stories and the narrator's point of view paramount, taking them as the source of all knowledge and the locus for action and social change.

Although it may be hard to believe in retrospect, we also had yet to figure out why women needed to get away in an emergency or that, when a woman told us she was escaping violence, anything more was involved than an individual relationship gone wrong. But the official agreement to be advocates prepared us to listen. Listening was now part of our goal, a self-conscious activity, not simply a method of getting information. We no longer hurried to get off the phone. Listening allowed us to discover what was really going on. When we focused on listening, women started talking about battering.

At first, we saw the common need simply as emergency housing. Then, the plain, painful truth of battering spilled out from our telephone log and from the women sitting around the kitchen table talking about their lives and trading stories. Instead of providing ready solutions, we asked each woman what she needed and wanted, and then advocated for her with various social and legal agencies, including housing, welfare, and legal aid and private attorneys volunteering their time, as well as medical, mental health, schools, and child welfare services. The stories made it impossible to deny a truth that seemed to come out of nowhere and, at the same time, to be common as the cold. It was by telling their stories that women put the truth of their experience at the heart of knowledge about battering.

The consciousness-raising group's original plan for Woman House, a retreat center for women wanting to get a break from their lives, folded in the crush of constant calls from women in crisis needing emergency housing. The women who had wanted the retreat house began to leave the group. By the time Women's Advocates was able to buy a house in 1974, it had become a shelter for battered women, pure and simple.

THE HOUSE

By 1973, pledges totaled $350 a month. We were determined not to seek funds from the government or private foundations because this meant indirectly supporting the war against Vietnam. But what we had was insufficient to buy a house for a shelter. We met to decide what to do. One person said, "We agree that money that supports the Vietnam War is 'dirty' money. But if we use money we raise for the shelter, it's 'clean' money, even if it comes from the government." And so we found a person to help Susan and me write our first funding proposal. An early grant came from the county Mental Health Program Board.

Our one volunteer with a professional degree was Karen Klinefelter, a social worker at the mental health center. Her director and another social worker supported us enthusiastically and sponsored our funding request. But when the Mental Health Program Board that actually issued the grants met, some board members were skeptical. One said that only trained mental health professionals could do this work. We said the women who came for shelter were not mentally ill—they needed safety, support, help getting housing, and whatever else. And they needed each other. We explained that we called women "residents," not "clients" or "cases." Another board member, the head of a large community social service organization, said, "If this was needed, we'd be doing it." When other board members talked positively about the proposal, he suggested that Women's Advocates come under his organization's umbrella. Our stomachs sank and we explained why we thought this would not be helpful. It was suggested that we change our name to something less inflammatory. After we rejected these suggestions, another board member insisted that we would surely need an executive director if we got the funds from the county, a real house, and a proper staff. Since we had none of these, not a house, a hired staff, or money for a shelter, when it was put this way, we caved in. The Ramsey County Mental Health Board gave us $35,000.

Our philosophy had been discussed and defined over the past 18 months and we had decided to work together as a collective. The two VISTA workers and the volunteers, about eight in all, shared the same title of advocate. At our meetings we adopted a consensus model of decision making. We managed to match the theory of our collective structure with the practice of egalitarian relationships with women calling on the phone and staying in our homes. Since Susan and I, as VISTAs, worked more than full-time, the reality was that we made many decisions ourselves. But the collective model meant everything to us. Coming from the women's liberation movement of the time, it signified a rejection of the model of male domination that defined so many organizations, even in the anti-war movement. The radical shift meant defining power as horizontal and shared rather than as power and control "over" others—of husbands over wives, for instance. Our vision was to extend the model to residents so that they would participate in decisions about running the shelter.

In that one moment—the mental health board meeting—we had abandoned the core principle of collectivity. While we were prepared to face and resist the inevitable pressures of outside agencies to mainstream us—in other words, prepared to resist being stripped of exactly what made us necessary—we were also vulnerable to those pressures and had to make some concessions concerning our future. We were learning as we went along. I applied for the director position and was hired by the board of directors. But after about six weeks, I couldn't see the point of the position and turned back the pay difference, becoming an advocate again and restoring the collective structure. The Women's Advocates Board of Directors agreed to disband to validate the collective structure and philosophy. To comply with state requirements as a not-for-profit organization, we needed officers. So we made the paid and volunteer advocates the board of directors, and three were selected (by consensus) to fill the roles of executive officers.

POWER PROBLEMS

As the shelter grew, we were repeatedly challenged to redefine power at every level of operation (method) and thought (theory), from working relations to personal relationships, and to replace the traditional model of hierarchical "power over" the battered women we served (and never to use the word "client") with a horizontal, shared-power model of "empowerment." We had no map to lead us out of the deep ruts of custom, authority, and male supremacy that had shaped so much of our lives to the hoped-for new ways of defining power and accountability.

The need to fundraise never abated. It became a political question that framed our vision of what we wanted the shelter to be and ultimately caused a split between the two VISTAs, Susan Ryan and myself. Susan had a true grassroots vision of a safe house in every neighborhood, a family's house, which had a small sign in a front window that said, "Battered women welcome here." Neighbors would take neighbors in, and the community would come together to enforce a community standard that would not allow women to be battered. This vision required community organizing rather than large sums of money. The vision I held of shelter required participating in various bureaucratic levels of government and other power structures, expending huge amounts of time that could be spent working with the women and children, being chronically understaffed and overextended, and struggling over compromising our principles and our ethics to convince the men in power (how many of them beat their wives?) to allow us to operate. Despite these challenges, I was convinced we would change the world.

Our differences came to a head one afternoon. We were meeting with staff of a large private foundation, sitting in the teak conference room underneath the oil portraits of the founders and explaining what we would do to end the battering of women if they would give us their money. In the middle of the conversation, Susan got up and left. She never returned. After taking the bus back to the shelter, she told me she was finished with fundraising. We continued to work together and maintained the fierce friendship our compulsive commitment to work created. But after a few months, she left and I stayed. It was a bitter time for us.

Like the relationship between myself and Susan, creating the shelter, the intensity of working there, and the emotional challenges of breaking new ground led others to form friendships that were both wonderful and terrible. We experienced both empowerment and traditional power. We believed in a model of shared power. But it was difficult to define how to make this model compatible with learning new skills or holding one another accountable for tasks or meeting deadlines. Almost everything was a learning experience. Although we were all "equal," we needed to be able to bridge differences between ourselves and the shelter residents. We claimed that all work was equally valued and paid. But no one wanted to clean the toilets and almost everyone wanted to do public speaking.

Whatever our ideal, we felt pressure when annoyed callers, usually officials or donors, would ask, "Well, who *is* in charge?" Problems with the collective structure included the lack of an organizational model, the need for a culturally diverse staff, and a time-consuming consensus decision-making process. The work to end patriarchy meant building an organizational structure that did not imitate patriarchy. But constant crises took us into the uncharted territory of not really knowing what equalized power was or how it worked.

BALANCING CONTRADICTIONS

Women's Advocates opened in the late afternoon of October 10, 1974. We were on the third floor, in an unfinished attic room under a sloping roof lined with silver insulation stapled to the rafters. Our board of directors was meeting; it was Friday and the telephone rang repeatedly with battered women seeking help, most wanting a place to stay and be safe. We were still renovating the downstairs and I was still the director. I remember saying or asking the others, "Let's just let these women come," and we did. By the end of the weekend, the house was filled.

We didn't want to have rules, except that the residents shared cooking and housework by signing up at the daily house meeting, which was also where they could discuss house problems, relationship problems with other residents, and problems with the shelter itself. They were to participate in decisions about the house and program and were invited to attend our weekly staff meetings, which no resident that I recall ever returned to a second time. Perhaps it was the sometimes lengthy consensus decision-making process that put them off, or just the mundane reality of shelter business. We thought rules recreated the situations the women had fled from. But when one woman said that if she couldn't bring some of her furniture her husband would destroy it and she had been paying on it for years, we said, "Bring it." Then the dining room was so crammed with chairs and tables that we had to climb over them to get to the kitchen. So we said, in the future, no furniture. That same weekend another woman said her cat would die if left alone. So the cat came with her and scratched a child, and so we said no pets. We decided on a rule against spanking children because it mirrored the violence done to women. So discipline should be nonviolent.

As the rules accumulated, the hardest questions involved defining criteria for not allowing a woman to come and when to evict a woman. Answering these questions became part of our self-institutionalization. We could say no if certain conditions were not met, such as remaining sober or being nonviolent in the shelter. Balancing individual rights with the well-being of the shelter community taught us hard lessons. One day I saw a young mother spank her five-year-old daughter and I told her this was not allowed. She looked at me with disdain and said, "Spanking is normal. It's how she learns right and wrong. If my kid gets in a fight, she has to know how to fight back. Spanking is part of that." She was talking about survival in a world of daily violence where our rule made no sense.

It was necessary to keep the doors always open, metaphorically speaking. Women called and arrived at all hours. It was hard work. A parallel priority stretched us to tell funders what they wanted to hear and yet at the same time create and lead a program modeled on empowerment. As we obtained local, state, and federal funds, as well as private foundation funds, pressure increased for us to meet bureaucratic regulations, raise money, and enforce necessary requirements such as keeping statistics, and writing funding proposals and financial reports.

BEYOND THE SHELTER

In the meantime, as advocates honoring each battered woman's experience, we took a comprehensive view of women's needs. As gaps in service became apparent to more people and interest grew in the shelter and the issue of battering, we called a public meeting, where about 100 battered women and social services workers came to hear a police officer, a social worker, a battered woman, and a shelter staffer talk about the issue of battering and what was needed. This led to the formation of a regional consortium comprised mostly of service providers from the community. By 1977, the consortium was working with state legislators and other groups to appropriate money for shelters and services and to pass laws that facilitated the arrest of suspected abusers.

Working with others, we persuaded the county hospital to have a social worker in the emergency room at night. We helped the St. Paul Police Department establish a protocol for domestic calls that included an immediate response to calls from the shelter. This policy change was the result of an incident that typified the ongoing risk at any shelter that an abuser's potential for violence will be realized. The front doorbell rang, and we could see through the door pane that it was a resident's abusive husband. It was mid-afternoon, and an advocate told him to leave and that his wife wasn't there. He covered the window with his jacket and smashed the glass. In the meantime, his wife and daughter left through the back door with an advocate. We called the police and took all the women and children up to the third-floor attic. Staff crowded into the office, a former closet. We could hear him rampaging through the house; he found the bedroom of his wife, smashed lamps, cut up her clothes, and then stabbed himself, causing a superficial wound. Twenty minutes later, the police came and took him to the hospital. When we complained to the police that they had not responded quickly enough to our call, they explained that it came during a shift change and was "just a domestic." A few days later we piled all the residents and children into cars and drove to City Hall, where we were met by a newspaper reporter we had contacted before-hand, explained to the children that just this time they did not need to be quiet, and demanded to see the mayor, which we did quite in short order. He agreed that the call had been an emergency, which should have been dealt with promptly, that any calls in the future would be high priority, as would all domestic calls the police received. The man who had come to the shelter later killed his former wife.

We had talked about having a security system in the house. Funds were scarce and someone proposed using an audio recording of a loud barking dog at the door. Instead, we covered the door window with a grill and installed an alarm system. One man threw a brick through an upstairs window where his family slept. Another husband, a police ser-geant, kept saying through the door that he just wanted to talk to his wife, who told us he always carried a gun. In this instance, police would not respond to our calls because, they said, no officer of equal rank was available. So we moved chairs into the room in front of the door, and all of us stayed there until he finally left. If he was going to come through, he would be facing every woman in the house except for his wife, who was hiding upstairs.

CONNECTING THE "ISMS"

As the movement continued to grow, the validity of the experience that had shaped it was challenged in two ways: first, by a need to diversify along lines of race, class, and sexual orientation; and, second, by the emerging expertise coming out of a growing network of institu-tions involved with battering.

Initially, we did not appreciate that we, being white, middle-class women, needed to address race and class as directly as we were begin-ning to address sexism. Our first step was to recognize the pragmatic need to have a racially diverse staff to do a good job of serving diverse residents. We were not yet ready for a political analysis of why white, middle-class women run the programs, comprise most of the staff, and assume that everyone thinks, lives, feels, acts, and responds they way we do. Our ignorance on this point reflected the way racism works in society as a whole, where the hegemony of white dominance masks itself so that white people hardly ever notice it in our daily encounters. At the same time, the real experiences of women calling and coming for shelter showed clearly how battering existed across systems of power and privilege that related to race, class, and gender oppression. Our own racism, classism, and homophobia were challenged as more women came to live and work at the shelter. It was an in-our-face les-son that we lived and learned.

Our early goal to include battered women as staff, volunteers, and advocates for other battered women helped us expand beyond our white, middle-class insularity. How deeply we were closed off in our narrow world was evident from questions raised about the meaning of what was going on. Before we opened the shelter, when women came to my house with their children and everything they could fit into green garbage bags, my daughter, who was about nine and going to a private school on scholarship, came home one day and asked, "I just want to know: are we rich or are we poor?" My next-door neighbor asked me one day, "What *is* going on in your house because some other neighbors asked me to sign something but I said no?"

We also began to find that violence cut across all classes. I was invited to speak about battering at the Women's Club. The elegant woman who welcomed me in the morning told me how wonderful her husband was—and at lunch how miserable she was from his abuse. Her social and financial status depended on her husband. Even with her wealth, she felt as trapped as the woman with far fewer options. Another time, I volunteered to serve divorce papers on an abuser in order to expedite the initial divorce hearing. I thought, no problem— he's a professor. I went to the house with his wife, and as I presented him with the legal papers, he punched me and gave me a black eye, then grabbed for his wife. We ran for our lives.

EXPERTISE

The second challenge, redefining expertise, began with callers asking to "speak to the director." "We don't have a director." Pause. "Well, who's in charge?" "We all are." We were "expert" advocates who created a new field of knowledge, employment, and organization by stepping in where the so-called professionals had failed. To fit this new role, the collective structure of the shelter had to be redefined and reconstructed and the hierarchical organization of power and authority, the traditional arrangement, replaced with our atypical organizational structure, a simple chart of a straight line across the page with the same job title, advocate, for each staff position. The collective organizational ideal was a brave experiment that went to the heart of the battering experience of power and demonstrated that giving up power for empowerment was itself a sophisticated form of expertise that could be applied by and to all of us, staff and residents alike.

This notion of expertise originated in the weekend retreat described earlier. Putting the stories of battered women at the center of our understanding and practice made them experts on their own situation and, conversely, made us, as listeners, experts on advocacy ourselves.

We were part of the early movement that named battering, and naming was a critical step in our development and understanding. The term "battering" did not come into popular use until there was something public to describe. Even then, the event seemed so distant from normal household life that a legal term for assault was borrowed, a term originally taken from the language of medieval warfare, in which the battering ram was used to break down the castle door.

Giving a name to battering opened a new frontier of knowledge, even as it acknowledged and focused what had been hidden in front of our eyes and ears. Each phone call pushed the definition closer to the surface, bringing the collective experience of women to the fore. The accumulation of stories practically created a social change movement by itself. Critical too was the attitude of openness that set the stage for us being there to listen, for our intuitive sense that what we were witnessing needed to be named. Talk pushed us to give a name to what women were saying; having a name allowed them to talk about their experience in ways that linked their stories to the stories of others in similar predicaments. And once named, the stories of "battered women" joined the stories of prostitutes and rape victims, to document the incidence, effects, and purposiveness of male violence directed toward shoring up and maintaining male control.

But if we were experts, were we also "professionals"? If a professional is one who follows a calling as a means of livelihood for the sake of remuneration, we were amateurs. In fact, most professionals were seen by some of us as part of the "Establishment" and therefore of a narrow-minded elite. Indeed, producing professionals seemed to be a major way the Establishment sustained itself, regardless of whether the related skill set did much good. With their college degrees and titles, they protected their turf from rabble like us. It was the social workers, nurses, doctors, lawyers, therapists, police, and corrections people, among others, who were the gatekeepers, along with the universities that produced them, who had failed battered women and their children.

Being professional meant the ability to make informed decisions. But our experience was that professional practices often took the form of victim blaming. For example, when women put their medications into a locked cabinet in the office on a daily basis, the sheer number of tranquilizers prescribed made it clear how battering had been made into a mental health issue. If "professional" pertained to requiring education with titles and letters after one's name, we had to educate almost everyone: funders, politicians, police, the medical profession, social workers, even educators. And yet these professionals seemed eager to appropriate our knowledge and claim it for themselves. If professionals learn how to not identify with "clients," we formed friendships and kept in touch with women after they left the shelter. Sometimes I even took children home for a weekend to give their mother a break. I became a foster parent for three sisters whose mother entered residential chemical dependence treatment after she left the shelter. Did this mean I was "unprofessional," or was it possible to be a professional and advocate at the same time? In the meantime, once battering was finally named, professionals turned it into "family violence" and rejected a political analysis.

But however much we distrusted professionals, we also needed them. We found there were professionals who supported and understood what we were doing, who came out of the thick of what could be called "the other side." Karen Klinefelter was a social worker with legitimately relevant training. Of all the volunteers, she worked most closely with Susan and me. At every juncture, allies came forward from within their institutions to refer women to us, bring them to the door, legitimize our work, and advocate for us through their steadfast support. And of course we learned from them as well. We understood that for battered women to be safe, the shelter had to be part of a coordinated community response. Community-wide effort was needed to make the changes in institutions, of laws, policies, and protocols necessary to end men's violence against women.

As the administration of the shelter became more complex, it required multifaceted expertise. The skills required included the multiple details of meeting safety and fire codes in order to stay in business, raising funds and managing bureaucratic funding requirements, public relations, and more—in addition to, rather than instead of, our original approach of empathy and egalitarianism.

The success of the shelter movement bred new challenges as woman battering evolved into a professionally, academically, and officially legitimized field and the problem was de-gendered by being renamed "spouse abuse" or "intimate partner abuse." As the term "domestic violence" replaced "battered woman" or "woman abuse," the underlying debate took new forms to accommodate new developments; giving credentials to advocates, for instance, pressure from men's rights groups, or policies that excluded women from shelters because their names appeared on "inappropriate" lists. Shelters are still at the mercy of funders; laws have been passed and weakened and repassed. Over the years, the field's "success" and the mainstreaming of local programs made it seem obvious to many that we had moved a long way from our origins.

Some research terminology continues to resurrect a woman-blaming approach; yet other research, programs, and coalitions are challenging biased research and practice and transforming society's response to woman battering in attempting to achieve equality between men and women. I saw these changes happening as I moved from Women's Advocates to the new Harriet Tubman Shelter when it opened in Minneapolis, then to the new state coalition for its first five years, and then produced a documentary public radio series: *Breaking the Silence: Voices on Battered Women*. I kept a foot in the door working overnight shifts at shelters through the 1990s as I completed graduate study. Now, I teach courses on community violence intervention and prevention at a state university, from the perspective of violence as socially constructed, including violence against women.

As we saw the women we sheltered discover their own strength mirrored in each other, I and those I worked with also learned to find strength in ourselves and one another, inspiring us to forge ahead with the shelter. Women stole silverware, sheets, and more; they argued, sometimes furiously, usually concerning children; yet the strength and determination of a woman just in escaping the violence, and the strength they drew from one another, were amazing. A woman would listen to another woman's experience, and the listener would say, "You did that? That took guts!" In retrospect, it seems clear that empowerment was our own work in progress as much as it was an aim of our advocacy.

But we were also empowered by what we learned, our analysis. From the start, women's stories presented advocates with a stunning paradox: that men's violence toward their wives and partners was inextricably bound up with intimacy. Perhaps the biggest achievement of the early battered women's movement was its discovery, taken from the accumulated wisdom of hundreds of stories, that this paradox, one of the more profound contradictions in personal life, could only be understood when it was viewed through the lens of sexual inequality and that its resolution lay not in the psyches of individual men or women but in the movement for change we—and they—had begun.

Chapter 2

The Evolution of the Shelter Movement

Deborah DeBare

During a 24-hour period in September 2007, a total of 53,203 victims of domestic violence received services from a domestic violence agency somewhere in the United States. Twenty-five thousand three hundred and twenty-one (25,321) victims were sheltered that night in one of the safe homes or transitional units because their own homes were not safe for them to sleep in.[1] It is hard to believe that a mere 35 years ago, there would have been no safe place for these individuals to go. The battered women's movement is a relatively young movement, having come into existence in the 1970s as an outgrowth of the struggle for women's rights in the United States. Reflecting back on the evolution of this movement is critical to understanding its vision, a future free from domestic violence, and the resilience and struggles of those at its base.

It is well known that domestic violence existed long before the first shelters developed, long before there was any reference to the problem on clinical psychology tests, and certainly long before the government recognized it as a crime. Women have been emotionally, physically, and sexually abused by their partners for millennia. But it remained an epidemic without a name. While the first shelter referenced historically opened in Chicago in the mid-nineteenth century, and both British and U.S. feminists referred to this issue in the late nineteenth and early twentieth centuries, it continued to be perceived as a private matter, not as a social problem. Without words to identify what was happening to them, many women understood their partner's abuse as "normal," "just life," or a result of "bad luck" in relationships. Perhaps they'd seen their parents use violence and were embarrassed to talk about it to anyone, or perhaps it was because they simply didn't know what "it" was. One woman reflected back on her relationship with her husband of 45 years. She confided, "When we were first married, it was in the 1950s. I knew I was being treated badly and I felt depressed that my husband treated me the way he did, but I didn't know what to do about it, or who to talk to about it, or what to even call it if I did want to tell someone about it."[2] Without language to identify what this woman was experiencing, it was difficult if not impossible to envision a different future. The first breakthrough for the evolution of the battered women's movement was actually naming the problem.

The battered women's movement learned a lot from the anti-rape movement in this area, since the anti-rape movement had been working to "name the problem" during the 1970s. Most of the early sexual assault organizations used the word "rape" in their name (such as the Philadelphia Women Against Rape, the Chicago Women Against Rape, and the Rhode Island Rape Crisis Center) to impress upon the public the importance of naming the problem. Susan Schechter details the emergence of the battered women's shelter in her book, *Women and Male Violence*, stressing how its history was shaped significantly in the 1970s by feminists, survivors, and community activists who "increasingly responded in a new way, providing emotional support, refuge and a new definition of 'the problem.'"[3]

Language, as many social movements have proven, is a key organizing tool. How we name a problem points toward certain solutions or interventions and away from others and allows those who have the power of naming to shape the social change strategies that follow. For example, early in the evolution of the domestic violence movement, the terms "battered wife" and "marital violence" were used, leading to an exclusive focus on husbands and their wives. As a result, most of the laws that were first passed to criminalize domestic violence were applicable only to married victims. Even today, there are a number of states in which unmarried (dating) partners are still not able to obtain civil protective orders because their state laws provide this protection only to married partners.

Between its founding in 1939 and 1969, the leading scholarly journal in the family sciences, the *Journal of Marriage and the Family*, made no references to "domestic violence," and when the *Archives of General Psychiatry*, a publication of the American Medical Association, started to discuss the issue in the mid 1960s, it used the term "wifebeaters."[4] Even the earliest feminist writings on the problem used the term battered wife. This narrow understanding of who was victimized shaped the early evolution of the domestic violence movement as well and carries on in many subtle ways today. For instance, even though all states finally eliminated the marital rape exemption, some states still include exceptions to these laws or penalize men who rape their wives less harshly than men who rape strangers.

Medical professionals (most often male) described the problem as being rooted in women's troubles relating to their husbands, or to psychological disorders related to frigidity or masochism. This view extended the age-old belief that women were men's property and that marriage gave men a contractual right to dominate their wives. Medical and mental health professionals were all too willing historically to collude with abusive husbands and suggest medication or even hospitalization if women refused their husband's sexual demands or "failed" to fulfill their "wifely duties" in other respects. When Anne Flitcraft, MD, and sociologist Evan Stark studied battered women who presented with complaints of injury at Yale–New Haven Hospital in the early 1980s, they found that battered women were often medicated inappropriately (with tranquilizers or pain pills, for instance) rather than properly identified as abused and that 85 percent of *all* pseudo-psychiatric labels attached to female patients (such as "hypochondriac") were applied to women who had been coming to the hospital with complaints related to abuse for years.[5]

The courts adopted a similar victim-blaming approach, convicting women who retaliated after years of abuse and chiding women in family court for "neglecting" their husbands or children if they pursued their independence outside the home. Added to widespread tolerance for physical violence so long as it did not result in severe injury or death, these responses from so-called helping institutions sent a strong message to other women to remain in their abusive relationships, keep silent, and not seek help. Changing the language used to describe abuse—giving it a name that clearly identified the abused person as "the victim" and the abusive partner as "the perpetrator"—opened the door for a range of new strategies to address the problem.

Thus, the "first wave" of a public response to domestic violence came during the rebirth of the women's liberation movement of the 1960s and involved significant efforts to "name the problem." Historians note that the first official battered women's shelter in the modern period opened in England, the Chiswick Women's Aid in 1971. Very shortly thereafter, battered women's shelters started to develop throughout the United States. Woman House in St. Paul, Minnesota, opened in 1974 (see chapter 1 in this volume), growing out of a consciousness-raising group for women. Rainbow Retreat, a shelter specifically created for battered women whose husbands were alcoholics, opened in Phoenix, Arizona, in 1973. The Bradley/Angle House in Portland, Oregon, started in 1975, and by 1976, when La Casa de las Madres opened its doors in San Francisco, California, there were shelters popping up all over the country. The stories of how these shelters started were very similar: without funding or any kind of formal strategic plan or business plan, women gathered around coffee tables in someone's home, set up a telephone line for women who needed help, opened up their own homes or found a house to rent, and started providing safety, shelter, and support for battered women.

Typically staffed by some combination of volunteers, VISTA workers (a domestic poverty program), or women supported under the Comprehensive Employment and Training Act (CETA), some projects received modest support from local municipal governments and a very few got money from the Law Enforcement Assistance Administration (LEAA), a federal justice program. But almost all programs raised the bulk of their funds through grassroots outreach, church donations, bake sales, yard sales, and the like. In *Battered Wives* (1976), one of the earliest books about domestic violence, Del Martin illustrated these humble and courageous beginnings: "La Casa was not funded; a coalition of thirty women just took the plunge, found a house and raised the rent.... At present, La Casa is completely dependent on donations—contributions of money, household furnishings, office supplies, time and energy."[6] By 1977, there were a total of 89 shelters for battered women in the United States, and they recorded that 110,000 calls for help had been received through the hotlines.[7]

Stories from the early days of the battered women's movement in Rhode Island echo those from other sections of the country. Women in rural communities like Hope Valley as well as women in the urban center of Providence, Rhode Island, came together in church basements or at a supportive college women's center and started hotlines by whatever means they could. Called "Safe Haven," "Transition House," "Interval House," "Independence House," or "Sojourner House," the names of the first shelters highlighted the need for safety, the focus on "women" as victims, the notion that shelters were merely a stopping point on the way to empowerment, and the history of the struggle for women's rights and equality. Many of the programs developed in the 1970s emerged from local chapters of the National Organization for Women (NOW), the YWCA, or a university women's center. In Rhode Island there were five organizations that developed during this period (1975–1978), each evolving from the passion and power of a small handful of committed volunteers. The Elizabeth Buffum Chace Center (named after one of the early suffragists in Rhode Island), Sojourner House (named after abolitionist Sojourner Truth), the Women's Center of Rhode Island, the Women's Resource Center of Wood River, and the Women's Resource Center of Newport established hotlines, safe homes, and support groups for women dealing with domestic abuse.

The advocates during this era felt like pioneers, and most were unpaid. Many had survived abusive relationships themselves, and the space created as the movement developed allowed open talk about the violence that had permeated women's lives and the lives of those around them. Sharing and building the movement were inseparable, and the bonds created gave even those who had not been abused a sense of crossing a frontier in women's experience of their power from which there was no going back. As Grace Mattern, the Coalition executive director from New Hampshire, recollects,

> *A group of us from New Hampshire rented a van from "Rent a Wreck" to drive out to the NCADV (National Coalition Against Domestic Violence) conference in Milwaukee together. I think it was 1983 or so. Sure enough, the van broke down and it was a longer trip than necessary. One remarkable moment on the trip was when one of the women told the story of her own, horrifically abusive birth family—how abusive her father was, how he continued to terrorize her mother, how damaged her younger brother had been by the exposure to abuse. Prior to that long van ride through the night, she'd thought she somehow wouldn't be taken seriously doing this work if people knew she was a survivor. Other women in the van began to tell their stories. Then we got to the conference and it was all about empowering survivors, of all kinds, to be part of the movement and to help shape how we approached our work together. We were literally breaking our own silences in order to help other women do the same, believing this was the first step in getting communities to take abuse of women seriously* (Courtesy of Grace Mattern).

At this point in time, there were few legal remedies in place. The need for safety was dominant. The women calling for help were often in such dangerous situations that the shelters that were created during the 1970s and early 1980s were built on a strict foundation of secrecy (about location) and confidentiality (about residents). It was also common during this era to have an "underground" network of volunteer homes in lieu of a stand-alone shelter where battered women could stay on an emergency basis. The safe home network established by Sojourner House in Rhode Island, for example, used a dozen private homes and maintained such a high degree of secrecy that even the organization's staff was unaware of where the victims were being housed. The homes were coded with the names of herbs, such as Rosemary, Sage, and Parsley, and only the victim and her volunteer advocate knew exactly where she was staying. When Sojourner House opened a free-standing shelter, they used extreme precautions to keep its location secret, even asking the victim to crouch down in a car when she was being transported to the facility for the first time, so that its exact address would not be revealed until after she had settled into the program.

During these early years of the battered women's movement, volunteers did most of the work of providing crisis intervention, shelter, and support services. Some shelters were successful in accessing grant or public funding, but, for the most part, paid staffing was minimal. Programs provided training for volunteers that focused on active listening skills, the philosophy of empowering abused women, and skills related to providing victim-centered advocacy. Advocates helped victims in ways that differed markedly from the approach taken by mental health centers, hospitals, or community service agencies. Where these traditional agencies adopted a clinical model based on treating "patients" or a top-down model whereby "professionals" counseled or delivered services to "clients," shelter programs were based on the belief that change would come about by providing peer support to victims of abuse, including support from other victims, and by breaking their isolation, building their self-confidence, and empowering them to make their own decisions, including decisions an advocate might believe were mistaken.

Apart from the particulars and despite the daily confrontation with situations that were frightening and could even be fatal, in these early years of the battered women's movement a reservoir of rage at the injustices women suffered was harnessed to hopefulness that a true social revolution was possible if women's collective strength could be mobilized. As one of the early activists and national leaders in the movement, Anne Menard reflected recently,

What motivated and energized my work to end violence against women was a keen sense of the incredible social injustice it represents. From a very early age, I was outraged that girls and women had to constantly compromise our freedom of movement and limit ourselves in response to too many men's sense of entitlement to rape, assault, and harass women. In response to men's violence, it was WE who had to stay out of parks and wooded areas, not walk alone at night, not talk to strangers, not venture into what were considered male enclaves. WE had to restrict ourselves in a million ways while the men who posed a risk to our safety moved about with no such restrictions. And it was we who, when we WERE attacked, were blamed and accused of "asking for it." This needed change. When I began this work in the early 70s, I joined grassroots organizations and worked with women who had been battered when there was no one to turn to, no support, and certainly no protection from the police or courts. They were the human face of women's strength, courage, and resilience and were so inspiring. We vowed together to do what we could to make the world different for our daughters and sons, and it was a bulldog belief that kept us going.[8]

The founders of many early shelters sensed that their work would radically change society, not just by providing safe havens for abused women but by altering the inequality and power differential that existed in male-female relationships. However, since the founders of shelters in most communities were disproportionately white and middle class, the solutions and strategies that developed often downplayed the needs of women of color and of other disadvantaged groups. Just as the language and the proposed solutions of the civil rights and peace movements of the 1960s and 1970s were skewed to reflect the interests of the men who dominated these movements, so did a gap develop within the battered women's movement between the needs of those people most directly affected by the problem and those whose class, race, or sexual orientation gave them positions of power to define the problem and identify and prioritize solutions.

Still, the shelter movement included large numbers of working-class and minority women from the start, particularly compared with the larger women's liberation movement. And in the early days, shelter residents ran the daily operations and women from disadvantaged groups comprised the majority of residents. Lesbian activists also played key leadership roles in the early movement. Because they too had been marginalized by mainstream society, many of these women felt closely identified with other disadvantaged groups. In some cities with smaller minority populations, racism in the shelters was pervasive. But in other cities, such as Hartford, St. Paul, or New York, the programs were developed by poor or otherwise marginalized women and reflected their perspectives. In fact, differences between the race, class, and sexual orientation of the battered women's movement and the mainstream women's liberation movement divided the two movements on a number of issues early on, both locally and nationally.

After the initial burst of energy expended in establishing hotlines and shelters throughout the United States, it became apparent that shelters alone could not eliminate domestic violence simply by offering a safe haven to victims and a confidential support group. By the early 1980s, most local shelters had some form of paid staff and were breaking out of their isolation by building bridges to other shelters in their own state. In Rhode Island, the 1980s was a decade where the shelters worked together to formalize the activities of the Rhode Island Council on Domestic Violence (now known as the Rhode Island Coalition Against Domestic Violence [RICADV]). Formed in 1979, the early work of the Coalition was to secure legal remedies for victims by advocating for legislative reform, and advocating with one unified voice for financial support for local shelters. The first significant success of the Rhode Island Coalition was to secure a $5,000 state grant for the five battered women's shelters in the state. At the time, this felt like a substantial triumph.

During this decade, advocates recognized that the same work that was being done on an individual basis with battered women (breaking their isolation and empowering them to make changes in their lives) needed be done within the battered women's movement as a whole. By banding together, individual shelters identified strategies to further their social change agenda and worked to bring other systems that impacted victims to the table. Early on, shelter meetings focused on where to get donated furniture or how to recruit and train volunteers for the hotline. Now, at least half of the time was spent developing strategies to criminalize domestic violence or pass protective order legislation. Without consciously planning it, the domestic violence movement had evolved in a relatively short time span of approximately 15 years from a loosely constructed set of individual emergency shelters to a network of organizations looking "beyond shelter." The NCADV was established in 1979 and dedicated its energies during the subsequent decade to networking among domestic violence advocates and survivors to help them learn from one another and break their isolation.

While the national movement may have grown slowly by today's electronic standards, given the limited technology and communications capacities that existed (e.g., most shelters did not even have fax machines in 1980), the national quilt of battered women's advocates had clearly been connected with strong fabric.

Although explicit federal funding for shelters was sparse, through the efforts of advocates many shelters were able to secure funding for staff through CETA (enacted in 1973) and other programs designed to support employment and training for the hard-core unemployed. When CETA was eliminated during the Reagan administration, some of these shelters lost such a disproportionate amount of their agency funding that they were forced to close. In Rhode Island, so many staff had to be cut when CETA funds were eliminated at Sojourner House in Providence that it ceased to operate as a free-standing safe house and had to find an alternate way to respond to the need for emergency housing. "I remember the feeling that we had been cut off at the knees when we lost that funding," recalls one of the shelter's former staff, "and we vowed never to be so reliant on one source of funding again." While the loss of this kind of financial support may have destabilized some programs and slowed the growth of others, it heightened the sense of urgency and the resiliency of the advocates throughout the United States.

By 1990 there were 1,200 battered women's shelters in the United States, and most states had established a coalition of these agencies. The National Network to End Domestic Violence (NNEDV) was originally established as the Domestic Violence Coalition on Public Policy in 1990, and then incorporated in 1995 as a formal membership and advocacy organization to impact national public policy on behalf of state coalitions. The daily operations of local shelters had changed significantly since the 1970s, as most organizations had been certified as nonprofit organizations, developed more formal ways of doing business, and were financially supported by a mix of public and private funds. The stability that this funding provided was often accompanied by requirements that the shelter be accountable to codes and standards set by their various funders. These ranged from state health and fire regulations to rules governing staff-resident ratios and standards of practice and employment. There was widespread pressure to professionalize leadership and staff and to add persons with legal, business, or related skills to shelter boards. Funders like the United Way also set limits in some communities on the amount and types of independent fundraising shelters could do. Dozens of shelters weighed the pros of financial stability achieved through outside funding against the cons of being accountable to groups other than the women's community and residents.

Many of the early advocates had been victims themselves or had good friends or family members who had been victimized or who came to the work from the more personal consciousness-raising experience of the women's movement. Now, a new cohort of advocates emerged who saw advocacy primarily as an employment opportunity or had learned about domestic violence in college through an internship or through activism or community service. New Jersey, Colorado, and other states developed certification programs for advocates, in order to develop the proficiency of staff as well as to demonstrate a level of professionalism comparable with other service providers in their community.

During this period of expanding services, widespread adoption of mandatory arrest policies, and broadened legal remedies, a stronger domestic violence movement could focus on shaping the federal and state public policy agenda. The 1990s was a decade in which the state coalitions assumed the major policy advocacy role formerly played by local programs and defined lobbying for increased funding and support as a major way in which they could "service" these programs. This allowed shelter advocates and local programs to reconnect to their base by expanding direct services to victims and their children and developing new, community-based programs in education and support. While state coalitions often succeeded in eliciting special funding streams for shelter programs and other incremental changes in law, the extent and means of this support differed markedly from state to state and were largely a function of continued and hugely time-consuming political mobilization, often in competition with other equally needy state organizations. Recognizing that national legislation was needed to compliment support from individual states, the NNEDV, the NCADV, NOW, and other national advocacy groups joined with key legislators in the House and Senate to craft federal legislation, an approach that culminated in passage and funding of the Violence Against Women Act (VAWA) as part of the Omnibus Crime Bill, signed into law by President Bill Clinton in 1994.

The original goal of the battered women's shelters was to serve victims, primarily by providing emergency and safe housing. During the 1980s and 1990s, the focus of the movement had expanded to include holding batterers legally accountable. State by state, advocates worked to pass legislation mandating arrest in domestic violence cases, lengthening the scope and duration of protective orders, and enhancing the facility of prosecution and the penalties for repeated abuse. VAWA reflected this shift on a national level, targeting the $1.2 billion appropriated for fiscal years 1995–2000 to improve the criminal justice system's response to violence against women and to expand community services and support for victims of domestic violence, sexual assault, and stalking. VAWA provided for the interstate enforcement of restraining orders (so-called full faith and credit provisions), made it a federal offense to cross state lines to violate a restraining order or injure an intimate party, and outlawed the possession of ammunition and firearms by persons subject to restraining orders. The act also provided significant penalties for a defendant found guilty of the new federal crimes of domestic violence and allowed victims to seek restitution in federal court for the full amount of losses. VAWA also established education and prevention grants to reduce sexual assaults against women and to establish a national domestic violence hotline. Based on the premise that these crimes are motivated by "animus" toward a victim's gender, a provision added by Senator Biden (and subsequently found unconstitutional) defined violence against women as a civil rights violation and allowed victims to sue for damages as a remedy. It was assumed that states would use VAWA funding to expand training programs for criminal justice personnel, refine criminal justice data collection and processing, and build bridges between law enforcement and domestic violence groups.

A VAWA funding stream dedicated to support state coalitions gave them real financial stability for the first time. Almost overnight, coalitions could replace part-time staff or volunteer workers from local domestic violence programs with full-time employees, expand their capacity to provide training and technical assistance to local programs, and participate nationally in public policy and advocacy work. From VAWA and other federal funding sources, justice agencies were also able to secure funding for specialized efforts dedicated to holding batterers accountable through stronger arrest procedures, dedicated domestic violence courts, and specialized prosecution units.

Despite its importance in helping a struggling movement establish a sound financial base, the sudden availability of federal and other funding and the ever-closer working relationships with state organizations these funds necessitated were a "mixed blessing." In the wake of their growing visibility on the national scene, state coalitions, and even many local programs, found themselves in fierce competition for funds with organizations that had very little history or expertise working in the domestic violence arena, faced a backlash from abusers, and became embroiled in internal debates about compromises local programs had made during the process of professionalization and in their relationships with the criminal justice system.

By 2000 there were more than 3,000 battered women's programs in the United States serving an estimated 3 million women and children annually and many additional organizations and programs vying for the limited funds that had been appropriated by Congress. Competition for funding with social services agencies provided the impetus for domestic violence shelters to develop a way to demonstrate their specialized expertise in the field, such as Advocate Certification programs, or licensing standards for programs. Some local programs have established service mandates and program rules or requirements that stray from the original philosophical foundation of the battered women's movement and have unintended consequences that some advocates feel diminish the sense of security or empowerment among shelter residents. One Midwest shelter, for example, required women to be searched each time they entered the shelter; another conducted random drug testing. Other shelters mandated that women attend professional counseling to remain in the facility.

Even when the intent of such rules is to protect residents or otherwise enhance their well-being, they can have unintended consequences for victims of abuse. Rather than modeling behaviors based on trust and independence or fostering individual decision making, these regulations can feel like another form of abuse and reinforce feelings of being controlled, distrusted, and/or infantilized, particularly for women who are trying to break away from a controlling partner who quashed any signs of independence and limited her access to money, transportation, or friends.

The overall impact of VAWA has been unquestionably positive. VAWA was reauthorized in 2000 and in 2005, and funds were appropriated to support a broad range of programs. These included local initiatives to encourage arrest, judicial training, legal assistance for victims seeking civil protection, transitional housing programs for victims, emergency services in rural or other underserved communities, specialized supervised visitation programs, and programs for victims with disabilities. In addition, VAWA funded specialized national resource centers and a national hotline. Since its passage in 1994, there has been a 51 percent increase in the reporting of domestic violence and an average increase in calls to the National Domestic Violence Hotline of 18 percent per year.[9] Some of the key provisions of VAWA 2005 included creating a national Resource Center on Workplace Responses to help employers make their workplaces safer, funding a tribal registry to track protective orders, and making technical corrections to existing immigration law to provide avenues for battered spouses and their children to leave their abusive families without jeopardizing their immigration status.

One important outcome of expanded funding is the capacity for communities to develop innovative programs to meet the specialized needs of victims who were not served or not adequately served before. One example is a shelter program with a kosher kitchen, so that observant Jewish residents do not have to choose between their religious beliefs and safety from their abuser. Another example is a program on an Indian reservation that utilizes traditional healing methods. Specialized programs have also been developed for the lesbian, gay, bisexual, transgendered, and queer (LGBTQ) and South Asian communities and to provide culturally competent services for Latinas. Emergency transportation funds have been set up so that victims who live in isolated rural areas, or on islands without a shelter, can access core and emergency services. Specialized trainings have been developed for leaders in faith-based communities, corporate settings, health care settings, and educational institutions.

Even with these and numerous other equally innovative programs and services, there is still a dearth of resources and programs to meet the needs of victims or to hold perpetrators accountable. A 2007 census of services during a randomly selected 24-hour period conducted by the NNEDV reported a total of 7,707 requests for service from victims of domestic violence that were unmet. Advocates have consistently recognized a huge gap between the needs of communities of color and the availability of culturally competent programs to service these communities. As a result, Congress approved a set-aside for 10 percent of the victim service funds to be dedicated to address this gap in the recent reauthorization of VAWA in 2005.

Funding alone will not cure the pandemic of domestic violence. Advocates have long recognized that domestic violence is rooted in social attitudes and norms that encourage tolerance for violence against women by their partners and positively sanction abuse of women in a number of situations. It is one thing to recognize the need to challenge these attitudes and norms, however, and quite another to develop a strategic or organizational capacity to do so.

Congressional designation of October as Domestic Violence Awareness Month in 1989 was the first federal recognition that educating the public and changing public attitudes about abuse merited a national focus. Throughout the 1990s, public awareness initiatives focused on getting the word out about the battered women's shelters and available services. Many coalitions sought to adopt this focus at the state and local levels. For example, the Rhode Island Coalition Against Domestic Violence identified the need to focus on advocacy work with the media, the pivotal system in shaping public attitudes. After the RICADV hosted a national conference for domestic violence coalition staff called "Media Matters" in 1992, many coalitions and local domestic violence shelters added full- or part-time staff dedicated to public relations and/or communications work. Just as the local shelters were broadening their service-delivery strategies to better meet the needs of underserved populations, so too were the coalitions broadening their advocacy strategies to look beyond the criminal justice system and have a significant systemic impact on decreasing domestic violence.

Nationally focused domestic violence organizations also adopted public awareness and public relations strategies. The San Francisco–based Family Violence Prevention Fund launched a public awareness campaign called "Coaching Boys Into Men," which focused on working with men to change social norms around domestic violence.[10] The NNEDV coordinated a national Communications Committee, engaged national corporate partners to support the ongoing work of developing national communications strategies and support for coalitions in this area, and worked with the Allstate Foundation and other groups to garner national polling data about perceptions of domestic violence.[11]

One of the most significant changes in the battered women's movement during the 2000s has been to make the prevention of domestic violence an important part of local and national strategies. In collaboration with local school systems, battered women's shelters in dozens of communities now offer classroom programs about nonviolent conflict resolution, dating violence, and abuse prevention targeting students at every level, from preschool to high school. In many districts, shelters also run school-based groups to help youngsters who are at risk of being exposed to domestic violence in their homes develop appropriate safety plans. Several coalitions are also working with their state's Departments of Education and their legislatures to incorporate standards for education about dating violence prevention into school policies or curriculum. Unfortunately, a tragedy is often the trigger that brings the issue to public awareness. This was the case in Rhode Island. After a teenager, Lindsay Burke, was murdered by her boyfriend, the victim's family and local advocates helped to pass the Lindsay Burke Act in 2007. This law requires all school departments to adopt policies designed to strengthen the prevention of dating violence. After giving Ann Burke, Lindsay's mother, the Attorney General's Justice Award, Rhode Island Attorney General Patrick Lynch successfully lobbied the National Association of Attorneys General to put the need for dating violence education on its policy platform.

Complementing pressure to make domestic violence prevention policies a priority within the battered women's movement is a drive to implement and evaluate primary prevention programming. Recognizing the importance of trying to stop domestic violence before it begins, the Centers for Disease Control and Prevention (CDC) took the primary prevention initiative in 2002 and funded efforts by 14 state domestic violence coalitions to prevent first-time perpetration. This program, called DELTA, focuses on reducing risk factors associated with intimate partner violence and promoting protective factors that reduce the likelihood it will occur. Because this program is science based, it has dramatically altered the way coalitions and local programs approach their work, highlighting the need to adopt evidence-based programs and to base prevention planning on behavioral health and social change theories. The hope is that the work of these 14 states and their local communities will benefit the battered women's movement as a whole by demonstrating the importance of an ecological model for prevention that includes individual, relationship, community, and societal factors and their complex interrelationships.[12]

Through the work of the DELTA initiatives and other local prevention programming, the battered women's movement has evolved to include language that would have felt "alien" 20 years ago. The acronym "IPV" (intimate partner violence) is commonly used today, whereas it would have been shunned a couple of decades ago as having been too "medical" in its tone and as not sufficiently targeting violence against women. As one director of a coalition that is immersed in the DELTA program recently stated,

> I've been doing quite a bit of Strategic Planning facilitation with local agencies and community teams, and without exception, prevention has been a vibrant part of the conversation about the future of our movement . . . imagine legislators talking about 'social ecology' when they are evaluating potential prevention initiatives![13]

Another paradigm shift that is taking shape within the battered women's movement involves recognizing the key role of engaging men in the work of ending violence against women. Historically, men have played significant roles in working with violent men as part of the domestic violence movement, often in alliance with local shelters. In Rhode Island, one of the founding member agencies of the RICADV was Brother to Brother, an organization that provided psycho-educational groups for abusive men. One of the earliest organizations that worked with batterers was based in Boston, called Emerge, which still exists and plays a leading role in this area.

Some domestic violence agencies have had men on staff and as volunteers for many years, working in outreach or education programs, helping with child care, in management positions, as board members, or as consultants. One coalition has a male executive director, and the NNEDV has engaged a man as a national spokesperson (Victor Rivers) to raise awareness of the issue from a male perspective. The RICADV elected its first male president of its board of directors 10 years ago. Various coalitions and numerous local programs have initiated campaigns to engage men in the work, such as the "white ribbon campaign" coordinated by Jane Doe, Inc. (the Massachusetts Coalition Against Domestic Violence and Sexual Assault) in 2008.[14] Men are emerging as role models for youth, mentors in local communities, and key advisors in the work to identify strategies to undo the damaging media and cultural fabric that has been established that associates masculinity with abusive behavior and violence.

In addition to emphasizing prevention and including men in the movement, national and local advocates are developing strategies that involve youth. In its DELTA programs and other domestic violence research efforts, the CDC has identified youth as a major population at risk for intimate partner violence as well as a major target for education and intervention. In addition, the Robert Wood Johnson Foundation recently set aside funding to support partnerships between domestic violence organizations, schools, and other youth-focused organizations and help them benefit from each other's expertise. Furthermore, one of the recommendations from a "Decade for Change" conference, organized in 2006 through 2007 by the National Domestic Violence Hotline, was to target prevention efforts toward youth. Suggestions included forming a Youth Advisory Board to help create a national communications campaign targeting youth. Other strategic suggestions that emanated from the conference were utilizing youth-Internet education opportunities, building alliances with stores that are popular with teens, developing peer-to-peer programs that train teens on the issue, creating allies within teen music culture for messaging, and creating partnerships with organizations that appeal directly to teens.[15]

The structure and organizational composition of the battered women's movement have changed significantly over the years to reflect the shifts in programming and strategy I have described. In the early years of the work, the boards of the state coalitions were made up of representatives from local shelters, all women. During the mid- to late 1990s, some coalitions changed their board structure to include prominent members of the public in addition to representatives from member programs, a trend that continues today. These changes reflect the changing landscape of the movement, the need to incorporate diverse voices and experiences in the governance and policy-setting arena, and the much broader public, private, and professional constituencies to which the battered women's movement is now accountable.

Many of the changes seen at the state and national levels began in local communities, where the needs for funding and political support as well as the expansion of program functions beyond emergency shelter and crisis intervention also necessitated the inclusion of parties and voices that were not part of the early movement. Whereas shelters were initially housed in a single facility and lacked the luxury of a distinct administration, let alone separate buildings, it is commonplace today to find that "the shelter" exists at multiple sites, with advocates in many states colocated at child welfare offices, courtrooms, police departments, one-stop justice centers, and so on. Meanwhile, many shelters run support groups for battered women at sites throughout the community, provide professional training as well as education, offer specialized services for children, and engage in community-wide service planning policy advocacy through a coordinated community response that often takes the form of a formal council that may be staffed by a shelter or by one of the new, integrated domestic violence courts. In any case, shelters and coalitions now regularly draw on and continue to work to engage expertise from men, communities of color and other underserved populations, educators, health care providers, corporate leaders, evaluators, researchers, criminal justice professionals, and others in all aspects of their work.

Needless to say, these changes have not come without challenges. One such challenge is figuring out how to address the tension between the need to strengthen and professionalize the movement while at the same time maintaining the integrity of the movement's foundation of social change and its commitment to make the safety and empowerment of battered women its principal goal. Reflecting on this dilemma, Grace Mattern, executive director of the New Hampshire Coalition Against Sexual and Domestic Violence, commented,

> *I believe we've held on to the centrality of victims' voices and experiences in our work, and that's how we'll overcome all the challenges we face—shrinking resources and budget deficits, difficulty retaining staff, attacks by the Mad Dads, professionalization, and becoming too much of a "system." When we remember we came together to do this work as a direct response to women's experiences of abuse and put those experiences back into the center of how we work, then it keeps us honest to all the principles of empowerment that are so key to what we do. We can't be co-opted if we are in it for the passion of making sure women and children are safe, and we know that addressing the trauma at the center of their lives is our best hope for making the world different in the future.* Courtesy of Grace Mattern.

Even as the battered women's movement has developed a more visible national face, the recognition remains widespread that the vitality of state coalitions, like the strength of local programs, requires that the organizational structure they adopt should reflect their unique history and politics and the dynamics of each state and locality rather than some master plan. Some coalition boards are made up entirely of member programs; others use a regional representational model. Some coalitions have designated slots on the Board for marginalized populations, with representation from groups like the Women of Color Task Force, Asian Task Force, Tribal Representatives, Survivors' Task Force, Lesbian Task Force, and Women of Diversity Committee. Some coalitions remain focused solely on domestic violence; others are organized around sexual assault as well as domestic violence. This organizational diversity has not kept the battered women's movement from addressing its overall goal with a unified voice. Sue Else, the current president of the NNEDV, puts it well:

> *The strength of the domestic violence movement comes from a breadth of knowledge and diversity. Though we might have different experiences and viewpoints that drive our individual efforts, we all work toward the common goal of keeping victims of domestic violence safe and providing them the resources to overcome abuse. From local service providers, to state and national organizations, our power lies in our ability to speak in one voice in order to create social change for battered women and children.*[16]

In 2001, the NNEDV surveyed representatives from all 50 state coalitions on a range of issues, including policy priorities, organizational structure, staffing patterns, membership, and achievements. Detailed information from the survey is described in the *Handbook of Domestic Violence Strategies*, edited by Albert Roberts. The responses highlighted the rich diversity among coalitions in terms of their operating structures, the range of issues they addressed, and the degree of success they had achieved. Importantly, reported accomplishments extended from successful legislative advocacy and improving the responsiveness of health and legal systems to domestic violence victims, to developing and enhancing domestic violence programs, designing and implementing training and public relations and information campaigns, and improving internal functioning.

The battered women's movement is clearly a "work in progress." Openness to new ways of intervening, providing services, and preventing domestic violence has been a cornerstone of the movement since its onset almost 40 years ago. If it still makes mistakes—some perhaps an inevitable function of growth, some possibly avoidable—the movement has proved capable of learning from mistakes. This ability, along with a continued willingness to "shake the boat" when necessary, is among its greatest strengths. There are few formal mechanisms by which advocates seasoned by 30 or more years of work pass on their accumulated wisdom to a new generation of advocates who bring an impatience for change to the table. Still, these experiences continue to meld in the daily work of providing support to women in trouble and their children, with the new cohort reawakening the optimism of old-timers while the veterans steel the courage of the young for the long march ahead. And, as the voices are heard of youth, of men and boys, of immigrants, of communities of color, of tribal nations, of people with disabilities, of elders or older abused women, and of other distinct and diverse communities, old programs may be replaced by new ones and new roads taken. New leadership and vision will undoubtedly bring us closer to ending violence against women. But how close? Interestingly, despite aging, there appears to be a resurgent commitment to a vision of change from which the battered women's movement was born. As Kristi Van Audenhove described it recently, "Our coalition level focus on prevention has provided an important foundation for re-committing to social justice work. Though dominated by a white male cultural bias, the analysis that has resulted has supported economic justice work, anti-racism work, and work to address gender equality."

Reflections from Susan Schechter that were written in 1982 ring true today:

> *The search for community solutions continues.... Future organizing work will proceed in numerous directions. Ingenuity and perseverance were the calling cards of the first movement activists and will be needed again.... Defeats, although numerous, will never negate the historic creation of so many safe spaces for battered women and their children. As long as women stay organized and visible, the soil for the next generation of activists remains fertile.*[17]

NOTES

1. National Network to End Domestic Violence, *National Census of Domestic Violence Services*, September 25, 2007, http://www.nnedv.org/docs/Census/DVCounts. This total figure includes reports from 69 percent of the existing domestic violence service providers in the country.

2. Quotes and anecdotes recounted in this chapter come from the 27 years of experiences that the author has had working in the field, first as a volunteer advocate, then as a shelter and agency director, and currently as the executive director of a coalition. Confidentiality of all victims is ensured by using different names and shielding any identifying information.

3. S. Schechter, *Women and Male Violence: The Visions and Struggles of the Battered Women's Movement* (Boston: South End Press, 1982), 56.

4. Schechter, *Women and Male Violence*, 21.

5. E. Stark and A. Flitcraft, *Women at Risk* (Newbury Park, CA: Sage, 1996).

6. D. Martin, *Battered Wives* (San Francisco: Volcano Press, 1976), 210–11.

7. A. Roberts, ed., *Handbook of Domestic Violence Intervention Strategies: Policies, Programs and Legal Remedies* (New York: Oxford University Press, 2002), 17–18.

8. From the author's correspondence/conversation with Anne Menard, director of the National Resource Center on Domestic Violence, May 12, 2008. Courtesy of Anne Menard.

9. See National Network to End Domestic Violence, http://www.nnedv.org; and for details on the provisions of VAWA 2005, see http://nnedv.org/docs/Policy/VAWA2005Summary.pdf.

10. See the Family Violence Prevention Fund's Web site for more information on this campaign at http://www.fvpf.org.

11. See the National Network to End Domestic Violence Web site for more information at http://www.nnedv.org.

12. For information about the DELTA primary prevention program, see the CDC's Web site at http://www.cdc.gov/ncipc/DELTA.

13. From communication and conversation with Kristi Van Audenhove, May 13, 2008, Virginia Sexual and Domestic Violence Alliance.

14. See the Jane Doe Web site for information about the white ribbon campaign at http://www.janedoe.org.

15. National Domestic Violence Hotline, *Decade for Change Summit Final Report* (2007), 27.

16. Quote from Sue Else from electronic communications with the author of this chapter, May 11, 2008. Courtesy of Sue Else.

17. Schechter, *Women and Male Violence*, 308–9.

Chapter 3

Changing from Victim to Survivor

Hilary Abrahams

I first met Jeannie and her two sons in an inner-city refuge (shelter) in 2003. She had left an abusive relationship with the father of her youngest child and felt depressed, angry with everything and everybody around her, and that there was no hope for her and her children. She talked to me about how she had felt while in the relationship:

> I reckon I would have either killed myself or killed him. I was that low. I felt like nothing . . . I couldn't even hold my head up on the street. I just felt like . . . I just felt like nothing, and then having someone telling you constantly you're nothing—you've got two different fathers for your kids, no one's ever going to want you. You're nothing, you've got nothing. You know, just destroying you. I mean what he did to me physically I can't even remember.

We met up again four years later. During that time she had had to move on again because of risks to her personal safety, been temporarily rehoused, lost the tenancy because of debts, and was now in a council-run hostel and living on state welfare payments. Life had not gotten any easier, yet her whole attitude had changed:

> She [support worker] really made me believe in myself again. You know what I mean? And mixing with other people that's been in the same situation as yourself. Talking to other people. And then just thinking that life has to go on. It has to go on. Whether you feel great or you feel like . . . you know. It has to go on. And don't get me wrong, sometimes I'll sit here and I'm just crying for the whole day, sometimes the whole weekend. I'm just like 'Oh my God.' But then I just get myself back up. I feel more positive. I just see things differently and I don't . . . like before I used to get angry a lot, quite quick as well and I've just learnt not to. I'm a lot more calmer. I'm not bitter. Before I was bitter, I felt . . . I was quite bitter, angry and bitter and I'm not any more.

Jeannie is typical of the women who have been talking to me over the past few years about their experiences of abuse and the effect it had on them. They told me about the changes they experienced within themselves as they recovered and what they saw as the best ways for others to offer support during this process. This chapter draws on these reflections to look at the reasons women like Jeannie are so down, explore the process of change that led to the "new" person Jeannie and other women became, and identify which approaches have helped women to change so dramatically. Hopefully, you too will hear their voices, as I did.

BACKGROUND

In 2000, I was asked by the Women's Aid Federation of England (whose members are the major providers of services to abused women in England) to look at the practical and emotional support needs of women who had come to refuges from relationships where they had been subjected to physical, sexual, emotional, and other forms of abusive behavior. Early UK research in this area had been designed to show policy makers and the general public why safe houses and support for abused women were necessary. There had been massive social, economic, and legal changes in the position of women generally since these studies had been done. For modern services for abused women to be effective, it was important to understand if the types of support women needed had changed accordingly. I published a book based on this research in 2007.[1] I also interviewed women who had suffered domestic violence and other forms of abuse as part of a government-funded study of supported housing for vulnerable individuals. In all, I heard the stories of 43 women across England—from the inner city to remote rural areas. The youngest was 21 when I first met her; the oldest was 68. They came from a wide variety of social and economic backgrounds and sexual orientations, and varied in their educational achievements and family circumstances. Most of the women were white and born in Britain, but the group also included black British and Asian women as well as women who had come to Britain from China and Europe. Some had physical or sensory impairments; a few had minor learning difficulties. Most of the women (65 percent) had children with them, and several were pregnant at the time of the first interview. I talked to support workers as well; to those who provided general support on practical and emotional levels, to housing and resettlement workers, and to those who provided support within the community and to specialist workers—play workers, children's advocates, and counselors. In carrying out these interviews, the most striking aspect for me was the women's unanimity about what had happened to them, the impact the abuse had, the process of recovery they were going through, and what kinds of support were most helpful.

ISOLATION AND CONTROL

Practically all of the women had suffered physical and sexual abuse, which had often permanently damaged their health and reproductive capabilities. But, like Jeannie, they remembered the emotional abuse most clearly, abuse that had stripped away their personal integrity, confidence, and belief in their own abilities as well as their capacities to conduct the ordinary business of daily socialization. In general, it had been a slow progression, as actions and words that initially seemed like loving possessiveness and care for their safety evolved into total control over every aspect of their lives and thoughts. In her book *Trauma and Recovery*, psychiatrist Judith Herman graphically describes this as a process of being "taken prisoner gradually, by courtship."[2] Women referred to the world "closing in on them" as they became isolated from family and friends. This could involve direct prohibitions, driving them away from others with insults and aggressive behavior, or, more subtly, restrictions on their access to cash or transport, so that visits were impossible. Not being allowed to use the telephone to make calls or to answer it if it rang was a common restriction. Sometimes, the instrument would be ripped out to prevent the woman using it at all. Sylvia captured how this process became more devastating over time:

> And I think as the violence and everything progressed I kind of . . . my world closed in and closed in and closed in. And then, unfortunately, outside of the children, he was my total center and yet he was the aggressor. So that's where that kind of became where you didn't speak, you didn't say. And all these things that people say when they see it on TV: 'What did that bloomin' stupid woman put up with that for?' you know. But they don't realize how your world . . . it takes a long time, it's over years, you know. They'll say something about one friend, make that friend feel uncomfortable and they'll drop off and drop off and drop off. And suddenly this center closes down and suddenly the person who's the worst is the only person you have left. So you start living in this kind of walking on eggshells scenario, you know, of just hoping that every day is going to be okay and don't say anything, don't tell anybody. You don't realize it and then when you've come out of it and you look back you think, 'Crikey, why on earth did I ever get to that point?' I'm an intelligent adult. You know, it's not like I'm stupid, it's not like I've got nothing, it's not like I didn't have independence and money and all the things that normal people have. It wasn't that I totally was dependent on him so I didn't dare do anything, you know. But, as I say, it is that shrinking world that is so slow a process, and then suddenly it's imploded on itself and now you've got to start building it back outwards again, you know.

It was not simply close relationships that were affected; connections with the wider community were also restricted or closed off, including interactions with everyone from neighbors to local shopkeepers. Shopping trips were timed, outings allowed only to places selected by the abuser. When women returned home, they would face lengthy interrogations as to whom they saw and what they did and told to provide precise details of every conversation. One woman was prevented from going to the hospital for her regular diabetic checks. Women had to quit their jobs because jealous outbursts and constant surveillance caused them too much embarrassment and shame at the workplace. As with Sylvia, so with many others as well: when supportive networks of friends, co-workers, or family members were shut down, women became more and more dependent on their abuser for communication. But this was almost always negative, involving chronic criticism and name-calling that targeted their appearance, ability, intelligence, education, and skills. Under this barrage of insults, women began to lose confidence in themselves and in their own judgment. Ultimately, they came to see the abuser's truth as their own, his reality as theirs. As they had so often been told, they began to think they were the ones at fault. The resulting feelings of shame and guilt further isolated them, keeping them from confiding in anyone who might have provided a different perspective. Amy said,

> Because you're isolated, you keep going over it, you're blaming yourself all the time. You see the man as the good one. Yeah, he's right. In the end, you are so down you think, well, it is all my fault. So, in the end, you're scared to talk to anyone. And I found myself thinking, they all know. They all know that ... they all think that 'it's my fault.'

In this way, the control originally exercised by the abuser was internalized and reflected back through the woman's own negative thoughts and self-image. Isolated, they had fewer and fewer outlets against which to test this negative self-image, and this destructive process was reinforced by the fear and uncertainty of their daily life.

LIVING IN FEAR

Fear also increased women's isolation. Once the first incident of physical, sexual, or emotional abuse had occurred, women lived in a constant state of anticipatory fear as to what might happen next. Although they might sense that an incident was imminent, it was never possible to predict the exact nature of what would happen or exactly when, or what the outcome would be. As a result, they lost any sense of physical or mental safety and yet had to be constantly "on" and ready for something terrible to happen. When almost anything they did was likely to be regarded as wrong by their abuser, there could never be a stable routine or framework for their everyday lives; no certainty, except the certainty of abuse. Even when they tried to please him, for instance by correcting a behavior that had been the butt of attacks in the past, the criticism would simply shift to a new ground. With this constant fear pervading their lives, women felt unable to trust that people around them would behave in a consistent and predictable way or would understand what was happening to them. Moreover, they felt less and less confident that anything outsiders would say or do could make a difference in their situation, further isolating them from potential sources of individual or professional support. Not only was their self-confidence significantly diminished, but also many women lost their sense of personhood, the feeling that they had their own ideas, ideals, or life projects. Perhaps the saddest thing about this situation was the way in which personal hopes and aspirations, the spiritual dimension of life, became crushed under the weight of emotional abuse. They no longer felt like persons with a future of their own or who could determine their future. Two lines of a poem Amalie wrote, expressing her sense of this deeper loss, still linger in my mind:

He took my hopes and my dreams
and my reach for the stars

As the abuse continued, women's confidence and self-respect for themselves was eroded further, until they no longer felt worthy even to exist. Barbara, who had endured emotional abuse for decades, spoke for many others when she said, "You have so many years of being told you're nothing—and you believe it." All that remained was the basic instinct to stay alive—to obtain food, water, shelter, and clothing. Even this posed stark alternatives for some women. Helga explained the choices: "I went through this for so many years, thinking I could either get beaten to death in a warm house or freeze to death on the street with nowhere else to go."

Yet even at this rock bottom, women did not see themselves as helpless. They clung tenaciously to survival, doing whatever they could to protect themselves and their children, within the narrow space they had to maneuver. As Sylvia said, they "walked on eggshells," monitoring their own behavior to avoid causing conflict and trying to defuse potentially dangerous situations, please and satisfy their abuser, and keep the home together. Whenever it was possible they tried to maintain links to others, using considerable ingenuity to cover their tracks and avoid confrontation. Recent UK research has shown that the intuitive assessment by women of the risk to themselves and their children and of alternative courses of action, such as leaving, are likely to be substantially accurate and need to be taken fully into account by any supporting agencies.[3]

A WAY OF UNDERSTANDING

The mental effects of abuse are often hard to discern, particularly for outsiders who have not been abused themselves. As Hayley told me, "You look alright, you look like you're alright and you're really a strong person. You know? But inside of yourself, you're not. But people can't see that." Nevertheless, chronic emotional abuse, whether alone or in conjunction with other forms of abuse (physical, sexual, financial, and so on), severely damages emotional health and mental well-being. Feminist mental health practitioners have argued that the physical and mental effects of domestic violence are similar to those reported by combat troops, hostages, and survivors of major disasters who carry a diagnosis of posttraumatic stress disorder (PTSD). PTSD, together with battered woman syndrome (BWS), has been successfully used, both in the United Kingdom and in North America, as part of a defense strategy by women who assaulted or killed an abusive partner, typically after years of enduring his abuse. Because the symptoms of BWS or PTSD may mimic the presentation of other psychiatric problems, these diagnoses can help practitioners understand that the woman's problems have an external cause and that advocacy as well as support and safety are critical pieces of the treatment process. They may also help her access needed mental health or professional services.

Without denying the value of the diagnosis of PTSD for the comparatively small number of women who need professional mental health services, it can be argued that there are major disadvantages in applying a blanket diagnosis of PTSD to all women experiencing abuse. Despite its good intentions, the term can be stigmatizing, both because many clinicians still identify it as a traditional psychiatric disease and because the woman herself and her immediate circle may interpret it as reinforcing the message that she is the one with the problem. Martha, for one, was far from happy at having to take this route: "It can be depressing to feel that you have to be diagnosed with PTSD in order to get help." It may also be seen as a drawback by potential employers or housing and other agencies, who might not fully understand the problems caused by situations of domestic abuse but can grasp the possible implications of a medical diagnosis. Significantly, it might also adversely affect legal and judicial proceedings for custody or residence orders. And many women, perhaps most, who suffer emotional abuse may never recognize it as reaching a level where they feel the need to seek assistance from mental health professionals. Indeed, this was true of all the women who talked to me, although they were well aware of the effect that abuse had had on their mental well-being. "He just messed with my head so much" was how they put it, but they did not see themselves as having the sort of mental health problems requiring professional medical intervention, nor did they want to become part of the medical system. This is in line with the point made by Herman that the majority of individuals who have endured traumatic events do not have access to or requirement for specialist medical help. They recover by "drawing on their individual strengths and the supportive relationships naturally available to them in their own communities."[4]

An alternative way of understanding the mental effects of abuse that may be more appropriate for the majority of women is to look at Abraham Maslow's ideas on human need.[5] While reserving the medical approach for those women who need it, using this paradigm captures the destructive effects of abuse in a way that is consistent with Herman's dictum, that women become the authors of their own recovery.

A close associate of Carl Rogers, a psychologist who founded person-centered counseling, Maslow believed that people have higher natures and needs and a spiritual dimension to their lives and that these needs formed a hierarchy that human beings wanted to move through. At the very base were the physiological needs that were needed for survival (food, water, clothing, and shelter). Once at least

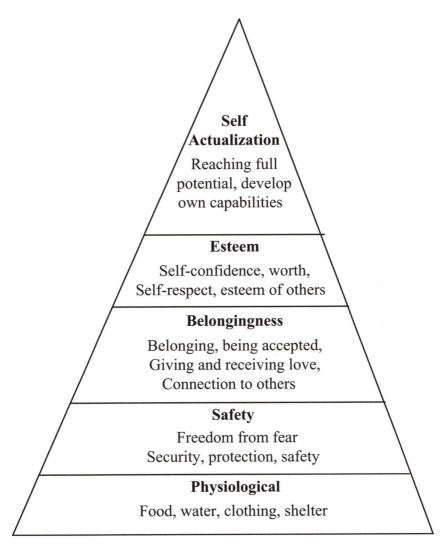

Figure 3.1. Maslow's Hierarchy of Human Need (1987, first published 1954). Based on the concepts in A. Maslow, *Motivation and Personality*, 3rd ed. (London: Harper and Row, 1954).

part of these needs had been met, individuals moved up to the next level of need and actively looked for some degree of safety and freedom from fear. After this had been supplied, they wanted to belong to a community, to connect, and to be accepted by those around them. With these needs satisfied to some degree, they wanted to experience feelings of self-respect, esteem, and self-worth, and, finally, they looked to develop their own abilities and inner capabilities. This hierarchy of human need is often described as a pyramid of building blocks. What stops people reaching upward like this are the social and economic disadvantages they encounter and past experiences that have blocked or damaged their innate ability to take action for themselves. For women who experience domestic violence, as their accounts show, abuse demolishes this pyramid by denying them hopes and dreams, destroying their sense of self-esteem and self-worth, isolating them from the community around them, and removing any sense of safety. Each of the building blocks are pulled out by their abuser, leaving only the basic survival needs, and for some women, even these could be at risk.

Reframing the effects of domestic abuse in this way removes any hint of stigma associated with labeling all women as suffering from PTSD or BWS. Instead, this approach holds that they are reacting in a completely understandable way to what has happened to them and that this reaction—isolation, loss of confidence, and fear and anxiety around personal safety—can make it more difficult for them to take action to end or fundamentally change their predicament. Using this concept also recognizes the positive way in which women do, indeed, try to take action to protect themselves and their children and to reach out to others, within the limits they face. It emphasizes self-help and the support role of the community in maintaining and meeting the needs of the individual and assisting them in rebuilding their lives. This role, which was of utmost importance to the women who talked to me, is played down in medical discourse.

GETTING OUT

To the uninitiated, there is an automatic connection between the severity of abuse women suffer and the reasonableness of their just leaving. In fact, in the face of the harms abuse inflicted on their confidence, personhood, and power of independent thought, making the decision to leave was extremely difficult for the women I interviewed. Indeed, leaving is often not the safest option. Homicide statistics in both the United States and the United Kingdom show that most women are killed by partners or ex-partners and that the danger is greatest at the point of leaving, as he tries to stop her, or just afterward, as he tries to find and punish her for doing so. Nor does the abuse necessarily stop even after a successful escape. For a substantial minority of women, verbal, emotional, or sexual abuse, stalking, and harassment may continue for years. This is particularly likely when there are issues around contact with any children of the relationship. Not only is this an opportunity to harass and abuse the mother, but also it may be seen as an opportunity to exercise final control over the family by killing the children, their mother, and possibly themselves. Women were well aware of the hidden agenda that might lie behind an abuser's (seemingly) natural wish to see his own children. Sally talked of the sheer terror and panic she felt when a contact visit was due: "I hate it. I really do hate it," she told me. "He makes me feel really ill when I see him. The night before, I can't sleep. I feel so ill and that."

For the women who talked to me, there were three main triggers for leaving: an awareness of imminent danger to their lives, an overwhelming feeling of anger, or the realization that the time had come to leave, that things were not going to change, despite all the efforts they had made to make the relationship work. Maddy talked me through her sudden decision to leave after 12 years of abuse:

Well, I'll tell you what happened. I went to work and ... he was being a bit ... funny, at the time. So I went to work. Well, they'd see'd me with a few bruises— I've been to work nearly three years and they've see'd me black and blue and they've said, 'It's about time you did summat about it.' I wouldn't take no notice. So, everyone said it was up to me. So I made my mind up on that particular day. So I went to work, did me work, came ... and I think they'd got an inkling that I weren't coming back. But it wasn't for them to say. So I went home, I got the kids, he was fast asleep. I'd got money upstairs from work. I just took me bag, the kids, no clothes nor anything. I walked. I had a mobile phone and I rang my oldest son and I said, 'I've walked out. I'm going.'

This was the first time most of the women I talked with had come to a refuge. Some had stayed for brief periods with family or friends, usually to shock the abuser into realizing what his behavior was doing and in the hope that he would change. This hope had not been realized and they had now decided that more decisive action was needed. Others had left several times previously, then returned, either because they believed their abuser had changed or because they felt overwhelmed by the obstacles they faced in trying to live independently. Still, they told me, each reversal had steeled their confidence in themselves and their abilities. This, they hoped, would be their final exit. Keira, whose last decision to leave had been in response to an impulse of anger, reflected on how she had changed with each refuge visit:

It was a long time. It wasn't the first refuge I'd been in, it was probably the fourth. But I knew, this time, I was ready to move on and make a life of my own. Several years ago, again with the younger children, I'd moved into a refuge and at that time I wasn't ready to move on. I think I knew that when I went. But this time ... You have to be ready yourself, don't you? I'd been in this violent relationship for

30 years. No one can tell you. You have to be ready in your own thoughts to do it. I think what it was, because I had become a different person.

It is not simply the physical aspects, the mechanics of leaving, that are hard to manage. It is also facing the prospect of material, emotional, and personal loss on a massive scale, loss that is likely to affect the family adversely for many years to come. On a material level, this might include a home that you have struggled against the odds to keep together, a regular income, and most of your possessions, right down to small personal items that can never be replaced—family photos, a CD that recalled a special occasion, a child's drawing. "When my little boy was about a year," said Jenny, "he did a little drawing and we had it, actually, up on the wall in a little frame. I'd love to have that. But it's gone."

On an emotional level, the immediate loss was that of the relationship, in which feelings toward the abuser might well be confused and difficult to understand. Many women still felt love for the individual who had abused them. Charmain explained how she had had to separate her loving feelings if she was ever going to get out of the relationship alive. "I kept saying to myself, 'I hate him.' I loved him but I hated him. I shoved the love to one side and kept thinking to myself, 'I hate him, I hate him. I'm getting out of here now.'" There could be other emotional losses as well, including breaking ties with older children because they had either adult lives of their own or needs that dictated staying in the family home. Pets who had to be left behind were a further cause of anguish, as were links to any remaining support networks. For many women, this had to include their parents or other immediate family members. It might be too dangerous for the woman, or for her family, to communicate for years to come, lest the abuser be alerted to where she was by a chance remark. Often, breaking off contact was motivated by a desire to protect the family from attack or harassment. As Tara explained, "They're getting on, do you know? They don't need the stress and strain and that. My dad is in bad health and that." And underlying these emotional leave takings, there was also the loss of a known environment—streets, parks, and houses they knew, however dangerous the familiar had now become for them. Women often sought safety by traveling considerable distances within the United Kingdom, but this meant adapting to a new area with new customs and probably a different dialect.

The women had already lost so much. These losses only come into perspective when we trace the development of control over their lives, their isolation from potential support, their mounting fear and uncertainty about their future, and the destruction of personal integrity. Even at their lowest point, however, the women I interviewed were trying to reclaim their lives and to keep going in the hope that things would improve. Making the decision to leave meant incurring further loss and hardship for themselves and their children. Yet, in listening to their stories, it was possible to see how, gradually, their attitudes and outlook were beginning to change.

THE JOURNEY OF RECOVERY

Many of the women saw this process of change as a journey, one that they knew was going to be difficult. Liz was being very realistic when she described it as "a long, hard road to go by." As they talked about what was happening to them as a process of emotional suffering and immense loss, I realized that, after leaving, they went through a process of recovery similar to that following bereavement. For those grieving the loss of a loved one, three phases to this process have been identified, each with different practical and emotional tasks and support needs: the initial shock, a period of transition and adjustment, and then the slow rebuilding of a new way of living.[6] The same phases appear to occur for abused women escaping to safety. To identify these phases in this context, I have called them reception, recognition, and reinvestment.

Phase 1: Reception

For women who left an abusive relationship, the initial phase started as they came to the refuge. Often they had only what they could carry, sometimes only the clothes they and the children were wearing. The effort of leaving and reaching a place of safety exhausted them, physically and mentally. They described being in a state of shock and feeling confusion and numbness, as if they were in a movie. Barbara said it was "very strange and very weird and very, very surreal. Like being in a Ken Russell film. You know, floating through it." This phase might last for days, weeks, and sometimes months after arrival and was experienced equally by women who had been to a refuge before and those who had come for the first time.

In addition to all the emotional turmoil they were feeling, they had to handle the practical activities of settling in, registering with the relevant authorities, and claiming benefits. This was extremely difficult for women who had not been allowed to act independently for some time. Although they needed intensive support and advocacy, their isolation made them reluctant, even fearful, to reach out.[7] Simply being in a place where the abuser could not get to them was crucial to starting the process of trust and recovery. Equally important to their sense of mental safety was the support of those around them. Harriet explained how the approach of the refuge workers helped give her the space and time she needed to take in all that had happened to her:

I was very emotionally bruised, let alone physically, and I felt that I'd arrived here and all the women that worked here just . . . just sort of picked me up and looked after me, really.

Support from the other residents also helped women realize they were not abnormal, weak, or stupid, as they had been told. This could be exhilarating. Val told me, "It was like a sigh of relief when I came from that house and came here and knew that there was other people in the same boat as me, that I could talk to."

Phase 2: Recognition

In time, women moved into a transitional phase that I have called recognition, in which they gradually came to terms with what had happened and recognized the need to take responsibility for themselves and their children. Looking ahead to an independent future was daunting. On a practical level, there were long-term decisions to make—finding accommodations and new schools, registering for medical services, initiating legal proceedings, and preparing to move into a strange new community. At the same time, they had to deal with the lingering emotional problems from the abusive relationship and from the losses, some temporary, some permanent, that these women suffered as a result of leaving. If they had initially felt numb, now their emotions felt raw and painful, with alternating waves of anger and sadness that could come on without notice. Even events they knew were trivial could set off these waves of feelings, overwhelming them, and making them feel fearful and out of control. Jenny felt exasperated by her own reactions:

It can be something and nothing. You might burn your tea or something and that could be it. You just feel, 'Oh God,' you know. It can be the smallest things, really . . . sets you into feeling very down.

When available, women found it helpful to participate in formal and informal therapeutic groups where they could discuss these issues. Some gained a great deal from formal counseling, although this was not to everyone's liking. Also important in this emotional reconstruction was interaction with others, healing the isolation forced on them during the abuse. At this phase of their process, women discovered it felt as good to give support to others as to receive peer support. Spending time with refuge workers was also very important, and they felt angry if other responsibilities, particularly administrative tasks or meetings, made workers less available to them.

A similar pattern of needing to deal simultaneously with intense emotions and practical difficulties has been associated with bereavement as individuals move between these twin sources of stress.[8] In addition to moving between these two challenges, women also moved forward and backward between the reception and recognition phases.

Sometimes they would stride forward confidently; at other times, the feelings of unreality and loss they had experienced on entering the refuge returned. Maryam explained,

Sometimes I just feel, like, on a high where I just do everything and I do it by myself, with no one's help. And sometimes I feel just on a low, when it's like . . . come on . . . you need that greater . . . push.

In dealing with this situation, workers needed to tread a fine line between encouragement and challenge, supporting independence and self confidence by allowing women to make decisions for themselves, even when they think these decisions are mistaken, but being available should a greater degree of support became necessary. As might be expected, given the pressures of refuge life, it was not always possible to gauge this accurately, and problems frequently arose when women felt they needed more help than workers considered necessary.

Phase 3: Reinvestment

Depending on when suitable housing became available, which might be as soon as three months, or, for some women, almost a year, women moved out of the refuge and needed to detach themselves from their supportive environment. I call this a time of reinvestment, as they turned at least some portion of their energy outward again, toward adapting and solving problems of daily living in their new communities and the society beyond. This period could also be extremely stressful. As a housing worker explained, "We take women so far, we support them so far in this safe environment. But then they go out, and it's cold. And there's no one there." Because of the effects of abuse on their confidence and self-esteem, women felt they needed practical and emotional help in setting up a home, in building bridges to the local community, and in developing new networks of friendship and support, so that they became less dependent on formal help. They wanted to know that support would still be there for them if they had problems they couldn't solve on their own, such as a legal issue or further difficulties with their abusive partner. Even if they never called on the refuge workers again, the knowledge that this support would be there if necessary gave them a feeling of inner strength. Many women told me that this reassurance, in and of itself, was what enabled them to manage alone.

Even with the added complexities of domestic violence, understanding the time spent in a refuge and immediately afterward as analogous to bereavement can help women make sense of what can otherwise feel bewilderingly chaotic and unintelligible. Moreover, like bereavement, the process of leaving an abuser, going to a refuge, and setting up on your own has an end point, the reestablishment of a "normal" identity wherein abuse, while always possible, is not the defining reality of everyday existence. The bereavement framework provides a structure for what can otherwise seem like a formless package of needs and support, in which the experience of abuse and the process of recovery can be located. It helps service providers and funders recognize that the needs for support will change over time, that emotional as well as practical help is needed, and that there are recognizable outcomes when it is reasonable to shift an investment of resources to those at an earlier stage of the process. However, to be complete, this framework has to include a more nuanced understanding of what support in the context of this staged process actually entails if residents are to transition from loss to recovery successfully.

REBUILDING THE ABILITY TO COPE

Listening to the voices of abused women is key if service agencies, refuges, and other community-based organizations are to serve victims and their families more effectively. I asked women to tell me what it was about their service encounters that most helped them work through their difficulties and move forward with their lives. Practical support, information, and advocacy were all regarded as necessary and helpful, but it was less tangible and measurable inputs that received the highest ratings, and there was no doubt about what these were. Amazingly, wherever I went, the women named the same six factors and rated them identically. Safety was the number one priority. They were clear that this meant not only physical safety but also mental security and a need to feel able to trust those around them. The remaining five factors were rated equally in terms of importance to them: respect, being believed, a nonjudgmental approach, time to talk and be heard, and peer support.

Being treated with respect was crucial in rebuilding self-worth, but was often very hard for women to accept since it was not something they were accustomed to, either from their abuser or, unfortunately, from many of the agencies they had approached for help. Many women had forgotten, if they ever fully understood, that they deserved respect whatever their situation. Barbara explained the problem:

> *People treating you as though you're a worthy person, that's really been something I found very, very difficult to get my head around ... that I am somebody that's worth being here, kind of thing. You get sort of emotional ... that's a shock and the fact that you're actually a worthy person and that your ideas and ideals matter and are important. And, you know, the respect.*

Respect meant more than simply "being nice." It involved treating women as responsible members of society, able to make their own decisions. This meant being open and honest, giving information about what was going on, and fully explaining choices that had to be made, even when the truth was likely to be unpalatable. Leanne appreciated this: "Other people sort of go behind your back, but they've always been up-front with me, told me exactly what they think, laid the ground rules down." Being believed, listened to nonjudgmentally, and trusted were also attitudes the women found unfamiliar, again largely because of their experiences of abuse and because of how they had been received by others to whom they had turned for support, professionals as well as some family members and friends. These facets of their reception helped to rebuild the trust in others that had been eroded by abuse, as well as their trust in themselves, and encouraged them to model nonjudgmental listening in their interactions with others in the refuge as well as with their children. Realizing they could say or do things that would not elicit a derogatory or humiliating response made them more able to be more honest and open about their situation and needs, facilitating more appropriate service and support.

Simply having the space and time to talk with someone really listening helped to end the isolation imposed during the abuse and so was another key element of support. Women highlighted three strands to these interactions. First were everyday conversations, no matter how seemingly trivial—chats about supermarket bargains or the latest episode of a TV soap opera. Then there was supportive talk—dealing with what had happened, sharing information, discussing options, and planning for the future. These strands were often interwoven: a conversation might turn from casual conversation to serious discussion and back again and might be with workers, specialist workers, or other residents of the refuge whose support, advice, and presence were vital in recovery. Finally, there was what might be termed "healing" talk, in which women reflected on their personal issues and dilemmas. This talk, too, might happen spontaneously in a casual encounter with other residents or workers, wherein a flash of insight might enable a woman to move forward or, more typically, in formal or informal group work or in individual counseling.[9]

Set in the framework of Maslow's hierarchy of need discussed earlier, the factors women identified as key to how they wanted to be supported show the natural progression they make from loss to recovery. For some women, even meeting basic physiological needs could not be taken for granted in the abusive relationship because such activities as eating, sleeping, or even toileting had been rigidly controlled and access used as a reward for compliance. It is commonplace, for instance, for abusive partners to awaken women repeatedly during the night, not let them sleep, force them to stand and be lectured ("the conversation is over when I say it's over"), or to get up to cook meals or provide sex whenever the partner wants. So for some of these women, simply eating, sleeping, and toileting on one's own was a step toward recovery. When I asked Jenny what the best thing about the refuge was, she confirmed how important meeting this need was:

The best thing . . . waking up in the morning without that person laid next to you, waking you up and, you know, go and do my breakfast, go and fetch this and go and fetch that and knowing that the day is just going to get worse and worse and worse and worse. Just knowing that you can wake up without all that.

The next basic building blocks toward recovery were first meeting their needs for physical and mental security and the freedom from fear that they found within the refuge setting, and then meeting their needs to feel loved and the sense of belonging they got from being accepted and connected to others within that safe community. As their sense of safety and belonging grew and they continued to be treated with the respect and the nonjudgmental trust described above, they began to develop a sense of self-worth and self-esteem. Having the space to talk through issues and feel that what they said and who they were mattered bolstered these feelings and gave them the confidence to move on with their lives. Women were realistic about the refuge—it was not all sweetness and light. There were conflicts about cramped conditions, different standards of cleanliness and discipline, and noisy children. Despite this, they recognized that, essentially, it provided a supportive community within which they could regain control over their lives.

It was clear that major changes had been and were taking place in the lives of the women who talked to me. Some of this can be ascribed to their own resilience and resourcefulness, once they were free of the constraints imposed by the abuser. But underlying this was the role of the workers and volunteers in creating an atmosphere in which the self-esteem and confidence described above (Maslow's fourth building block) could be rebuilt through being treated with respect, believed, and not judged. Women, like Jeannie at the beginning of this chapter, were deeply appreciative of their efforts. "They were always there for me" was often said, and Dido went further: "It turned my life around, because they *cared*."

At the apex of Maslow's assessment of human need is the development of the self, what he termed "self-actualization," a stage associated with such traits as creativity, spontaneity, acceptance of self, and a capacity to problem solve. Toward the end of their stay or, in some cases, soon after they had left, many women developed a positive and proactive attitude toward their lives and a palpable respect for themselves as individuals that resonated with this phase of self-development. I've called this stage "realignment," to reflect their changed perception of themselves and their role in society. Lindy was aware of this change in herself:

It's made me find myself, what I want and what I don't want. . . . I'm the boss. I don't know where it comes from, something just appears I think. If I could bottle it, I'd sell it. Yeah!

It seemed that this was, as Maslow suggests, a natural progression for women who had been given time and support to recover from abuse, adjust to a new way of life, and develop their own abilities. Similar personal development and growth of awareness have been noted in other situations where self-help and support groups for women have existed.[10] Recognizing the passage women go through in these situations should help both those going through the process of change and those who support them gauge their progress and adapt expectations and resources needed accordingly.

FIVE YEARS ON

Material from both of these studies provided unique and valuable insights into women's needs. What was missing was any insight into longer-term outcomes. A grant from the British Academy permitted me to reinterview the women I'd talked to originally to see where they are at in their lives, what support they have needed in their new communities, and what they now thought about their time in the refuge. Proceeding cautiously, with the safety for women who have moved out into a new community paramount, we located about half of the original interviewees and talked to the 12 women who responded to the invitation. They gave three main reasons for responding. For some, talking to me again marked the end of a chapter in their lives. I had seen them at perhaps the lowest point of their lives, soon after they had left the relationship, and again as they moved into fresh accommodations. Now they were moving on with their lives and wanted to mark this in some way.

Many also wanted to show me what they had achieved—the effort and ingenuity that had gone into making a pleasant home for themselves and their children. They also wanted to talk about educational achievements, finding a job, holidays, and perhaps a new and nonviolent partner. As Keira told me, "Everything that I wanted to achieve for myself has really happened ... to set up home, to make sure the children are secure and safe and feel happy. That I got my life back on track." And finally, they wanted me to tell other women that they could do it, too; to tell them that, although it was hard work, there was light at the end of the tunnel; and to encourage them to keep going. There were also a very small number of women who were still struggling to make a successful transition to a new life. They wanted to share their experiences so that other women could learn from them. Amber saw this clearly:

> I will not wreck this experience. I have to make something good come out of it, otherwise I suffered for no reason and that's not acceptable to me. I lost so much and it's ... yeah, I can't waste that experience, I do have to do something with it. And right now, I'm not able to, but you can. So I have to share anything that could be put to use for other people.

Not all of the women I met again had been permanently rehoused—some were still in temporary accommodations, and others had made several moves before settling in what they hoped would be a permanent home. Often they had had very little choice about the housing they were offered, the standards were variable, and they often had to battle to get basic repairs and maintenance. Although independent living was scary, having a place of their own, where they could close the door and feel safe, was very important. "A front door of my own" was a phrase they often used to convey this sense of safety and separateness. Instead of being the place where they lived in fear, trapped by their abuser, it was a creative space where they could express their new sense of autonomy. These expressions often reflected a unique facet of how their abusive partner had controlled them. Color was very important in Briony's transformation, for instance, because her partner had had firm ideas about what color was appropriate in the home—everything was painted in magnolia. Briony's response was to turn her new home into a rainbow palette of every shade—except magnolia!

A quarter of the women were economically active, and two others were going to school or in job training. Some were limited by ill health, the lack of affordable child care, and negotiating the complexities of the state welfare system. Others reported that they had decided to stay home out of concern for their children, who had witnessed and sometimes experienced abuse and who needed the reassurance that their mothers would be there for them. Many of these women said they would return to work only when the children were less traumatized. A number of them commented that they would have liked support for their children, as well as for themselves, after leaving the refuge, but this was rarely available or accessible. For most of them, money was a continuing problem as was managing on a tight budget, particularly with growing children. Some had taken on debt through trying to make a nice home for themselves and their children, or to provide them with the small treats, holidays, and the additional things that their peers were enjoying.

In the first round of interviews, the women had been unable to look beyond day-to-day survival, the next task or battle, and sometimes even the next day. The follow-up interviews revealed women who felt more positive about their lives, had gained in self-confidence, and were better able to cope with problems. More importantly, most had plans for the future. Illustrating this new capacity to look beyond their personal or immediate situation was that 10 of the 12 women were working to help others in some way. This might involve paid or voluntary work with disadvantaged or vulnerable groups and individuals, mentoring young people, or actively sharing their experiences with other women, helping them to identify what was happening to them and to take action. They didn't make a big deal out of this, but it was clear that it was important to them as a way of giving something back.

Their past still casts a shadow over their lives. For instance, safety remained a major concern—even those who had changed their names or moved long distances away felt fear and anxiety on occasion, and they all talked of looking over their shoulders when they were out of the house. Most would not go near major city centers or to areas where they felt they might accidentally be seen by their abuser. This limited their ability to move around freely or to contact friends and family in their home areas. All of the women, as Jeannie indicated, felt emotionally vulnerable, tearful, and lonely at times. And there were things about the abusive relationship even when their heads told them that they had done the right thing. Briony knew "if I stayed, I'd be dead," but she also remembered tenderness and a sense of closeness: "I miss the cuddles." The trust and sense of being part of a community that had been destroyed by the abuse and had partially been regained during their time in the refuge were only being restored slowly within their new communities. In part, this was because the women found it very difficult to trust others in any capacity. This affected their relationships with agencies and organizations and also made them immensely wary of forming new intimate relationships. Even those who had found loving and nonabusive partners said that they were still likely to react adversely to any situation that had previously been a trigger for abuse, and this was difficult for the new partner to understand.

MAKING IT

As with the original interviews, support in settling in was seen as the key to making a successful transition to independent living. These needs fell into two areas in particular: preparation for moving out, when the skills for independent living and the emotional challenges they would face could be discussed, and adapting during the first six months of their new lives. Women felt they needed fairly intensive support during this period and wished they had had personal or phone accessibility to this support 24/7. Those who were on their own with their children found that they were able to be strong for them during the day, but that the evenings, after the children were in bed, were a particularly difficult time, with fears and memories flooding in and with no one around to provide support.

Because their confidence had been undermined by the abuse, they also wanted help making contact with other agencies and organizations, rather than simply being given a list of telephone numbers and left to get on with it. The importance of long-term support of this nature and from a variety of sources after being rehoused, or moving back into a community, has also been highlighted by findings from much bigger studies carried out by researchers at the Universities of Warwick and York. When I asked what they valued most about the support they received, the essential elements remained the same as when I had interviewed them earlier: being respected and treated as responsible members of society; agencies and individual workers who took time to listen to their concerns and believe their accounts of their experiences without judging them; and finding supportive friends within the local community. Contact with the women they had met and grown close to in the refuge had gradually diminished as these other friendships developed, or the differences in the way they lived or their approach to disciplining their children became more apparent. If contact continued it was only with one or two women, often by phone or with text messages. But continuing links with the support networks of the refuge *were* vital, particularly the outreach and helpline services. The knowledge that they had been strong enough to leave and stay away, that, if they needed it, support and understanding were available and that they would not be rejected was often what kept them going in the darker moments. Looking back at their time in the refuge, it was clear that it had marked a turning point in their lives; it had given them a safe space to recover, reflect, and begin to restore their sense of personal integrity. Keira said, "It gave me the 10 weeks that I needed to sit back, to reflect on everything that was being done and take a completely different course in my life. Yes, definitely."

CONCLUSION

One question I had in interviewing women was whether their support needs had changed since the early days of the women's movement. The aims of the first refuge workers had been to provide a safe environment and appropriate practical and emotional support to help women to change their lives. I found that very little had altered. There was a need to understand ever more complex statutory regulations and a requirement for greater awareness of the other agencies that now offered support, but it was still the safety of the refuge and the emotional support that enabled women to rebuild their lives. Understanding the process women go through in doing this, the steps through which they reconstruct their sense of self, and their capacity to direct their lives is useful not only to women who enter a refuge and those who choose to remain within their own communities but also to all of those who hope to provide them with support, both in and out of the refuge movement. Knowing that it is possible to recover from the loss incurred when a woman leaves a long-standing abusive relationship may also help those who, for whatever reason, go back to the abusive relationship or choose not to leave.

The joy and relief experienced by women who have taken back control over their lives in this way are best expressed by Sylvia:

I said to my mum, I said, 'I sometimes feel like a spring flower.' She goes, 'Why?' I goes, "Cos the bulb sits in the earth so long closed in on itself and then suddenly Mr. Sun comes out, Mr. Showers comes down and out he bursts with all his glory, you know, and says, 'Hello world, here I am." You know. And I says ... it is that real feeling of rebirth ... and at 46 it's a bit old to be reborn.

ACKNOWLEDGMENTS

My thanks go to the residents and former residents of the UK refuges in York, Birmingham, Penzance, Derby, Devizes, and Alton who took part in this research and who wanted to share their experiences to help other women; to the workers, volunteers, and managers who participated so enthusiastically; and all the members of Women's Aid who helped to shape this research. The original research was a collaborative project between the Violence Against Women Research Group, School for Policy Studies, University of Bristol, and the Women's Aid Federation of England. It was supported by a grant from the Economic and Social Research Council. The evaluation of supported housing was commissioned and funded by the Office of the Deputy Prime Minister, United Kingdom (now the Department for Communities and Local Government). The longitudinal study was supported by funding from the British Academy (grant no. SG 41644). The quotations from interviews and the notes to this chapter are reproduced with kind permission of Jessica Kingsley, Publishers.

NOTES

1. H. Abrahams, *Supporting Women after Domestic Violence: Loss, Trauma and Recovery* (London: Jessica Kingsley, Publishers, 2007). Reproduced with kind permission of Jessica Kingsley, publishers.

2. J. Herman, *Trauma and Recovery*, 2nd ed. (London: Pandora, 2001), 82.

3. A. Robinson, "Risk Assessment and the Importance of Victim Intuition," *SAFE: The Domestic Abuse Quarterly* 21 (Spring 2007): 18–21.

4. J. Herman, *Trauma and Recovery*, 2nd ed. (London: Pandora, 2001), 241.

5. A. Maslow, *Motivation and Personality*, 3rd ed. (1954; reprint, London: Harper & Row, 1987).

6. C. Murray Parkes, M. Relf, and A. Couldrick, *Counselling in Terminal Care and Bereavement* (Leicester, UK: British Psychological Society, 1996); and S. Shuchter and S. Zisook, "The Course of Normal Grief," in *Handbook of Bereavement: Theory, Research and Intervention*, ed. M. Stroebe, W. Stroebe, and R. Hansson (Cambridge: Cambridge University Press, 1993).

7. Advocacy can have multiple meanings, depending on its context. As the term is used here, advocacy means acting from a belief that an abused woman is entitled to support from a variety of organizations, agencies, and statutory

bodies; that she may not, for a variety of reasons, have the knowledge, expertise, or confidence to fight for her rights or to receive a fair hearing; and that it is the advocate's responsibility to work with the woman to remedy this situation and provide additional impetus.

8. M. Stroebe and H. Schut, "The Dual Process Model of Coping with Bereavement: Rationale and Description," *Death Studies*, no. 23 (1999): 197–224.

9. "Counseling" is used here to describe a formal, explicit, and agreed upon relationship between two people to meet, in private, at set times, within clear boundaries and with a mutual understanding of confidentiality, to work on specific aims connected with self-understanding and personal growth. Counselors are usually trained and belong to a professional body with a code of ethics to which they are expected to adhere.

10. M. Hester with J. Scott, *Women in Abusive Relationships: Groupwork and Agency Support* (Sunderland: University of Sunderland, 2000).

Chapter 4

Evaluating Community-Based Services

Cris M. Sullivan
Tameka L. Gillum

Although somewhat difficult to believe today, community-based services designed specifically to assist women with abusive partners were rare to nonexistent in the United States before the mid-1970s. During those early years, if battered women fled their homes they generally found themselves in the same shelters as catastrophe victims, alcoholics, and all other homeless individuals because their only options for shelter were the Salvation Army, church homes, and shelters for homeless people. These assistance centers not only were few and far between but also were often full and rarely made provision for children. Furthermore, health controls of infectious diseases were few, most of the shelters included men, and often the shelters were unsafe. Most were also insensitive to the needs of women with abusive partners, often blaming women for their victimization.[1]

In the United States, the first shelters specifically for women with abusive partners developed out of the feminist movement of the 1970s, during which time consciousness-raising groups led to women talking, often for the first time, about the abuse they were experiencing in their homes. Feminists, community activists, and formerly battered women began organizing to develop new ways to meet the needs of battered women and to define the problem of domestic violence. Early shelters often involved no more than women opening their homes to battered women and their children, and none relied on governmental funding. Later came shelters that often shared facilities with local YWCAs or utilized institutional settings such as motels or abandoned orphanages. Many of these shelters were in large, older buildings where women and children often shared space with other women or families because of limited space. The average shelter capacity of the early facilities was 15, and the average length of stay was two weeks. By 1980, 65 percent of shelters received some government funds, usually in the form of grants through the Comprehensive Employment and Training Act (CETA).

Times have certainly changed since those early years. Today, there are approximately 3,000 domestic violence programs across the United States and approximately 3 million women and children receive services from community-based shelter programs annually. Funded largely by federal, state, and local dollars as well as private contributions, most of these programs provide emergency shelter, 24-hour crisis lines, and numerous support services. Unfortunately, the number of programs available is still much lower than the need, with the discrepancy between need and availability greatest in urban areas and disadvantaged communities. Although shelter funding has increased substantially in recent years, particularly since the original passage of the Violence against Women Act (VAWA) in 1994, many shelters still struggle financially to remain open. For every woman who receives shelter, another is turned away for lack of space.

THE SHELTER EXPERIENCE

Although domestic violence shelter programs are not all alike, most programs share certain basic characteristics. Typically, a shelter stay begins with a telephone call to a local shelter or crisis "hotline," either from a woman who has just been assaulted or fears an assault or from a service worker at a facility that screens for domestic violence. Since a woman can only call when it is safe to do so, the proximity of a call to an actual threat or assault varies. The hotline volunteer or staff person who answers the call is trained to quickly assess the emergent nature of the situation, to provide emotional support, and to arrange immediate assistance for the caller. This might mean coming to the shelter, but it could also entail receiving medical attention at a local hospital or going to the home of a neighbor, friend, or relative.

If, after hearing the worker's assessment and the conditions of a shelter stay, the woman decides shelter is the best option, arrangements are made for her to get there safely. Few shelters pick up women at their homes because doing so could endanger both the woman and the worker. However, some women do not own or have access to cars and may also not have money for public transportation. In these cases, arrangements can be made for pickup. Because of safety concerns, many shelters will only meet callers outside their homes. Others have agreements for transport with bus or cab companies. In some communities, police will make emergency pickups.

Most women choose to enter shelter programs only as a last resort. The woman may have experienced a traumatic event and be suffering both physical and emotional pain. If she has children, she is trying to comfort them and think of their needs as well as her own. Few women look forward to entering a new environment that is often crowded with strangers, involves living collectively with many other women and children, offers little to no privacy, and includes numerous restrictions that come with such a living condition. If they can stay with friends or relatives, secure their own homes so that they feel safe living there, or afford to move either temporarily or permanently, these choices are generally deemed more desirable and less traumatic for women and their children. Unfortunately, many women lack the social and economic resources to choose any of these options, and for them a shelter is their best alternative.

Policies Regarding Adolescent Boys

Shelter programs differ in their policies regarding allowing women's adolescent children to stay as residents as well. Although most shelters allow all children younger than ages 12 or 14 years to stay with their mothers, some ask that women find other accommodations for their male adolescents. This regulation was created for a number of reasons. First, some boys have already grown quite tall and muscular by early to mid-adolescence and look more like men than children, frightening some residents. While most adolescent males pose no threat, some have a history of violence against their mothers or against other women. In some cases, shelters have created special facilities to house adolescent males or can place families with adolescent males in a free-standing apartment or motel room.

Rules regarding the older male children of residents illustrate a general dilemma to all shelters—how to balance the safety needs of residents while respecting and preserving the integrity of the mother and her children. One approach is to deal with situations on a case-by-case basis, talking directly with the adolescent male (who may actually be happier to stay with friends or relatives) and making exceptions to the rule when enforcing it means a woman will simply not come.

Other Shelter Rules

The "typical" domestic violence shelter resident is younger than 35 years of age, with two children, little income, and few options. When she arrives at the shelter she is likely to be assigned to a room with at least one other woman and her children. Bathrooms are often shared, and residents are expected to complete household chores to keep the shelter running smoothly. These chores might include cooking, vacuuming, dusting, or helping with child care. Women are responsible for the whereabouts of their children at all times, with some shelters providing more respite from constant child care than others. Typically, children have bedtimes and adults must be in the shelter by a certain time at night unless they call and notify the staff. This way staff know if beds are available when new women call needing help.

While some rules are no doubt necessary to accommodate communal living arrangements for a diverse array of families, many shelters are now reexamining how their rules may make women's lives unnecessarily difficult or might result in women being denied services they desperately need. For example, many shelters will deny services to women who admit to having an alcohol or drug problem, or who suffer from some form of mental illness. While these decisions have been made to consider "the greater good" of all shelter residents, this has also meant that some of the women with the most complex needs are being denied services that could keep them safe.

Rules governing day-to-day living in the shelter can also prove more detrimental than helpful. For example, some shelters mandate that women get out of bed at a particular time, participate in mandatory shelter services, and complete chores in a particular way at a particular time. Whatever their original intent, these rules can also have had the unintended consequence of making women feel controlled rather than empowered. In response to this concern, at least one shelter in the United States has only one rule: "If it's illegal out there, it's illegal in here." All other rules are negotiated by those living in the shelter at any time, with input and support from staff.

Assistance Received

The typical maximum length of stay at a domestic violence shelter in the United States has been 30 days, although most programs offer extensions as needed and many are now moving to longer stays given the lack of housing and other resources available in communities. During their stay, women are provided with much more than beds, meals, and laundry facilities. "Counselor advocates" work with women to identify and meet the family's unmet needs. This might include making arrangements with their children's school, negotiating a leave from work, finding employment or training opportunities, or obtaining health care. Women are also informed about their legal rights and are assisted in obtaining protection orders and legal assistance, if desired. Most shelters also run educational as well as support groups, where women receive both factual information about available services and a conceptual framework—such as the Power and Control Wheel—to help them understand what they've been through. These formal sessions are complemented by the informal opportunities to talk with other women that arise in the normal course of a day. Safety planning is also a core service offered to women and their children in a shelter.

Residents themselves rank domestic violence shelter programs as one of the most supportive, effective resources for women with abusive partners. Most programs provide all services free of charge or at minimal cost and are philosophically committed to empower and respect women. More and more communities are recognizing the importance of domestic violence shelter programs and are either establishing or expanding such services in their communities.

Although shelters receive high "effectiveness" ratings in general from their residents, not all women feel that shelters are options for them, others are denied services (often because of mental health or substance abuse issues), and some are distrustful of the experiences they might have there. Lesbian women, for example, are much more likely to have negative shelter experiences and/or to believe that shelters are for heterosexual women only. If lesbians are less likely to report discrimination by staff or residents today than in the early days of the shelter movement, certain lesbians—those identified as playing the "male" role in a relationship, for instance—still report discrimination. Others fear shelters would be unsafe because their abusers, also being women, could gain entry into the shelters more easily than could male batterers. Finally, the distinctive dynamics of abuse in lesbian relationships are often not understood even by well-meaning shelter staff, leading to inappropriate services (see the chapter by Ristock in this volume). These issues of safety and discrimination are beginning to be addressed in many shelters, and a limited number of services have been developed that target lesbian survivors. However, the complexity of the problem still makes it difficult for most lesbian survivors to receive adequate assistance.

Two other groups that are underserved by shelters are abused women younger than age 20 and older women. This reflects in part the failure of shelters to accommodate the special needs of these populations and in part the perception by these groups that shelters are not for women "like me." Although domestic violence may actually be more common against younger women than any other group, teens 16 to 18 often fall between the cracks because they are too young for adult protective services, yet too old to be protected by child welfare, even though they may technically be the responsibility of Child Protective Services. But teens younger than age 18 are excluded by law from shelter in many states unless they are legally emancipated or have a child. Even when they are technically eligible, older teens do not access shelter services for a host of reasons. They may not identify as being "battered" or "abused," they may assume that shelters are for married or cohabiting women only, or they may believe that their abuse will not be taken as seriously as abuse against older women. There are also special problems because they may still be in school. Safety planning with teens has become a regular part of many shelter services, but many gaps persist.

The problems facing older battered women who try to access service are also widespread. In some cases, the same barriers apply to older women that limit shelter use by lesbian women and teens. They may not identify themselves as "battered," assume the shelter is for younger women with small children, or be unaware that shelters exist since services were nonexistent when they were younger.[2] Some may have more embarrassment or shame about discussing their abuse because of their membership in a generation that didn't talk about such things as freely. Other barriers reflect the limits of shelter programs. Some shelters are not fully accessible or otherwise able to cope with the special health or physical ability needs of older women. As importantly, services suited to younger women (such as job training or receipt of welfare) may be inappropriate for older women; levels of noise or activity in the facility may make older women uncomfortable; physical or mental conditions may limit their ability to complete work assignments; the time limits on a shelter stay may be too short to resolve the more complex problems presented by older women; and the substance of support groups for younger women may not apply to the experience of older women. In Wisconsin and several other states, shelter programs have partnered with advocates from the Office of Aging to form multidisciplinary teams that greatly enhance the appropriateness of service to older battered women, leading to a substantial increase in shelter utilization by this age group.

From the start of the battered women's movement, women of color have used shelters at a higher rate than white women. This utilization reflects a number of factors, including the higher poverty rate in the United States for women of color, greater rates of physical violence in low-income communities, the location of many shelters in inner-city neighborhoods, and the dearth of housing and other alternatives for low-income women of color. Nevertheless, some communities of color have had more difficulty accessing shelters than others, and some women of color, regardless of age, sexual orientation, or ethnicity, also hesitate to use shelters that are predominantly staffed by white women. While the shelter movement has struggled to overcome its race bias almost from the start, women of color are still underrepresented in leadership positions at shelters as well as on the staff at many facilities.

Language barriers remain a major barrier for women seeking shelter, as do shelter policies that feel more comfortable to those from the majority culture (e.g., chores needing to be done at specific times and the ban on corporal punishment of children). Migrant women are often working far from their homes and face multiple language, cultural, and structural barriers preventing their use of shelter programs. They are by necessity very transient and unable to stay in one location for an extended period of time without losing their livelihood. Their children often work alongside them and may be prevented from fleeing with women by the abusive partners.

Immigrant women face language, cultural, and sometimes legal barriers to accessing services. In addition, immigrant women may face dietary problems in shelters and may also fear that their privacy will be compromised by shelter staff from their communities. Many women have reported that when resources were not respectful of their ethnic, cultural, or religious background, they either did not use the services or used them for only a brief period of time. It is important to understand the context of experiences of partner abuse by varying cultures, particularly in the area of service delivery. In addition, women from majority cultures need to educate themselves about the different needs of *all* shelter residents, and shelter staff need to reflect the population whom they are serving.

DOMESTIC VIOLENCE PROGRAMS BY, WITHIN, AND FOR COMMUNITIES OF COLOR

In response to the need for culturally specific services for survivors of domestic violence, an increasing number of domestic violence shelter programs are being designed specifically by and for women from their own communities. One example is the Asian Women's Shelter in San Francisco, California. The first domestic violence center to specifically serve the Asian and Asian American community, they offer, among other things, a multilingual access model that addresses the issue of language barriers that many Asian women face in seeking services from other shelters. Their services also are respectful of the values and traditions held by many Asian and Asian American women. For some Asian women, leaving an abusive man means leaving her children, family, and entire social network, and she may not be respected by her larger community. Because of this, some programs designed specifically for South Asian women (such as Manavi in New Jersey or Sakhi in New York City) emphasize advocacy and support rather than emergency housing.

Another example of a culturally specific family violence intervention program is Asha Family Services, Inc., in Milwaukee, Wisconsin. Many programs developed and staffed by white women specifically exclude any programs directed toward male perpetrators. Some in the African American community, however, believe it is important to employ a holistic family approach, meaning that services are available for survivors, children, and batterers, and services are designed to promote the healing of mind, body, and spirit. Founded in 1989 to meet this need of the African American community, Asha Family Services is a nonprofit, spiritually based family violence intervention and prevention agency. The program strives to provide effective and comprehensive family violence intervention and prevention services. The agency also holds a state license as an outpatient mental health and substance abuse treatment facility.

Programs have also been designed to more adequately meet the needs of the Latina community. One of the best known such programs is Casa Esperanza (House of Hope), founded in St. Paul, Minnesota, in 1982. In addition to offering direct services to survivors, Casa Esperanza provides technical assistance to help other shelters improve their cultural sensitivity and works on a range of community issues related to abuse within the Latino/a community. Another such program is the Latina Domestic Violence Program of Congreso de Latinos Unidos, Inc., located in Philadelphia. This program also offers a range of services to Latina survivors of domestic violence, including counseling, assistance in accessing legal services, and community education and dating violence prevention education for youth. It is important to note that interventions designed to target the Latina community often also have services available for perpetrators, in addition to services they offer to women and children. This is important because the Latino/a community, in general, is very family centered. Respect and loyalty to the family, as well as family unity, are strong values in this community. Hence, programs serving this community must recognize and be respectful of these values and provide services that are inclusive of the male perpetrators for those Latinas who need or want their partners to be involved.

One program that provides support services specifically to Native American battered women and their children is the Lac du Flambeau Domestic Abuse Program of Lac du Flambeau, Wisconsin. This program offers emergency transportation to and shelter at the statewide Native American shelter, support groups, individual counseling, advocacy, a 24-hour crisis line, restraining order assistance, community education, a Children's Services project, and transitional living. All services are provided by Native Americans, honoring the traditions and strengths of the Native community.

These projects are just a sampling of the culturally specific domestic violence service programs across the United States. However, there is still great need for increased funding and cultural awareness so that such programs may expand in number and in scope.

THE MULTITUDE OF SERVICES OFFERED BY DOMESTIC VIOLENCE SHELTER PROGRAMS

Many people believe that domestic violence programs offer only crisis lines and residential (shelter) services. In fact, most domestic violence programs offer an array of services for women with abusive partners, including but not limited to support groups for women who are not residing at the shelter, advocacy services, individual and group counseling, programs geared specifically toward children, referrals to other community-based services, and financial assistance.

One common program provided within domestic violence shelter programs (and sometimes through other community-based organizations) is the *support group*. These groups were initially created by shelter programs as a forum in which women could discuss their experiences and share information about resources with other survivors. While generic support groups still operate at many shelters, their function has expanded to both target specific populations of abused women (e.g., Latinas, lesbians, and mothers) and focus on particular circumstances (groups for women still in the relationship, for example, or for women who are no longer being abused but who still seek support with dealing with the aftereffects). Evaluations of such groups have been quite limited. However, one study evaluated 12 "closed" support groups (i.e., not open to new members once begun) for survivors. These commonly offered groups typically focus on safety planning, offering mutual support and understanding, and discussing the dynamics of abuse. After surveying 76 women before, immediately after, and six months after the group, the researchers reported significant improvements in women's self-esteem, sense of belonging, locus of control, and overall stress.[3] The study was limited, however, because fewer than half of the original 76 women completed the six-month follow-up assessment, and there was no control or comparison group.

The benefits of support groups were corroborated by a more recent study that did include an experimental design.[4] The eight-week group was led by a trained nurse and focused on helping women increase their social support networks and access to community resources. At the end of the eight weeks, the women who had participated in the group showed greater improvement in psychological well-being and reported higher feelings of social support than did women who had not participated in the group. Taken together, these studies offer promising evidence that support groups are effective in helping women feel more connected with others and less distressed over time.

In response to the lack of affordable housing in most communities and the understanding that many survivors continue to need support and services over time, a number of domestic violence agencies now offer *transitional housing*. Transitional housing programs are designed to help survivors and their children transition from a domestic violence shelter to a more permanent residence. The units often are apartments in which women can live for a set period of time or until they can obtain permanent housing while paying only a small percentage of their income for rent. Some programs only allow women to stay for two months, but it is more typical that women and their children can stay for 18 to 24 months. Many transitional housing programs include other support services such as counseling, housing assistance, and employment assistance.

One model transitional housing program is Middle Way House, Inc., in Bloomington, Indiana. In 1998 they opened a 28-unit facility for low-income battered women and their children. Each family that enters the program is assigned a case manager with whom they work throughout their stay. Additional services offered through this program include support groups, 24-hour child care, legal advocacy, parenting workshops, employment assistance, and community activities. Families can stay for up to two years, and rent is determined by a family's income.

Another innovative program that some domestic violence agencies are now providing is the visitation center. One of the ways many batterers are able to maintain contact with women to continue their abuse after a relationship has ended is through access to the children they have in common. Abusive men often are legally entitled to visit with their children and can use those visits to harass and harm their ex-partners. In response to this, a number of domestic violence programs have opened visitation centers, through which they can minimize contact between the parents and also protect the children involved. These centers are designed in such a way that women do not have to have contact with their abusive ex-partners. Often the women enter through one entrance of the building while the fathers enter through another. There is a neutral mediator (usually a center worker) who takes the children to the visitation area and later returns them to their mother. All exchange between the two parties takes place through the center workers.

The Duluth Visitation Center, a model program that opened in 1989, is located in a YWCA building and includes family rooms, play areas, and a gym. In cases in which abusive men have been granted unsupervised visitation by the courts, the visitation center can serve as a drop-off and pickup site for parents. Women can bring their children in one door, while men use a separate door in a different section of the building. Staff oversees the exchange of the children and helps ensure that perpetrators and victims do not have contact. In cases in which batterers have been granted supervised visitation by the courts, staff remain in the same room with fathers and their children and are available to intervene if necessary to keep children safe.

EXPANDING SERVICES TO CHILDREN OF WOMEN WITH ABUSIVE PARTNERS

As mentioned earlier, the majority of women using domestic violence shelter program services have children accompanying them. Until recently, however, many programs had no services available specifically targeted toward children's needs. Lack of funding and human resources forced many domestic violence programs to focus exclusively on the women using their services. This has changed significantly. Today, many domestic violence agencies have comprehensive children's programs, including support groups, counseling, play rooms, and educational resources. The Women's Center and Shelter (WC&S) of Greater Pittsburgh is one example of a program that offers an extensive array of services to children. Their children's program provides services to children of both shelter residents and nonresidents. These services include child care, age-appropriate support groups, school enrollment assistance, information and referrals to other agencies, individual counseling, after-school and summer recreation programs, and individual and systems advocacy.

A common intervention program for children exposed to domestic violence is the domestic violence *support and education group*. Groups generally run 10 to 12 weeks, and the curriculum is age appropriate. Sessions include serious topics as well as fun activities and snacks, and children learn about labeling feelings, dealing with anger, and honing their safety skills. One evaluation of such a program revealed that children learned strategies for protection in times of emergencies and regarded their parents in a more positive light. Mothers also reported a positive change in their children's behavioral adjustment.[5] A similar study, based on 371 children who attended a program over a four-year period, found that children improved their self-concepts, understood that violence in the home was not their fault, became more aware of protection planning, and learned new ways of resolving conflict without resorting to violence.[6] Although the majority of support and education groups for children are currently being operated within domestic violence programs, most are open to children regardless of whether they are staying at the shelter.

NONSHELTER-BASED COMMUNITY SERVICES FOR BATTERED WOMEN AND THEIR CHILDREN

Not all grassroots domestic violence programs are shelter based. Many provide support and advocacy within the community but refer women to other programs if emergency housing is needed. Rural areas, especially, are likely to have non-shelter-based domestic violence services. Women either receive services by phone (especially in more remote rural or frontier areas) or go to an office for in-person assistance, or, in some instances, advocates will go to women's homes and work with them there.

HOME-BASED ADVOCACY PROGRAMS

The idea of working with women in their own homes and communities is gaining popularity in many areas. One research study used a true experimental design and followed women for two years in order to examine the effectiveness of one such program. In this case, advocates worked with women 4–6 hours a week over 10 weeks, in the women's communities. Advocates were highly trained volunteers who could help women across a variety of areas: education, employment, housing, legal assistance, issues for children, transportation, and other issues. Women who worked with the advocates experienced less violence over time, reported higher quality of life and social support, and had less difficulty obtaining community resources over time. One of four of the women who worked with advocates experienced *no* physical abuse, by the original assailant or by any new partners, across the two years of postintervention follow-up. Only one of 10 women in the control group remained completely free of violence during the same period. This low-cost, short-term intervention using unpaid advocates appears to have been effective not only in reducing women's risk of reabuse but also in improving their overall quality of life.[7]

Many services for battered women and their children are being offered, not just within free-standing domestic violence programs but also within a variety of systems throughout communities. Programs are growing in health care settings, in police stations and prosecutors' offices, in family service organizations, and on college campuses, just to name a few.

PROGRAMS IN HEALTH CARE SETTINGS

By the late 1970s, researchers had shown that domestic violence was the single major cause of injury for which women sought medical attention; that after the onset of abuse, battered women suffered a significantly elevated risk of a range of medical, psychosocial, and behavioral problems; and that health personnel neither identified the problem nor treated its victims appropriately. Starting in 1977 at hospitals in Boston and Seattle and building on hospital-community collaborations in establishing rape crisis teams, the earliest medical responses to domestic violence relied on multidisciplinary hospital-based teams of volunteer nurses and social workers. Since this time, virtually every major professional medical and nursing association has made domestic violence a priority; hundreds of hospitals have adopted screening protocols backed by referral networks for emergency shelter and other services; domestic violence training for clinicians is widespread; and domestic violence education has been widely introduced into the medical school curriculum.

Advocacy for Women and Kids in Emergencies (AWAKE) was the first program within a pediatric setting to link assistance for battered women with clinical services for their children. The program has its own satellite office in the Family Development Clinic at Children's Hospital in Boston, Massachusetts. Through this program battered women and their children are paired with an advocate who assists them with everything, from legal issues to safety planning. Additional services include assistance with emergency housing needs, individual counseling, and weekly support groups offered in both English and Spanish. The program also provides training to medical staff as well as in the community.

Another early domestic violence program to be established in a public hospital was the Hospital Crisis Intervention Project (HCIP), founded at Chicago's Cook County Hospital in 1992. Staff and volunteers offer immediate assistance to battered women in the hospital and also train hospital staff to properly identify and treat domestic violence victims. In response to the cultural diversity of the patient population in Chicago, a multicultural staff is available to provide services in several languages. In New York City, each public hospital is assigned a "domestic violence coordinator" responsible for taking domestic violence referrals, training clinical staff, and implementing programs to improve services to victims.

The Medical Advocacy Project out of Mercy Hospital in Pittsburgh, Pennsylvania, is unique in that the hospital offers an apartment on hospital grounds for survivors when local shelters are at capacity. In addition, all women who come through the emergency department are screened for domestic violence, and a full-time advocate is on staff to assist survivors.

Programs Located within the Criminal Legal System

As laws and policies pertaining to domestic violence have improved, more women have contacted the criminal legal system for help in protecting themselves and their children. In response to this, some communities have created programs within police stations, prosecutors' offices, or legal offices to reach women in need of legal assistance.

One such program is *legal advocacy*, through which a highly trained domestic violence legal advocate offers information, support, referrals, and direct assistance to women through all stages of the civil or criminal legal process. Research on the effectiveness of legal advocacy efforts, however, is limited. The only published evaluation of such a program to date found that women who had worked with advocates in Washington, D.C., reported decreased abuse six weeks later as well as marginally higher emotional well-being, compared with women who did not work with advocates. Their qualitative findings also supported the use of paraprofessional legal advocates. All of the women who had worked with advocates talked about them as being very supportive and knowledgeable, while the women who did not work with advocates mentioned wishing they had had that kind of support while they were going through this difficult process.[8]

Another program is the *first response team*, which, like legal advocacy, can but does not necessarily need to be housed within the criminal justice system. One typical first response team, the Capital Area Response Effort (CARE), has been operating in mid-Michigan since 1995. When arrests are made in cases of domestic violence, the police call CARE and two volunteers go to the home of the victim to offer immediate support and assistance. Depending on the need, volunteers can refer women to local shelter programs, inform them about the legal process that has begun, offer referrals, or simply provide immediate emotional support. As needed, CARE volunteers also provide advocacy and accompaniment through the legal process. CARE is housed within a police department but staffed by domestic violence advocates. The staff is overseen by an advisory board composed of police, prosecutors, service providers, and others from the community.

Another example of a citizen-based response is the Domestic Violence Response Team (DVRT) in New Jersey. The DVRTs were authorized in 1987 through that state's Prevention of Domestic Violence Act to provide comfort and consultation to victims of domestic violence after police respond to a domestic violence call and secure the safety of the victim and other family members. DVRT volunteers come from all walks of life and are specially trained to provide critical information so the victim has a clear understanding of her options. A similar program in New York City was experimentally evaluated, and the researchers found that those survivors who had received the information and education were more likely to call the police during the next 6 months compared to an equally revictimized group of women who had not received the intervention.[9]

Although a first response team can provide immeasurable assistance to women after the police have been called, such help is limited if the police, prosecutors, judges, and probation officers are not cooperative in holding perpetrators accountable for their behavior. In response to this, an increasing number of communities have designed what the Minneapolis Domestic Abuse Project first termed community intervention projects (CIPs). Under many different names across the country, these projects involve coordinating criminal justice system and community efforts to respond more effectively to domestic violence. The police agree to contact the CIP after responding to a domestic violence call, and perpetrators are held in jail for a set period of time (usually at least overnight). The CIP then sends female volunteers to the survivor's home and sends male volunteers to visit the perpetrator in jail. Survivors are given information, referrals, and transportation to a shelter if needed, and perpetrators are encouraged to accept responsibility for their actions and to attend a batterer intervention program.

Prosecutors agree to aggressively pursue domestic violence charges, and judges agree to order presentence investigations and to mandate jail time and/or batterer intervention if the perpetrator is convicted. Probation officers also play an important role in this coordination. They agree to incorporate the perpetrator's violent history and the survivor's wishes in the presentence investigation, and they hold perpetrators accountable if they do not obey the judge's mandates.

There is some evidence that CIPs do result in increased safety for survivors of domestic violence. One study found that CIPs resulted in increased arrests, increased successful prosecutions, and a larger number of perpetrators being mandated into batterer intervention programs.[10] Another study found that when police action was coordinated with other systems—a critical component of coordinated community intervention—perpetrators were significantly less likely to reoffend.[11] Equally important, when police action was *not* coordinated with other components of the system, perpetrators actually seemed to *increase* their use of violence against women.

Not all CIPs are identical across the country, and some are much more comprehensive than others. Not all communities have gained the cooperation of all necessary players (police, prosecutors, judges, probation officers, and advocates), but thousands of communities have adopted components of this model, with varying degrees of success.

Programs Developed through Family and Social Service Agencies

As more community members learn that domestic violence is a social problem requiring a comprehensive community response, programs are developing through a wider network of social service agencies. In 1980, for example, Dove, Inc. (Decatur, Illinois), a nonprofit social services agency organized by area churches as a cooperative community ministry, began its own domestic violence program. This program has developed an array of projects and services for battered women and their children, including but not limited to shelter, counseling, legal advocacy, parenting assistance, and an abuse intervention program for teens who have abused dating partners and/or family members. The program also houses an intervention program for abusive men.

Programs Developed through Universities

In 1994, Michigan State University (MSU) became the first university to establish and fund its own on-campus domestic violence shelter and education program. One of the largest campuses in the country, MSU recognized that universities are communities unto themselves and as such experience the same social problems that other communities face. Their program, which includes shelter services, advocacy, counseling, support groups, and community education, serves as a prototype for other academic settings.

CONCLUSIONS

Community-based services for battered women and their children have expanded exponentially in the last 30 years. As our knowledge about this complex issue has grown, as funding has increased, and as more community members are accepting responsibility for ending intimate male violence against women and children, community-based services have developed that reflect this growth.

Though evaluations of many of these programs are quite limited, there is evidence to believe that these services are making a significant difference in women's lives. Women seem to be most helped by those services that are offered in an individualized and empowering manner by staff who are also actively collaborating with other community-based and legal agencies.

Today, most communities have at least some programs available for battered women and their children. Nonprofit domestic violence service programs offer an array of services to women and children, whether or not the family needs residential services. Many communities also have services provided through health care systems, the criminal justice system, and/or social service systems. Efforts have improved to ensure that services are culturally appropriate and respectful of the complex obstacles facing women with abusive partners. However, no community can be said to be doing enough. There are still too many survivors receiving insufficient help, and too many communities providing uncoordinated or inadequate assistance. Although funding has substantially increased for domestic violence services during the past 30 years, it continues to be woefully inadequate.

We have clearly come a long way, but our journey is far from over. Domestic violence victim support services will continue to develop and expand to meet the changing needs of women and children. At the same time, advocates nationwide eagerly anticipate the day when such support services for battered women and their children are no longer necessary.

ACKNOWLEDGMENTS

This chapter is a modified and updated version of a chapter from C. M. Sullivan, "Interventions to Address Intimate Partner Violence: The Current State of the Field," in *Preventing Violence: Research and Evidence-Based Intervention Strategies*, ed. J. R. Lutzker (Washington, D.C.: American Psychological Association, 2005), 195–212. Copyright © 2005 by the American Psychological Association. Adapted with permission. No further reproduction or distribution is permitted without written permission from the American Psychological Association.

NOTES

1. S. Schechter, *Women and Male Violence* (Boston: South End Press, 1982).

2. L. Vinton, "Battered Women's Shelters and Older Women: The Florida Experience," *Journal of Family Violence* 7, no. 1 (1992): 63–72.

3. L. M. Tutty, B. A. Bidgood, and M. A. Rothery, "Support Groups for Battered Women: Research on their Efficacy," *Journal of Family Violence* 8, no. 4 (1993): 325–43; and L. M. Tutty, G. Weaver, and M. A. Rothery, "Residents' Views of the Efficacy of Services for Assaulted Women," *Violence against Women* 5, no. 8 (1999): 898–925.

4. R. Constantino, Y. Kim, and P. A. Crane, "Effects of a Social Support Intervention on Health Outcomes in Residents of a Domestic Violence Shelter: A Pilot Study," *Issues in Mental Health Nursing* 26 (2005): 575–90.

5. P. G. Jaffe, S. K. Wilson, and D. A. Wolfe, "Specific Assessment and Intervention Strategies for Children Exposed to Wife Assault: Preliminary Empirical Investigation," *Canadian Journal of Mental Health* 7, no. 2 (1989): 157–63.

6. R. J. Gruszinski, J. C. Brink, and J. L. Edleson, "Support and Education Groups for Children of Battered Women," *Child Welfare* 67 (1988): 431–44.

7. C. M. Sullivan and D. I. Bybee, "Reducing Violence Using Community Based Advocacy for Women with Abusive Partners," *Journal of Consulting and Clinical Psychology* 67, no. 1 (1999): 43–53; and C. M. Sullivan, "A Model for Effectively Advocating for Women with Abusive Partners," in *Domestic Violence: Guidelines for Research-Informed Practice*, ed. J. P. Vincent and E. N. Jouriles (London: Jessica Kingsley, 2000).

8. M. E. Bell and L. A. Goodman, "Supporting Battered Women Involved with the Court System: An Evaluation of a Law School-Based Advocacy Intervention," *Violence against Women* 7 (2001): 1377–404.

9. Davis, R. C. & Medina, J. (2001). Results from an elder abuse prevention experiment in New York City (NIJ Research in Brief). Washington, DC: US Department of Justice, National Institute of Justice.

10. D. J. Gamache, J. L. Edleson, and M. D. Schock, "Coordinated Police, Judicial and Social Service Response to Woman Battering: A Multi-Baseline Evaluation across Three Communities," in *Coping with Family Violence: Research and Policy Perspectives*, ed. G. T. Hotaling, D. Finkelhor, J. T. Kirkpatrick, and M. Straus (Newbury Park, CA: Sage, 1988): 193–209.

11. M. Steinman, "Lowering Recidivism among Men Who Batter Women," *Journal of Police Science and Administration* 17 (1990): 124–32.

Chapter 5

Intimate Partner Violence and Economic Disadvantage

Claire M. Renzetti

During the 1970s, when the women's movement was trying to draw public attention to the problem of intimate partner violence (IPV), a common theme was "It could happen to anyone—to you, to someone you know and love." Revelations that celebrities, such as Tina Turner, had been abused and popular television movies such as *The Burning Bed* sent the powerful message that wealth and status are no protection from victimization. It is true that women in all social classes are victims of IPV, but we now know that economic disadvantage significantly increases a woman risk for IPV victimization. Women who are poor are much more likely than their wealthier sisters to be abused over the course of their lives.

This chapter will first summarize what we know about the relationship between social class and IPV as well as the consequences of IPV for poor victims. I will then consider what dimensions of economic disadvantage contribute to an elevated risk of IPV victimization among poor women. These dimensions include physical and mental health problems as well as substance abuse, community and neighborhood violence, employment issues, and weaknesses in social support networks and social services systems such as Temporary Assistance to Needy Families (TANF), commonly known as welfare. Linkages among these problems are tracked to show how they, as well racism and sexism, collectively impact IPV victimization. The chapter concludes by exploring some of the ways that the IPV victimization of poor women may be reduced through changes in public policy and social services.

HIGH ABUSE RATES: IS RACE OR SOCIAL CLASS TO BLAME?

Since the early 1980s, researchers have reported higher rates of IPV among African Americans than among whites. Large national surveys, including the National Family Violence Survey (NFVS), the National Crime Victimization Survey (NCVS), the National Survey of Families and Households (NSFH), and the National Violence Against Women Survey (NVAWS), indicate that African American women are at greater risk of being violently victimized by their intimate partners than are white women.[1] Studies that have examined IPV rates by race typically included only two racial groups: African Americans and whites. More recent research that has included Hispanics has produced inconsistent results, with some studies showing elevated rates of IPV and others showing either comparable or lower rates than those of whites. These inconsistencies are likely due not only to differences in samples and measures but also to the diversity across Hispanic ethnic groups. Similar inconsistencies occur in research with Asian American samples. Studies of Native American women, however, consistently show them to have the highest IPV victimization rates of any racial or ethnic group of women.[2]

Some experts think that culturally specific factors may contribute to a higher rate of IPV among African American couples, including beliefs about marriage and fidelity as well as negative stereotypes of African American women.[3] But even though these ideas have received some empirical support, research that has examined both race/ethnicity and social class has shown that when social class is controlled, differences in IPV rates between African Americans and whites are significantly reduced or completely disappear.

For example, in an analysis of data from the NSFH and the 1990 U.S. Census, Michael Benson and his colleagues found that the influence of race is far less important than the type of community—or what they refer to as the "ecological context"—in which individuals live in accounting for IPV rates.[4] These researchers discovered that IPV rates are comparable for whites and African Americans who live in similar communities. IPV rates are highest in communities characterized by severe economic disadvantage and lowest in affluent communities. Findings such as these indicate that socioeconomic status has a greater influence on women's risk of IPV victimization than does race or ethnicity. The elevated rates of IPV for African American women are one of the outcomes of residential segregation; a disproportionate number of African Americans live in economically disadvantaged neighborhoods. Additional studies show that the lower a woman's income, the more likely she is to say she has been abused.

Poor women are not a homogenous group, however. For example, some poor women are housed and some are homeless, living on the street or in temporary shelters. Some poor women are employed, albeit in low-paying jobs that typically have no benefits, and some are unemployed or receive public assistance. Data indicate that while all poor women are at elevated risk of IPV victimization, it is the poorest of the poor who suffer the highest incidence. For instance, Susan Lloyd surveyed 824 women in an economically disadvantaged Chicago neighborhood and found that, although women in all income groups in this neighborhood had high rates of violent victimization, women with the lowest annual incomes (between $2,500 and $7,000) reported experiencing severe violence three times more than women with higher annual incomes.[5] Numerous studies have documented the extraordinarily high rate of violence against women who receive welfare. Lifetime rates of physical abuse by a male partner—referred to as "prevalence rates" as opposed to "incidence rates"—range from 28 to 63 percent in welfare samples, but most estimates are between 40 and 60 percent. These figures are especially startling when compared with statistics from recent, nationally representative surveys, such as the NVAWS, which estimated that 1.5 percent of women had been physically abused by an intimate partner in the preceding year and 25 percent have been victimized at some point during their lives.[6]

Poor women have higher rates of all forms of violent victimization during the course of their lives. For instance, the Worcester Family Research Project (WFRP), conducted between 1992 and 1996, was a longitudinal study of 216 housed, low-income, single mothers and 220 homeless single mothers, which included questions about the women's lifetime trauma histories. The sample included non-Hispanic white, African American, and Hispanic women; the average age of the sample subject was 27 years. Only 16 percent of these women had *not* been physically or sexually assaulted in their relatively short lifetimes. In addition to reporting a high incidence of severe physical violence by a current or most recent intimate partner (nearly 33 percent), including death threats (about 20 percent), 60 percent of the women reported physical violence perpetrated by a male partner during adulthood, 63 percent had experienced severe physical violence by a parent or caregiver during childhood, and more than 40 percent had been sexually molested during childhood. As the researchers note, "For many respondents, categories of victimization overlapped with different types of experiences and assailants in their lives. The majority of women in both groups had experienced only brief periods of safety."[7]

Although homeless women are usually seen as being at an increased risk of violent victimization relative to housed poor women, the women in both groups in the WFRP had such extensive histories of abuse that they were considered to be at comparable risk. Moreover, these two groups tended to experience different types of violence. In the year preceding the study, women in homeless shelters experienced more instrumental aggression (i.e., violence to achieve some end, such as money or drugs) from a range of perpetrators, including strangers as well as people they knew. Housed women, in contrast, experienced more hostile aggression (i.e., violence accompanied by anger or rage with the sole objective of hurting or injuring the target) perpetrated by intimate partners. However, the women in shelters were more likely to have been raped in the previous year—rape was classified separately from instrumental and hostile aggression—and although they reported fewer incidents of major physical violence, they were significantly more likely to have incurred serious or life-threatening injuries when they were violently victimized.[8]

Thus, poor women are at an increased risk of experiencing multiple victimizations across the life span by multiple perpetrators, a point to which we will return shortly. It may be argued that poverty and violent victimization are reciprocally related: that is, women's violent victimization experiences not only are one of the consequences of living in extreme poverty, but also serve to entrap women in poverty. In the sections that follow, we will consider some of the factors that contribute to this reciprocity.

PHYSICAL AND MENTAL HEALTH PROBLEMS

Women who have experienced IPV have more physical health problems than women who report no IPV victimization, and the more severe the abuse experienced, the higher the reported rates of health problems. These problems include chronic fatigue, insomnia, and recurring nightmares; headaches; chest pain; back pain and other orthopedic discomfort; stomach and gastrointestinal disorders; respiratory difficulties, including hyperventilation and asthma; and gynecologic problems, such as chronic pelvic pain and menstrual disorders. When the abuse is reduced or ended, the women's physical health symptoms diminish.

Women who are poor are more likely than nonpoor women to report health problems. The elevated risk of ill health for poor women is due to a number of factors, including living in substandard housing, greater exposure to communicable diseases, higher exposure to environmental toxins, and other stressors related to poverty. Compounding the problem of ill health is their lack of financial resources, which makes it difficult, if not impossible, for poor women to obtain treatment, or they postpone treatment until the condition becomes severe. Compounding the problem, ill health may preclude employment or allow only intermittent employment, putting jobs that provide health insurance benefits out of reach for these poor women.

In considering the difficulties faced by poor women who have also been victimized by IPV, the question arises as to the extent to which their physical health problems are due to their poverty or to their IPV victimization. In a study designed to address this question, Cheryl Sutherland, Cris Sullivan, and Deborah Bybee interviewed a community sample of 397 women about their income, their experiences of physical abuse, and their physical health.[9] They found that, regardless of income, abused women reported more physical health symptoms than did nonabused women and that women's experiences of IPV had a significant effect on their physical health beyond that explained by income. That is, when income was controlled, significant differences in physical health symptoms for abused and nonabused women remained. And the poorer the women, the more likely it was that IPV would have a negative effect on their health.

Mental health symptoms have also been correlated with both poverty and IPV in numerous studies. The stresses associated with living in poverty seem to lead to elevated risk for various mental health problems among the poor, including depression and anxiety disorders. Women in abusive relationships also show a high incidence of these and other mental health impairments, such as posttraumatic stress disorder (PTSD). The relative contribution of poverty and IPV to lowered psychological well-being has not been measured, but one mental health factor related to both poverty and IPV that has been studied extensively is substance abuse, a topic to which we turn now.

SUBSTANCE ABUSE, INTIMATE PARTNER VIOLENCE, AND POVERTY

That drug and alcohol use figure prominently in many IPV incidents has been well established by research. The nature of the relationship between substance abuse and IPV is far less clearly understood. It is commonly assumed that substance abuse causes IPV because it lowers inhibitions and impairs judgment in perpetrators, raises the emotional states of both perpetrators and victims, and makes it more difficult for victims to protect themselves or escape. However, studies of substance abuse and IPV perpetration and victimization have not yielded consistent findings. Indeed, available research indicates that the linkage between these two problems may be quite complex and may be mediated by a number of other factors.

One question that has been raised with regard to victimization, for example, is whether women who abuse substances are more likely than women who do not abuse substances to become involved with violent intimate partners. Some studies have shown that substance abuse is a risk marker for IPV victimization among women—that is, the incidence of IPV is higher among women who use drugs than among women who do not; other studies have found that drug use *following an incident of IPV* is more common among some groups of women, including, for instance, women with no history of recent drug use. For example, it has been estimated that the lifetime rate of IPV among drug-abusing women is 60 to 75 percent compared with estimated lifetime rates of 17 percent for non-drug-abusing women. The research indicates that, after controlling for social and psychological factors associated with a history of physical violence and/or drug use, women with a history of adult partner violence are significantly more likely to subsequently use illegal drugs than are women who do not experience such violence. Additional research shows that women often increase their substance abuse after IPV incidents.[10] Thus, substance abuse may be a way that women self-medicate in an effort to cope with the trauma of abuse.

The self-medication hypothesis is further supported by research showing that poor women with a history of child abuse, especially child sexual abuse, are significantly more likely to use drugs as adults than are those without a history of child abuse of any kind. The incidence of PTSD is particularly high among women who were abused as children, and a combination of a history of child sexual abuse and PTSD appears to have a far greater impact on adult drug use among poor women than does *either* a history of child sexual abuse *or* PTSD alone. Among poor women, however, IPV predicts adult drug use regardless of a woman's history of childhood sexual abuse or PTSD, but "accumulated traumas" may contribute to both women's likelihood of using substances and their risk of violent victimization.

A number of recent studies have linked the lifestyle associated with active substance abuse to increased risk for violent victimization. Not surprisingly, substance abuse may interfere with employment. Poor women who use drugs often also sell drugs and engage in other types of illegal behavior, such as prostitution, in order to survive. These activities are dangerous and pose a significant risk for violent victimization, often putting the women in life-threatening situations. For example, women may trade sex for drugs, but this exchange may include extreme physical and psychological abuse of the women.

Sociologist Jody Miller documents the extraordinary amount of victimization experienced by the young women, perpetrated not only by strangers but also by intimates, relatives, and acquaintances.[11] Similarly, research with female public housing residents in Camden, New Jersey, found that the majority of the women reported high levels of fear of crime and that their typical safety strategies included not going out alone, especially at night; securing the doors and windows of their residences with multiple locks; and not making eye contact or speaking with strangers. Nevertheless, the women reported multiple incidents of violent victimization at the hands of intimates and acquaintances, more so than from strangers.[12]

Women who use drugs also experience social isolation in that the people with whom they socialize or to whom they turn for support, including intimate partners, are often abusing drugs themselves. If her intimate partner is violent, the woman's dependence on him—financially as well as emotionally—may make it extraordinarily difficult for her to get help, for the substance abuse and the violence, or to leave the relationship. Women may also find themselves working to support their abusive partner's drug habit. And, as we will discuss next, when women live in neighborhoods with high rates of community violence and a weak sense of social cohesion among residents, the social relationships they develop may be more harmful than beneficial.

NEIGHBORHOODS, COMMUNITY CONTEXTS, AND SOCIAL NETWORKS

The importance of community context and neighborhood characteristics has been central to the sociological study of crime since the early-twentieth-century research of the Chicago school. "Social disorder" refers to various social incivilities—for example, public intoxication, drug dealing, and street prostitution—that may take place in public areas of a neighborhood. Social disorder tends to be accompanied by community violence, such as robberies and muggings, gang fights, and arguments that escalate to assault and sometimes murder. Social disorder may occur in any neighborhood, but it is characteristic of economically disadvantaged or impoverished neighborhoods because they lack critical institutional, political, and economic resources. Without such resources, social disorder can flourish.

In her study of urban inequality and gendered violence among adolescents in impoverished neighborhoods in St. Louis, Missouri, Miller heard complaints from residents about the physical deterioration of their neighborhoods, the simultaneous problems of police harassment of residents as well as under-policing of the neighborhoods, and a strong sense of social isolation and mistrust among neighbors. The woeful lack of resources in these neighborhoods makes it difficult, if not impossible, for residents to develop strong collective efficacy—that is, community or neighborhood cohesion based on mutual trust and a willingness to intervene on behalf of the common good. Residents may be highly fearful of the crime they see around them, but they are unable and/or unwilling to monitor, intervene in, and combat this social problem. Importantly, Miller's work also shows that the experiences and effects of this community context are gendered. The young men whom she observed and interviewed were more active and embedded in neighborhood activities and networks, whereas the young women stayed indoors more, especially at night, and went out in groups or accompanied by young men. This, Miller argues, is the primary strategy the young women use to stay safe in their neighborhoods, although it is often unsuccessful.

Joining Miller, a number of researchers have argued recently that community structure and context are central in explaining elevated rates of not only property crime and community violence in disadvantaged neighborhoods but also IPV. Neighborhoods characterized by a high concentration of poverty, a high male unemployment rate, and widespread family disruption also have a higher rate of IPV than do other neighborhoods. One explanation for this relationship draws on cultural norms of hegemonic masculinity and how they play out at the micro or individual level in these communities. The social structural context in which people live helps shape their values and norms, including gender norms. Being unemployed or underemployed is associated with high levels of stress among men because one's work and income from employment are measures of masculine success in our society. Unemployed and underemployed men living in neighborhoods of concentrated disadvantage certainly cannot draw on the breadwinner role as a measure of masculine success. They can assert dominance, however, through violence—against one another, against those who disrespect them or cross them in some way, and against women.

Economically disenfranchised men associate with one another in male peer support networks that collectively devalue women and regard them as legitimate victims who deserve physical and sexual abuse. Sexual conquest and asserting social and physical control over women are sources of power and measures of success for powerless men who are unsuccessful by the traditional measures of white, middle-class culture. In some ways, this is no different from the devaluation of women by men in more affluent peer networks, such as fraternities. But some have argued that among poor men, sexual dominance of women, sometimes expressed through violence, is an alternative route to claiming success as a man, given that other avenues to such success are blocked.

Social support networks, then, are an important factor in explaining men's perpetration of violence against women. At the same time, several researchers have begun to explore how women's social support networks may factor into their risk of IPV victimization. Daniel Rosen, for instance, has studied the importance of social support networks in the lives of poor teenage mothers who are also IPV victims.[13] Rosen emphasizes that when social support is scarce, young women's options are highly restricted, which may force them to remain in unsafe and insecure situations. Young women with a parent or caregiver who offered emotional, educational, and financial support fared significantly better than young women without such support, who, out of fear of becoming homeless, were sometimes trapped in abusive relationships. Similarly, Susan James and her colleagues found that social support networks played a central role in poor women's substance abuse as well as their vulnerability to IPV. James and her colleagues report that the majority of the women in their study were initiated into drug use by people in their neighborhoods and by immediate family members, including parents and older siblings.[14] These networks served to encourage women's drug use by defining it as a "shared social activity," supplying the drugs or a place to use drugs and covering for the women (e.g., watching their children) while they were on drugs. Moreover, the women depended heavily on their intimate partners, many of whom were abusive. Because the women were not in school and were unemployed, their likelihood of expanding their social networks was slim, and many reported that their partners actively kept them from making new friends.

The concept of social networks is closely linked to collective efficacy, since both deal with those in one's immediate environment on whom one can count to intervene or help in a crisis. Research with poor women in public housing developments in Camden, New Jersey, found collective efficacy to be low. Most of the women said they could not count on their neighbors for help when a problem or emergency arose for a number of reasons: their neighbors were often a *source* of problems for them, or they felt their neighbors had so many of their own problems they wouldn't want to get involved. But most often, the women said they didn't know their neighbors and didn't want to get to know them because, as one woman put it, "people are too nosey," and she didn't want them "in her business." While some of the women said they could rely on a relative who lived nearby, on a clergy person, or on their case-worker, many women said they relied on no one but themselves.

Interestingly, in my interviews with women in Philadelphia housing projects, I found that collective efficacy was relatively strong, *except with regard to IPV*. More specifically, the majority of women in the Philadelphia study said that they could count on their neighbors to look after one another's children, call the police if a suspicious person is hanging around the building, or call the police if rowdy teenagers are causing trouble. But few thought people in their development would call the police if a neighbor was being abused by her husband or boyfriend. Such findings raise the question of whether IPV, unlike the other problems mentioned, is considered a "private" problem, in which case people are reluctant to get into "other people's business." Indeed, Christopher Browning reports that high collective efficacy reduces IPV when it is *coupled with* community norms that support intervention into intimate relationships.[15]

Chitra Raghavan and colleagues' research speaks to this issue as well. They examined the extent to which poor IPV victims were involved in social networks in which those from whom they sought support were IPV victims themselves. The researchers found the level of IPV victimization in the women's social networks to be high and, among the women in their sample, network IPV increased a woman's personal experiences of IPV victimization. Raghavan and her colleagues speculate that high rates of IPV among women's social support networks may cause such violence to become part of the women's "cognitive landscape," normalizing such behavior so that it is seen as neither abnormal nor abusive.[16] Further, such norms may promote self-blame and exonerate abusers, so that women are encouraged or compelled to remain in violent relationships. And although support group members are often sympathetic to IPV victims, they may not have the resources to provide tangible assistance in the form of money or temporary shelter if a victim wishes to leave her abuser. Their own situations may preclude them from providing tangible assistance.

This final point once again underlines the importance of women being able to attain financial independence in order to free themselves from abusive relationships. A primary means to financial independence is employment, the topic to which we turn next.

POVERTY, EMPLOYMENT, AND INTIMATE PARTNER VIOLENCE

Given the relationship between poverty and IPV that we have discussed, one would expect that women who are employed and, therefore, acquiring financial resources may be at lowered risk of IPV victimization. The research indicates that the relationship between employment and IPV victimization is less straightforward, however. For example, some studies report that women with a history of IPV victimization do not differ in their current employment status and in their desire to work from women without a history of IPV victimization. At the same time, IPV victims are more likely to miss days of work, suffer mental or physical health problems that can impair their ability to work, and report periods of unemployment in the past and a lower likelihood of sustaining employment over time. If IPV interferes with work, there is considerable evidence that many batterers sabotage their partners' efforts to obtain and maintain employment. Documented tactics by abusers include damaging or destroying women's work clothes or books and other items associated with job training, inflicting facial cuts and bruises to keep them from going to work, promising to care for the children but suddenly becoming unavailable to do so, demanding sex or initiating a lengthy discussion just as they are leaving for work, calling the women repeatedly while they are at work, or showing up at the workplace and creating disturbances. Of course, such tactics can undermine the careers of women in lucrative positions, too, reminding us that while living in poverty may increase a woman's chances of IPV victimization, IPV victimization may also cause some women to lose their jobs or give them up, choosing safety over work, and consequently become poor. It is estimated that women lose nearly $18 million in annual earnings because of IPV.[17]

For some women attempts to work precipitate or aggravate their partners' abuse and efforts to control them. This is likely because working is a pathway to independence for women and it increases their status while reducing the power inequality in their intimate relationships—facts that some men, particularly men who are themselves unemployed or underemployed, may find very threatening. As Anita Raj and her colleagues found in their study of IPV in a sample of low-income African American women, receiving income from a male partner reduced a woman's likelihood of being abused by that partner. The more economic power a woman had, the more likely her male partner was abusive.[18]

Nevertheless, employment can have a protective effect for some women experiencing IPV. It can provide opportunities for women to expand their social networks, thereby reducing social isolation, an important correlate of IPV as previously noted. Employment can also raise women's self-esteem and equip them not only financially but also psychologically with the resources needed to leave an abusive relationship. Lisa Brush, for instance, found in her sample of women in a Pennsylvania welfare-to-work program that PTSD symptoms were diminished among women who were employed.[19]

The issue of employment is especially salient for poor women, since if they cannot find or maintain work they must rely on public assistance, commonly referred to as welfare. In 1996, Congress passed and President Bill Clinton signed the Personal Responsibility and Work Opportunity Reconciliation Act (PRWORA), representing the legal embodiment of the federal government's pledge to "reform" welfare. The former means-tested federal entitlement program, Aid to Families with Dependent Children (AFDC), was renamed Temporary Assistance to Needy Families (TANF), but the changes in the program were more substantial than nominal. Although AFDC could hardly be considered generous in benefits, TANF established time limits as well as low family caps on aid receipt. The PRWORA limits lifetime receipt of cash assistance to five years, although states are permitted to impose even lower limits. TANF applicants who are single mothers are required to cooperate with child support agencies, assisting them in establishing paternity, locating the absent parent, and obtaining a child support order. Such requirements are especially onerous for battered women, putting them at further risk of victimization by, for example, making abusers aware of their location or angering abusers with orders for child support.

Undoubtedly, a major objective of PRWORA was to reduce the number of people on welfare, not the number of people living in poverty. Nevertheless, the government stated that a primary goal was to move people from welfare dependency to financial self-sufficiency through work. Studies show that state welfare rolls did decline dramatically following enactment of the PRWORA, and that more poor women, most of whom are single mothers, are employed and are remaining employed longer than before PRWORA.

Women themselves recognize the potential benefits of employment. Many poor women state quite emphatically that they want to work. But it is important to keep in mind that employment is not necessarily sufficient to raise these women out of poverty, given that the jobs they obtain typically pay low wages and have few benefits (e.g., health insurance). At the same time, the women incur the costs of transportation to and from work, and they may earn just enough money to lose Medicaid and child care subsidies, thus incurring those costs as well. They also have the care of their children to worry about, given that safe, affordable child care is rarely available to them. Poor, battered women have even greater obstacles to employment, not the least of which, as we have seen, is the escalation of violence by their intimate partners when they seek job training or work outside the home.

Congress was made aware of the particular barriers to work that IPV victims face and that trying to meet TANF requirements could jeopardize their safety. Consequently, included in the PRWORA is the Family Violence Option (FVO), which was crafted to ensure that women would not be unfairly denied public assistance because IPV prevents them from meeting TANF requirements. States that adopt the FVO may give IPV victims temporary waivers or exemptions from TANF requirements as well as provide referrals to battered women's services. Most states have adopted the FVO but, contrary to critics' pre-adoption warnings, large numbers of women in these states have not taken advantage of FVO provisions and services. In fact, studies show that a minority (0.5–3 percent) of TANF clients disclose IPV to caseworkers, request an FVO waiver or exemption, or utilize domestic violence victim services, even though it is estimated that 20 to 30 percent of applicants are eligible for exemptions and services.[20] Research indicates that this discrepancy may be due in large part to the failure of TANF caseworkers to adequately and sensitively screen clients for IPV.

Women who have obtained FVO waivers report that they are helpful in that the waivers give them extra time to pull their lives together after abuse and prevent them from losing TANF benefits if their abusers interfered with job training or work. But many poor, battered women do not see the waivers as the best way to address their multitude of needs, in part because they face other problems they consider more serious than IPV. When I interviewed IPV victims living in public housing in Philadelphia, many told me that they could "handle" their intimate partners' abuse because it was intermittent and often not "that bad." Instead, they wished for assistance with what they perceived as the unrelenting problems of daily life in poverty: getting a job that paid enough for them to support themselves and their children; access to safe, reliable, and affordable child care; safe and reliable transportation to and from work; and safe and affordable housing. This suggests that effectively responding to the needs of poor, battered women requires multidimensional, collaborative strategies that simultaneously address the intersecting problems and consequences of poverty and IPV. This chapter concludes with suggestions for such strategies.

STRATEGIES FOR ADDRESSING POVERTY AND INTIMATE PARTNER VIOLENCE

Poverty and IPV are major problems that are both multifaceted and often approached with a sense of fatalism. As we have suggested, however, to paraphrase Miller, they don't "just happen." They are the products, at least in part, of policy decisions and, to some extent, individual choices made within the constraints of specific structural conditions. Consequently, solving these problems requires first the deliberate will to recognize their seriousness, to stop blaming the victim, and to develop and implement policies and programs that help both communities and individuals. I certainly do not suppose that I have *the* solutions to these problems. But here are some suggestions informed by research as to directions we should be taking to mount a more effective response.

As discussed previously, the community contexts in which people live generate behavioral norms or "cognitive landscapes," which govern social interaction. Therefore, these community contexts must change. Resources must be committed to making neighborhoods where poor people reside more livable and stable. For example, when Miller asked her research participants how their neighborhoods could be made safe, a common response was to clean them up. Research shows that reversing the physical deterioration of these neighborhoods—by, for instance, stepping up municipal services, enforcing building codes, renovating housing, investing in businesses—not only makes them better places to live environmentally but also helps reduce crime and build collective efficacy.[21] When neighbors look out for one another, and especially when intervention norms develop, communities become safer places for *all* residents, including women.

Of course, neighborhood residents cannot be expected to handle all disturbances or crises in their communities themselves. Even if collective efficacy is relatively strong, a response by "authorities" is safer and more effective in some situations. Resident intervention might entail calling police, for instance; but for that to happen, they must have trust in the police, something that is in short supply in disadvantaged neighborhoods. On one hand, they are frequently targeted by police suspicion and subjected to police harassment, including frequent stops, verbal abuse, and the use of unnecessary force. On the other hand, when they or someone they know calls the police for help, the police are often unresponsive. Some scholars believe there is a greater tolerance for crime among the poor and others argue, as noted earlier, that violence, including violence against women, may become normalized in impoverished communities. Yet most residents of disadvantaged neighborhoods tell researchers they want better law *enforcement* and police *protection*. These are not contradictions: legal cynicism can contribute to a cognitive landscape in which violence is normalized, a part of everyday life with which one has to cope. Consequently, improved community policing and police-community relations, so that residents feel they are treated fairly and respectfully and that the police are present to actually "protect and serve," are critical in reducing all forms of violence, including IPV, in disadvantaged neighborhoods.

Given the downward slide of the U.S. economy in recent years, the problems of both poverty and IPV may worsen. The economic downturn will undoubtedly have a negative impact on already reduced municipal, state, and federal budgets for social programs at a time when the need for funding and services is increasing. Service providers in various arenas—domestic violence, welfare, health care, housing, and legal advocacy—need to resist the temptation of competing with one another for scarce resources to address discrete social ills and instead develop collaborative working relationships that recognize the interconnections among the various problems they each address. A starting point is universal screening for IPV of clients who present for service, with referrals to appropriate providers with whom each agency has a memorandum of agreement. This approach assumes that all agency staff—from administrators to supervisors to front line workers—receive training in best practices for IPV screening; recognize IPV as a serious, widespread problem; and are motivated to respond sensitively and effectively. For example, battered women often seek medical attention not only for injuries from abuse but also for health problems that do not appear related to an injury or a predisposing health condition. Routine, universal screening by health care professionals who show interest, empathy, and sensitivity could result in early detection of abuse and allow for appropriate referrals to other services, such as counseling and legal assistance, as well as begin the process of documenting a woman's abuse history. One advantage of universal screening is that it resists further marginalizing the poor. Although IPV seems to be more prevalent among poor women, it is not a problem only of "those women." Universal screening breaks down stereotypes and has the potential to benefit all women.

Of course, screening is irrelevant if services are not available for women who are identified as needing them. Poor minority women may be unaware or suspicious of victim service agencies, seeing them as intrusive and racist. It is critical for victim service providers to be culturally competent. As Tameka Gillum found in her research, African American women who sought help for IPV from a culturally specific agency said they felt more comfortable speaking with African American staff, who they thought could better understand them and their experiences.[22] They also appreciated an Afrocentric environment, which made them feel more welcome and safe. Moreover, the women praised the agency for incorporating norms, expectations, and attitudes that African Americans value into their programming, including family centeredness and spirituality. Given limitations on funding and personnel, it is impossible to establish a culturally specific agency for every racial or ethnic group present in a community. Nevertheless, Gillum's research highlights the need for all service providers to be attentive to culturally specific factors in the client populations they serve. Racial and ethnic diversity of staff as well as cultural representation of diverse groups in the agency environment are critical to effective outreach and service provision.

Evidence of the role of religion in buffering IPV or its effects has produced mixed findings, with some commentators pointing to the pervasive sexism as well as sexual harassment in black churches. In general, though, religiosity has been shown to have a protective effect for women, with women reporting higher levels of religiosity also reporting less IPV. Interestingly, this effect seems to be stronger for African American men and women and Hispanic men than for whites or Hispanic women. Such findings, along with Gillum's, indicate the need for greater involvement of faith-based groups in IPV prevention and intervention programs.[23]

As job losses continue in communities throughout the country and the number of home foreclosures mount, it seems likely that increasing proportions of women will become poor and seek not only IPV services but also welfare. Welfare "reform" went into effect when the economy was robust and job growth appeared steady. Still, even with the recent severe economic downturn, it is unlikely that politicians will turn away from their commitment to addressing poverty through employment rather than government-funded financial assistance. In fact, some analysts predict that mandatory work requirements associated with welfare receipt could become even more stringent. It is imperative, therefore, that victim advocates and advocates for the poor lobby together for policies that help women become financially stable and independent while receiving services to address other serious problems in their lives, including IPV and substance abuse. One proposal is to amend the federal Assets for Independence Act of 1998 (AFIA) to specifically include abused women. As Christy-McMullin points out, economic security and independence derive not only from income, which for the majority of poor people is spent in full each month, but also from asset accumulation.[24] The AFIA allocates revenues to fund, through matched government contributions, individual development accounts (IDAs) for individuals and families, thus providing them with structured assistance to accumulate savings, similar to incentives provided middle-class and wealthier individuals and families (e.g., tax credits for child care expenses, Keogh plans, and tax deductions for mortgage interest on owner-occupied homes and on property tax on owner-occupied homes). The money saved may only be used for first-time home purchases, small business capitalization, and postsecondary education, but it may be transferred to eligible family members, including spouses and children. Although Christy-McMullin identifies specific problems AFIA presents to battered women, she argues that these difficulties can be overcome, and she proposes that Congress "mandate states to direct a significant portion of the funds that are being 'saved' from the decreased number of TANF recipients back to abused women via matched government contributions into individual development accounts (IDAs)."[25]

Proposals such as Christy-McMullin's are innovative, but they are likely to impact only a small number of poor abused women, most of whom will continue to look to employment as their means to self-sufficiency. Employers must also be enlisted to protect and assist their female employees who are experiencing IPV. Employers have a vested interest in this effort, since studies indicate that IPV-related injuries to women cost about $5 billion each year in terms of medical expenses and lost productivity, and of this amount, more than 50 percent is born by the private sector in the form of payments for health insurance and sick leave benefits.

Despite such statistics, employers have been slow in responding. In fact, research indicates that male employees who perpetrate IPV report that their employers support them by, for instance, posting their bail and testifying on their behalf in court. IPV often spills over into the workplace with batterers stalking their intimate partners at work and sometimes assaulting and murdering them at work. There are few easily implemented steps employers can take to address IPV and increase their female employees' safety while helping them maintain their jobs. They can reprimand employees who are arrested for abuse and encourage or require them to complete a batterer intervention program, for instance, or offer a female employee who is being victimized paid leave or a job transfer to another company office or plant in a different state. Moe and Bell offer the example of a female employee whose partner kept her computer, which was necessary to her job. Had her employer simply provided her with another computer, she could have kept her job. As Moe and Bell point out, these formal and informal efforts on the part of employers benefit abused employees by maintaining their primary source of income while also increasing their safety. They also allow employers to retain knowledgeable employees and generate loyalty and goodwill among employees generally.[26]

Finally, in designing or implementing any policy or program for battered women, be they poor or not, the women themselves should be consulted. In my own research and that of many others, one consistently striking finding is the level of resiliency to their troubles IPV victims display. They are active problem solvers, and they know through their lived experience which programs will be most helpful and which may reduce rather than improve their safety and the safety of their children. They are not a homogenous group, and what is beneficial for some may be less beneficial for or potentially harmful to others. Just as there is no single solution to either the problem of IPV or poverty, there is no one-size-fits-all program or policy for battered women, poor or otherwise. Therefore, one of the most important services anyone can provide to battered women is to *listen* to them and recognize them as skilled decision makers in their own lives. They are, after all, the true experts on IPV.

NOTES

1. L. A. Greenfeld, M. R. Rand, D. Craven, P. A. Klaus, C. Perkins, G. Warchol, et al., *Violence by Intimates: Analysis of Data on Crimes by Current or Former Spouses, Boyfriends, and Girlfriends* (Washington, D. C.: U. S. Department of Justice, 1998); and R. L. Hampton and R. J. Gelles, "Violence toward African American Women in a Nationally Representative Sample of African American Families," *Journal of Comparative Family Studies* 25 (1994): 105–19.

2. E. N. Luna-Firebaugh, "Violence against American Indian Women and the Services-Training-Officers-Prosecutors Violence against Women (STOP VAIW Program)," *Violence against Women* 12 (2006): 125–36.

3. T. Gillum, "Exploring the Link between Stereotypic Images and Intimate Partner Violence in the African American Community," *Violence against Women* 8 (2002): 64–86; and R. Staples, *Black Masculinity* (San Francisco: Black Scholars Press, 1982).

4. M. L. Benson, J. Wooldredge, A. B. Thistletheaite, and G. L. Fox, "The Correlation between Race and Domestic Violence Is Confounded with Community Context," *Social Problems* 51 (2004): 326–42.

5. S. Lloyd, "The Effects of Domestic Violence on Women's Employment," *Law & Policy* 19 (1997): 139–67.

6. P. Tjaden and N. Thoennes, *Prevalence, Incidence and Consequences of Violence against Women: Findings from the National Violence against Women Survey* (Washington, D. C.: U. S. Department of Justice, 1998).

7. A. Browne, A. Salomon, and S. S. Bassuk, "The Impact of Recent Partner Violence on Poor Women's Capacity to Maintain Work," *Violence against Women* 5 (1999): 393–426.

8. J. Tucker, S. L. Wenzel, J. B. Straus, G. W. Ryan, and D. Golinelli, "Experiencing Interpersonal Violence: Perspectives of Sexually Active, Substance-Using Women Living in Shelters and Low-Income Housing," *Violence against Women* 11 (2005): 1319–40.

9. C. A. Sutherland, C. M. Sullivan, and D. I. Bybee, "Effects of Partner Violence versus Poverty on Women's Health," *Violence against Women* 7 (2001): 1122–43.

10. A. Salomon, S. S. Bassuk, and N. Huntington, "The Relationship between Intimate Partner Violence and the Use of Addictive Substances in Poor and

Homeless Single Mothers," *Violence Against Women* 8 (2002): 785–815; J. A. Inciardi, D. Lockwood, and A. E. Pottieger, *Women and Crack-Cocaine* (New York: Macmillan, 1991); S. James, J. Johnson, and C. Raghavan, "I Couldn't Go Anywhere: Contextualizing Violence and Drug Abuse: A Social Network Study," *Violence against Women* 10 (2004): 991–1014; J. Raphael, *Listening to Olivia: Violence, Poverty, and Prostitution* (Boston: Northeastern University Press, 2004); and J. Raphael, *Freeing Tammy: Women, Drugs, and Incarceration* (Boston: Northeastern University Press, 2007).

11. J. Miller, *Getting Played: African American Girls, Urban Inequality, and Gendered Violence* (New York: New York University Press, 2008); and see also Jody Miller, *One of the Guys: Girls, Gangs and Gender* (New York: Oxford University Press, 2001).

12. C. M. Renzetti and S. L. Maier, "'Private' Crime in Public Housing: Violent Victimization, Fear of Crime and Social Isolation among Women Public Housing Residents," *Women's Health and Urban Life* 1 (2002): 46–65.

13. D. Rosen, "'I Just Let Him Have His Way': Partner Violence in the Lives of Low-Income, Teenage Mothers," *Violence against Women* 10 (2004): 6–28.

14. S. James, J. Johnson, and C. Raghavan, "I Couldn't Go Anywhere: Contextualizing Violence and Drug Abuse: A Social Network Study, *Violence Against Women* 10(2004): 991–1014.

15. C. R. Browning, "The Span of Collective Efficacy: Extending Social Disorganization Theory to Partner Violence," *Journal of Marriage and the Family* 64 (2002): 833–50. Browning's research shows that community norms supporting nonintervention into partner conflicts are associated with an increased risk of IPV.

16. C. Raghavan, A. Mennerich, E. Sexton, and S. E. James, "Community Violence and Its Direct, Indirect, and Mediating Effects on Intimate Partner Violence," *Violence against Women* 12 (2006): 1132–49.

17. A. M. Moe and M. P. Bell, "Abject Economics: The Effects of Battering and Violence on Women's Work and Employability," *Violence against Women* 10 (2004): 29–35; and J. Raphael *Saving Bernice: Battered Women, Welfare, and Poverty* (Boston: Northeastern University Press, 2000).

18. A. Raj, J. G. Silverman, G. M. Wingood, and R. J. DiClemente, "Prevalence and Correlates of Relationship Abuse among a Community-Based Sample of Low-Income African American Women," *Violence Against Women* 5 (1999): 272–291 [the quotes is from p. 285]; and see also R. MacMillan and R. Gartner, "When She Brings Home the Bacon: Labor Force Participation and Risk of Spousal Violence against Women," *Journal of Marriage and the Family* 61 (1999): 947–58.

19. L. D. Brush, "Effects of Work on Hitting and Hurting," *Violence against Women* 9 (2003): 1213–30.

20. T. Lindhorst, M. Meyers, and E. Casey, "Screening for Domestic Violence in Public Welfare Offices: An Analysis of Case Manager and Client Interactions," *Violence against Women* 14 (2008): 5–28.

21. R. J. Sampson and J. L. Lauritsen, "Violent Victimization and Offending: Individual-, Situational-, and Community-Level Risk Factors" in *Understanding and Preventing Violence*, vol. 3., ed. A. J. Reiss and J. A. Roth (Washington, D. C.: National Academy Press, 1994): 1–114.

22. T. Gillum, "The Benefits of a Culturally Specific Intimate Partner Violence Intervention for African American Survivors," *Violence against Women* 14 (2008): 917–943.

23. A. Raj, J. G. Silverman, G. M. Wingood, and R. J. DiClemente, "Prevalence and Correlates of Relationship Abuse among a Community-Based Sample of Low-Income African American Women," *Violence Against Women*, 5 (1999): 272–291; and C. G. Ellison, J. A. Trinitapoli, K. L. Anderson, and B. R. Johnson, "Race/Ethnicity, Religious Involvement, and Domestic Violence," *Violence against Women* 13 (2007): 1094–112. See also M. H. Whitson, "Sexism and Sexual Harassment Concerns of African American Women of the Christian Methodist Episcopal Church," *Violence against Women* 3 (1997): 382–400.

24. K. Christy-McMullin, "An Analysis of the Assets for Independence Act of 1998 for Abused Women," *Violence against Women* 6 (2000): 1066–84.

25. Christy-McMullin, "An Analysis of the Assets for Independence Act of 1998 for Abused Women," 1068.

26. A. M. Moe and M. P. Bell, "Abject Economics: The Effects of Battering and Violence on Women's Work and Employability," *Violence against Women* 10 (2004): 51.

Chapter 6

The Trapping Effects of Poverty and Violence

Jody Raphael

When we think about the relationship between domestic violence and poverty, what comes immediately to mind is this: poor women, lacking the economic means to escape, are more prone than more affluent women to be permanently trapped by the abuse. This image makes sense. Abusers make a special target of poor girls and women, who can more easily be controlled because they lack education or work skills and may have fled households mired in domestic violence, sexual assault, and substance abuse. As a result of their vulnerabilities, poor women are more likely to stay in abusive relationships too long and to rely on coping strategies that facilitate disassociation, such as drug abuse, which further limit their options.

Poverty also traps women in violent relationships in other important ways that only recently have become understood. Already marginalized by their economic situation, when these women are further isolated by their abuser and shamed by the violence, they can become completely invisible. They are, however, all too visible in certain institutions like the welfare and criminal justice systems, which further punish and stigmatize the women because of how they cope with abuse. To this extent, society colludes with abusers to maintain institutional practices that further trap women in violence.

Americans love success stories. But women who suffer the double penalties of poverty and abuse are so stigmatized that no one wants to hear their stories, let alone acknowledge their plight. During a recent speaking engagement in southwest Virginia, I met a survivor of domestic violence and sexual assault who told me her church was organizing a program on domestic violence. When she told her pastor that she wanted to tell her story, he responded, "Oh no, we wouldn't want to traumatize the congregation."

If we are to respond humanely to women trapped by poverty and abuse, we must learn to hear their stories. Over the past 10 years, three biographies have been published of three Chicago women whose lives illustrate the complex relationship of poverty and violence.[1] Direct quotes in the following sections are excerpted from this work.

Unfortunately, the experiences of these women also demonstrate the disinterest, and even contempt, that mark our responses. In the end, it is we who should be ashamed, not them.

BERNICE

Bernice Hampton, a 27-year-old welfare recipient, came to the West Side Chicago welfare-to-work program desperately seeking job training and employment. Only over time did the program learn that Bernice had been living with an abusive man since she was a teen. The mother of two, Bernice's father was also an abuser who had burned his son to death and threatened to kill his wife if she testified against him. After Bernice's aunt testified in court against her father—her mother was silenced by her husband's threats—he went home and shot at Bernice's mother seven times; he was shooting at Bernice's sister when her mother crawled down to the first floor to alert the neighbors. Bernice's mother was in the hospital for 11 months. When she left, she became an alcoholic.

At age 14, Bernice met Billy, a handsome and charismatic junior at the high school. It seemed like the perfect solution to her problems at home. Two years later, she dropped out of school and left her family to make the "perfect home" with Billy. Billy turned out to be a violent abuser himself. Although Bernice saw it coming, she chose to ignore the signs and symptoms because she clung to her fantasy of the perfect nuclear family.

Billy's violence wasn't impulsive or rooted in mental illness. Instead, he carefully calibrated his abuse to prevent Bernice from education, training, and work. Bernice says he knew that as only a sporadic worker he had little to offer Bernice and the children. She explained his thinking:

If I work, I am going to interact with people. I am going to make money, develop skills. I am going to have confidence, be dedicated to something other than him. People will be allowed to have input. I will start to come alive, I will care about the way I look, the way I dress, and ultimately I will want something different outside of my current life. Billy knew that our life was nothing. If I went to work, he would have lost me. He knew it, and that was what he was afraid of. He was right. If I had been able to get a job, I would have been gone.

Bernice was intent on helping her family get out of poverty by finding employment and getting off welfare. But every time she tried to either work or leave the relationship, Billy's violence escalated. He began burning her with cigarettes and an iron and hurting her with a broom. He also bought a gun. Bernice could not envision how she could go to work or leave Billy and be alive to tell the tale. To cope with the anxiety and the bleakness of her days and the lack of a future, Bernice turned to drugs, which Billy was only too happy to supply.

Ultimately, through a job training program, Bernice enrolled in a course to become a licensed practical nurse, a job that could support her and the children. Bernice's welfare check didn't even cover the amount needed for monthly rent in Chicago.

She was 15 weeks from graduation.

I was so proud of myself. I was motivated. I had been offered a job, my life was about to change. I had one more course to go through as well as the final exam. I didn't tell Billy how close I was to graduation, but unfortunately he overheard me on the telephone talking with my sister, as I was very excited to be offered a job. The weekend before the final exam he made sure we fought all weekend. He knew how important this test was for me. He wouldn't watch the children, he wouldn't feed them, he wouldn't let me study, he would take my books from me. I never got a chance to either sleep or study.

Around 2 a.m. on Monday morning, Billy raped Bernice. Exhausted and sleep-deprived, physically and mentally beaten down, she nonetheless dragged herself to school and took the final exam. Not surprisingly, she failed the test and was dropped from the program. Although her case manager appealed the decision to the head of the program and to its board of directors, the school categorically refused to reconsider or let Bernice retake the examination, or even re-enroll in the program.

Several months later, Bernice left Billy and took the children to her mother's. Billy came to the apartment, broke the windows, and threatened to kill Bernice's mother if she didn't return, which she did.

Billy also threatened to physically harm Bernice's case manager. This was an effective means of control because she was one of the few sources of support Bernice had.

One day, when he made the threat again, I said, "Go ahead and kill her then." He pushed me down on the floor, and he put a broom across my neck and he had a gun in his hand and he was holding the broom down in the other hand and his knee was on my throat. He said, "You know, I could just kill you right now," and as he talked he moved the gun to my neck. I said, "Well, go ahead, take Denise out, and you might as well take me out, and take yourself out too." He got up and said, "I wasn't doing anything but playing with you. Even if I pulled the trigger nothing would have happened." It so frightened me that I was still on the floor. He took the gun and put it in the closet and said, "You'll always know where this is at."

I stayed in the house for three months after that and I didn't get dressed. I wouldn't go out, I wouldn't feed the children. I just sat there in front of the TV all day, and I said, "This is what you wanted. You wanted me to be a vegetable, not to have a mind of my own, how do you like it?"

Billy was right. If I had been able to get a job, I would have been gone.

Bernice finally escaped by entering a battered women's shelter. She found a job and got her own apartment with the two children. Soon afterward, Billy located Bernice and stalked her for one-and-a-half years. When the stalking failed to convince her to return, he upped the ante and sued for custody of their son. As her son wanted to live with his father, Bernice decided not to contest the action, hoping that if Billy "won" this victory, he might conclude his revenge was complete and end his threats to her and her young daughter. Happily, that proved to be the case.

With the small amount of money from her monthly welfare grant, Bernice was unable to financially survive on her own and so couldn't leave Billy. But the welfare was just enough to make her an attractive target, particularly when combined with her lack of work experience. Bernice explains another way in which welfare colludes with abusers.

As a welfare recipient, I knew that society didn't accept me. I was in a different class. An untouchable class. Women on welfare know that they are an untouchable class; that is how they are seen. Because they are already suppressed by being on welfare, these women are already there. All the abusers have to do is to maintain the situation. We have nothing, and we don't know how to stand up for ourselves. That is why abusers encourage welfare usage. With welfare, you are being given something, but that something really stigmatizes you in society. That stigma lowers your self-esteem and keeps you in line.

Research just before the 1996 federal welfare reform demonstrated that 25 to 30 percent of all women on welfare were current victims of domestic violence.[2] Since federal welfare reform, which mandated work and time-limited welfare receipt to 60 months, the percentages of those left on the rolls who are current violence victims has risen. In one recent California study, a total of 37 percent of women welfare applicants reported recent, serious domestic violence.[3] In research conducted between June and November 2001 in California with a fairly large sample of applicants, almost 30 percent of those applying for the federal welfare program, and almost 40 percent of single women applying for the state General Assistance program, had experienced domestic violence within the past year. For those applying for the federal program, about a third of it was serious violence. Almost 13 percent of General Assistance applicants, and 6 percent of the federal applicants, had experienced sexual assault, rates that are 10 times the national average.[4] These data are significant because in Michigan, longitudinal welfare-tracking research measuring the effects of welfare reform in the state found that recent domestic violence and chronic, severe domestic violence were associated with greater reliance on welfare and an inability to comply with mandatory work requirements.[5]

Sabotaging Bernice's completion of job training was one way to keep her on welfare. Another way her abuser prevented her from working was interference with her birth control. Billy actively encouraged her pregnancies and sabotaged her birth control arrangements. Bernice had a tubal ligation after her last pregnancy and told Billy about it afterward. Being constantly pregnant meant that Bernice wasn't likely to be attractive to another man, leave the relationship, or even be able to handle employment. But Billy also sabotaged her birth control because of jealousy. Once on birth control, a woman could have sex with another man and never get caught.

Bernice explains that there is no way one can overstate the importance to abusers of seeing their wives or girlfriend become pregnant and give birth to their child. Years after the relationship ended, Bernice's tubal ligation was still on his mind. "There is one great thing," he gloated to Bernice. "Another man can't give you a baby." Recently, research with teen girls has identified birth control sabotage by abusive intimate partners as a major cause of teen pregnancy that has been totally overlooked; one recent study in Massachusetts found that over a quarter of the girls who were involved in violent relationships reported that their partners were actively trying to get them pregnant by manipulating condom use, interfering with birth control use, and making explicit statements about wanting them to become pregnant.[6]

It is also important to note that the criminal justice and legal system were unable to assist Bernice in any meaningful way. She obtained an order of protection as well as a felony stalking charge against Billy, but he got out on bail or on probation each time, which sent him a signal that he could get away free. And upon his release, the physical abuse escalated. One time he even attacked Bernice on the stairs as they left the courthouse. Since Billy was never locked up, Bernice's use of the criminal justice system simply made everything worse.

Bernice's story teaches us the many ways in which the intimate partners of women on welfare use violence to sabotage their efforts to work. When the criminal justice system failed to adequately respond, Bernice found herself trapped both on welfare and in a dangerous, abusive relationship. Ironically, at the same time, she found herself labeled by society as an indolent dependent person who, by failing to take responsibility for herself and her children, needed to be mandated into work.

OLIVIA

Olivia's family background resembled Bernice's. But her journey through abuse took a very different direction.

Olivia's father brutally abused her mother physically, and the two were both alcoholics.

Punching, slapping, kicking, throwing her against the wall, dragging her by her hair. We kids would huddle together during these two-hour episodes. We lay in bed hearing it and we would go to sleep hearing it. We didn't know what to do as kids. We talked about calling the police, but we thought that would make it worse.

Olivia started to drink at the age of eight or nine as a method of numbing herself; alcohol became a means to disassociate and get to sleep when the sounds of violence became intolerable.

When I tasted booze, I liked it. For many reasons. I wouldn't be as fearful at night when my parents started fighting. The drink desensitized me to what was really going on. I would see a glass and sip the drink. It would calm me and make me pass out, or it didn't devastate me as much.

At very young ages, Olivia and her two sisters were also asked to dance at the drunken poker parties her parents attended. Olivia and her sister are pretty certain that they were sexually abused at these parties.

I saw a hand. I was a real little girl lying on the bed. I saw a very young child's private parts, and a man standing over her. I could never get to the face. I have often wondered if it was my father, or one of his friends. I don't doubt that something happened. Everybody's drunk, the kids are in the room asleep, the door was never all the way closed. My sister thinks that she may have been too, and we both can't be wrong. It was probably so early on that subconsciously we just buried it.

There was to be no Prince Charming for Olivia. Having seen what happened to her mother, she was determined to take a totally different path. No man was going to save her; *she* was going to take advantage of men. So what does a 16 year old do to make a living on the street? A girlfriend suggested that the petite and beautiful Olivia join her at a downtown Chicago strip club. To get the job, Olivia had to lie about her age. Initially, she believed she was hired to dance at the facility.

I really thought of it as a dancing job. Within 30 days I found out the real dynamics of these clubs.... I remember my first routines. The older dancers must have thought, she is some joke, she will learn real quick. I did all these modern dance routines, and I really thought I was hired because I was a good dancer. You find out it has nothing to do with the dancing, or whether or not you can dance. It's your willingness to take your clothes off, to be seductive. The alcohol helped me to enjoy that part of it because I saw the rewards. The alcohol helped me to get through it, the money reinforced the benefit of it. I said, this is the easiest money in the world.

So Olivia danced, she flirted, she got customers to buy drinks. And she became persuaded, little by little, to do more and more at the club, including providing sex in the back room. Olivia was continually disgusted by the physical contact with the men.

They reach up and put money in your G-string, and they ram their fingers into you. A lot of groping. Within 30 days the awful reality sets in. There are 50,000 hands touching me, you begin to feel dirty, the guys are smelly, they are usually drunk. Some of them sit and drink so much until they are physically sick. Even talking about it now, I can still smell them. That is the most disgusting part. They were animals.

So why did she stay at the club? The combination of the money and the glamour was irresistible for the young girl. "This is such an easy way," she said to herself. "Can I deal with this?"

For Olivia, alcohol became the way.

It is a myth that any woman can get up there and do that and not have something in her. It doesn't have to be hard-core drugs, but you have to take something to help you deal with it. Alcohol is probably the easiest because it is so accessible in the clubs. Before I got to work, I would drink anywhere from a pint to a fifth. I found out that a couple of drinks would take off the nervousness right away. I then had the courage to get up there and take my clothes off. I was able to disassociate totally, totally. I did not have to be presently there, but I could do my job.

So Olivia made the fateful decision to stay in the business. And her alcohol consumption increased. She began to drink throughout the entire night. Sometimes she drank so much she had blackouts and had to be awakened in the dressing room after she had missed her set. Or she would be found with her head in the toilet, violently vomiting. And slowly but surely, Olivia began to be enticed into doing more and more at the club. From lap and table dancing, she graduated to dancing in a private room.

Slowly you are lured into doing more. Each step, there was more involved, and more money involved, and more drinking; drinking was almost around the clock by this time. It was pretty disgusting, but alcohol cured it for me. When I'd feel a moment of disgust, I'd drink a little more and I would get less inhibited, it didn't seem as bad. If I woke up and thought, "Oh my God, I did this in front of people, I gave a blow job in front of six other guys," for a minute I would feel ready bad about it, but again, I rationalized it a lot. I made it make sense. You make sense of the world around you, and that is what I did. You say, "At least I got the damn fool's money."

Over time, the party began to wind down.

Eventually you feel the self-loathing and the shame. Jacking these guys off, I'm letting them spill on me, I'm sitting on their laps, they are breathing on me, you can feel their whiskers touching you when they put their face close to you. It was totally against me morally; somewhere deep inside, I felt it was wrong. I knew it was. I began to see myself: "Oh my God, you will do anything, you will let guys do anything." The drinking, the drugs help you find a way to feel better about what has happened to you and what you are doing to yourself. There are glimpses of yourself that frighten you, that tell you this isn't right, you shouldn't be living like this, and you feel sad for a minute. But if you drink enough, or get enough in you, you can push it far, far away.

Ultimately, the sex became humiliating for Olivia.

I definitely felt degraded most of the time. I showered. I washed over and over because I felt unclean. You feel so degraded doing some of these acts or even accepting being talked to in that manner. You know it is wrong, but there is nothing else you can do about it.

Heroin, to which a fellow stripper introduced her, helped Olivia continue to do the job. But when the heroin habit interfered with her remaining on an eight-hour shift, she switched to turning tricks in hotels and on
the streets, where conditions were a bit more dangerous. So she relied on
Strych, short for his longer nickname "Strychnine," her drug supplier
who soon became her boyfriend/protector and pimp, because he soon
started living off her earnings. With his six-foot-three, 230-pound frame
and his quickness to anger, fueled by alcohol and drugs, people on the
street feared Strych and left Olivia pretty much alone.

But Strych turned out to be an abuser. He broke Olivia's ribs, hit her
on the back, and stomped on her. He threw an ashtray at her back that
damaged her kidneys. He hit Olivia with baseball bats. She was beaten
on the street, all to make sure she obeyed his commands to turn tricks
every night. At the same time, Olivia suffered verbal abuse, violence,
multiple rapes, and gang rapes from some of her customers.

Olivia did not exactly know how to ask for help. Several times, tired
and beaten down from all the drugs and the violence, she sought assistance from area hospital emergency rooms. Several times she even pre-
tended to be mentally ill so that she would be kept overnight at the
hospital as a kind of respite from Strych and the streets. Unfortunately,
no one in any of the hospitals talked to her about her problem or
referred her to available treatment programs. Every single time, she
was patched up and sent back to the streets, often with a prescribed
narcotic for the pain.

> I would just be so tired. I remember walking into a hospital and saying that if they
> didn't keep me, I was going to kill myself. Again, they let me see a psychiatrist who
> kept me for stabilization for something like three days, and that was it. Between the
> Librium or Valium and whatever else they gave me, I didn't get drug sick right
> away. I was so tired. I slept. And after I rested up a couple of days, I was right back
> out on the street. It just shows you how hospitals fail. Either they didn't care
> because I didn't have insurance, or they weren't real sure what to do with me. You
> are talking about people that nobody wants anything to do with.

In October 1990, Olivia, down to 90 pounds and nearly dead, was res-
cued by an outreach worker on the street and sent to a special house for
women in prostitution. She agreed to go only because she simply could
not continue what she was doing any longer. Olivia had no hope of a better life; she thought of the recovery home simply as an end station.

> I didn't have an ounce of hope. I never thought in a thousand years that it would
> work. I was just tired, tired, and vulnerable enough to be willing to stay. That is all
> that I wanted for that moment, never knowing, because I didn't know there was
> anything better. I thought that was it. I was going to die that way, either from a shot
> of dope, a trick killing me, or a pimp killing me. I wasn't looking for a better way or
> wanting to change. I didn't know change would be possible, or that you could
> change. I thought that after you became something, that is what you were.

To her astonishment, she was able to get off heroin after 19 years and safely leave prostitution, although Strych stalked her for some time. Today, Olivia has her college degree and works for a social services program, helping other women exit lives dominated by drugs and prostitution.

Olivia is typical of the majority of girls and women in the sex trade industry in North America. Research shows that almost 90 percent are victims of childhood sexual assault. Although not all victims of childhood sexual assault are involved in prostitution, the strong connection makes sense; experts believe that the sex trade industry provides a structure that girls and women think enables them to seek power and control over men, which has been removed from them by sexual assault.[7]

Olivia knows now that she had a need for a sense of power and control that involvement in the industry at first addressed.

It met some need that I was not even aware of at the time. I had no idea that I had other needs that were being met or even needing to be met. I was really caught up in it. I had control of these guys, I could make them eat out of my hand.

Olivia's story illustrates that the sense of power and control she felt was illusory. Her participation in the sex trade industry became a highly dysfunctional strategy to cope with her earlier exposure to domestic violence and sexual assault.

Research has also demonstrated that, like Olivia, a large proportion of women in the sex trade have begun sex work on a regular basis as teens. One research sample from Chicago found that over 60 percent first exchanged sex for money before the age of 18, with 32 percent starting between the ages of 12 and 15.[8]

To meet an ever-growing demand, the industry relies on recruiters, like Olivia's girlfriend, and very often pimp boyfriends, who offer love, protection, and money to poor and vulnerable teen girls who need to leave home and then exploit them by persuading them to enter the industry. Many are held in the sex trade industry through violence and coercion, as Olivia was by Strych. And the number of girls and women involved in the sex trade industry is not insignificant. In Chicago alone, research has shown a minimum of 15,000 girls and women active on any given day.[9]

Childhood sexual assault and domestic violence led Olivia into the sex trade industry, where she was further physically and sexually assaulted. Heroin and alcohol, the self-medications that enabled her to continue in the business, sealed her off from reality and kept her from escaping. Olivia's trajectory turned her into a subhuman walking zombie. It is hard to find words to describe the extent of her isolation and disconnection from the world. As an institution, the worldwide sex trade industry facilitates this violence and abuse of poor and needy girls and women, most of whom have already been abused. Stories of women like Olivia make a compelling case to eliminate the sex trade industry in our midst.

TAMMY

Tammy's story illustrates how childhood sexual assault and domestic violence can actually make a person poor. Tammy came from a middle-class home in southwest Michigan. Unlike her other siblings, she developed an angry, aggressive personality early and in her teens acted out sexually and became dependent on alcohol. Only later did Tammy link these early behaviors to childhood sexual assault. From the time Tammy was two until she was five, her godfather, a church minister, regularly sexually molested her in his home.

> *I can see it like it was yesterday. My mother would dress me in these frilly dresses and he would put his hand under there and play with my genitals. Every time I would stand there and cry while he did it until he got finished. This went on forever, as long as I can remember, years.*

It's not that Tammy forgot about the sexual molestation, but to continue to function she had to stop thinking about it. Even today, it is painful for her to dwell on it for very long.

> *If I'm asked whether I'm a victim of violence, I've said "no" repeatedly. I haven't accepted it. That's everybody else. That wasn't me, I had a beautiful childhood. There are horrors that I completely blocked out. A therapist would have brought them out very early and I would have been able to deal with them. I never had any help.*

Her godfather gave her candy afterward.

> *It would explain the voluntary teen prostitution. Grabbing power back. I could always be more powerful with these worthless men, so I would go after that crowd. I can be more powerful than them.*

Tammy's anger motivated her to leave home the day she graduated from high school. She came to Chicago and hit the ground running. But the youngster with no skills unfortunately found a job working for a small businessman who, sensing Tammy's vulnerability, required her to dispense sexual favors to him during the lunch hour. Because Tammy didn't want her mother to know that her efforts at independence had not worked out, she just grit her teeth through these approximately 30 different encounters.

Tammy was more than ready for the protection afforded by her first husband. A former minister, he had become a gang leader involved in robberies, drug sales, and prostitution. He also introduced her to heroin. She was physically abused by the handsome but alcoholic security guard who became her second husband. He was a dedicated womanizer who beat Tammy so that she would flee their home, leaving the coast clear for his liaisons with other women. On one occasion, he assaulted Tammy while she was bathing, forcing her to run naked to her neighbor's house. Another time, he beat her so badly while she was hiding in a closet that blood splattered over the walls and her eyes were closed shut, making escape difficult. Often she spent the night in the bathroom of the neighborhood gas station.

With this history, it was not surprising that Tammy, like Olivia, developed a 19-year heroin habit. The heroin helped to calm Tammy down, making it possible for her to continue to live without confronting her traumatic childhood. In addition to suppressing the pain of her earlier abuse and the coincident feelings of anger and powerlessness this abuse elicited, heroin also obliterated her sense that she had wasted her life, in no small part because of her addiction to narcotics.

I knew I was wasting myself. I had a lot of regrets, a lot of disappointments. But the drugs make it go away. You don't feel anymore. It masks those feelings of unworthiness. It was like a fight going on there, where the drug made me feel like I was winning over the other part that said, "You're really nothing, you are really the dregs of society."

While in drug rehab, Tammy met Maurice, the man who became her third husband. Tammy succeeded in getting off heroin for good, but Maurice simply could not quit. To finance her husband's drug habit, Tammy agreed to let her drug dealer store his drugs in her home. Although Maurice was verbally abusive, he had never physically attacked Tammy. But one day he did so when high on drugs, and she called the police. When the officers arrived, Maurice told them about the drugs in the home. Unfortunately, the drug dealer had just replenished the heroin stash the day before. Maurice's betrayal ultimately led to Tammy's conviction for heroin possession with intent to sell and a two-year incarceration. Thus, coping with and enabling her abusive husband's drug addiction became Tammy's pathway to crime.

During her incarceration, Tammy retreated to dissociation, an old survival strategy, though this time without the help of drugs. Her 12-year old son Terrence had to stay with his aunt, but eventually his own anger disrupted her home to such an extent that she had to ask him to leave; that move left her son effectively homeless. When Tammy called her sister's house, she could see how hard her son was working to be bubbly and jovial, but she knew how he was struggling and how much he was hurting, all due to her actions; mother and son had been extraordinarily close.

Tammy became preoccupied with thoughts of suicide. She started to buy and hoard medication from other incarcerated women.

I knew that I had money in my inmate account and that I could buy anything that I wanted. And I wanted to buy. I didn't want to live without my son. I didn't want to live here, in that prison. When I was talking to Terrence and I knew how sad he was, it was more than I could bear. It was more than I could take on, it was so horrible for me.

Eventually Tammy realized that for her to commit suicide would make life far worse for her son, who would be dealt another cruel blow from which he might never recover. So to survive her time in prison, Tammy numbed herself. She simply had to put off dealing with any feelings until she got out.

I had to numb myself without drugs because I was going to kill myself otherwise, and I knew it, I prayed to God to take all feelings away. I had to numb myself to the fact that my son was out there by himself, I had to numb myself that my family was acting like they were ashamed of me, I had to numb the fact that I was homeless now and had nowhere to go. I remember the day, to this day, that I did it. I was on the top bunk and it was like a knife in my heart and I knew I wouldn't make it, and I told God, "Take every feeling out of my body, I don't want to feel anymore, it hurts too much, I'm not going to live." And I got off that top bunk and I never felt anything after that. I postponed feeling until I got out.

Like Olivia and Bernice, Tammy responded to her inner sense of futility and the daily challenges of incarceration by disassociation. Disassociation is a common psychological adaptation for battered women and, once it becomes a habitual response to stress, it is hard to set aside despite its adverse repercussions on women's abilities to cope with the vicissitudes of life.

When Tammy emerged from prison, she found the stigma she experienced the hardest thing to bear. As a person convicted of a drug offense, she was ineligible for welfare benefits. And no one wanted to hire her because of her felony record. Both she and her son were in danger of becoming even more marginal to mainstream society.

But Tammy persevered. She graduated from college, got her master's degree, and works today in a drug program in Chicago's south suburbs. After weathering a suicide attempt, her son is now a senior in college. Tammy believes the societal stigma attached to her time in prison will stick with her always, and represents the worst part of her entire experience.

We feel like we are in a box that will never have the lid taken off, never, because of that imprisonment. Society makes you pay for the rest of your life. You never stop paying. There is no cap on it. You pay for the rest of your life. One crime and you will pay for the rest of your life.

In addition to feeling rejected and despised by society, Tammy experienced her own self-esteem problems. She had internalized the stigma. At one point, she stayed in her house in a complete state of depression.

I was still in the dark. I was hiding so the world couldn't see me. Same thing as being on drugs, only I didn't have the drugs. Trapped forever. It was all the same ball of despair and degradation and embarrassment and humiliation. I was encompassed in that circle, and I couldn't break through that circle, so everywhere I looked I felt that humiliation, I felt the degradation, I felt the embarrassment.

I relived every minute of it. I relived the wasted years, the wasted time with Terrence. I relived how much could have happened to him because I wasn't there. I relived all the humiliations, the worse of which were at Cook County. When you are sitting there and reliving all of that, it is like a self-fulfilling prophecy. I felt worthless. So how could I get up and make things better when I felt worthless?

Psychologist Craig Haney calls what Tammy went through "internalizing the prison experience":

[P]risoners may come to think of themselves as the kind of person who deserves no more than the degradation and stigma to which they have been subjected while incarcerated. This degraded identity may be difficult or impossible to relinquish upon release from prison, especially if prisoners return to communities where they continue to be marginalized or stigmatized by others.[10]

Tammy's story is all too typical, reflecting the current practice of incarcerating low-income female drug users. In 2004, 104,848 women were incarcerated in the United States, the bulk for nonviolent offenses, a 740 percent increase in women's imprisonment since 1980. And it's a startling fact: the increase occurred in the final two decades of the last century.[11] The number of female prisoners increased at mid-year 2006 to 111,403. Between mid-year 2005 and 2006, the female prison population increased by 4.8 percent, compared with a male increase of 2.7 percent.[12]

According to The Sentencing Project's analysis of women's imprisonment, drug crimes account for half the rise in the number of women held in state facilities between 1986 to 1996.[13] Only 20 percent of women in state prisons, 12 percent in jails, and 7 percent in federal prisons in 2004 had committed violent offenses, with property, drug, and public order crimes making up the rest.[14]

The majority of women incarcerated in the nation's jails and prisons are victims of childhood sexual assault and domestic violence. The U.S. Department of Justice's study in the mid-1990s found that 57 percent of women in state prisons and 48 percent in jail were victims of violence; almost 40 percent of prisoners in jails and state prisons have been sexually abused.[15] Research at specific jails and prisons yields even higher percentages; a study of new admittees to the Bedford Hills, New York, Maximum Security Correctional Facility for Women found that 59 percent reported some form of sexual abuse during childhood or adolescence, with 75 percent victims of severe physical violence at the hands of intimate partners in adulthood.[16]

In the criminal justice system, women drug addicts are viewed as women gone bad who have abdicated their responsibility to be good mothers. That these women are already abused cuts no ice. Displaying the poor judgment to hook up with and stay with abusers further demonstrates their weirdness. As one prison warden explains,

Women degrade themselves.... There is no sense of self-respect, of dignity.... There is something wrong on the inside that makes an individual take up those kinds of behaviors and choices.[17]

So the answer is to try to get through to the women through hard and punitive prison conditions, designed with the toughness and alleged immorality of women drug users in mind. Tammy's story shows just how our current approach to incarceration retraumatized an already abused woman, dangerously lowering her self-esteem and almost causing her suicide.

FOUR ASPECTS OF THE INTERRELATIONSHIP OF VIOLENCE AND POVERTY

The stories of these three women also share four important characteristics that can lead us to more humane and effective societal responses.

First, disempowered by violence and sexual assault, the young women left home too early, seeking a sense of control over their lives, but their youth and experiences of violence limited their choices and compromised their success.

Domestic violence and sexual abuse caused the three to leave home early. All had passionate yearnings to be somebody, to be self-sufficient, and to achieve recognition, natural tendencies made even more potent because the girls had power stripped from them by the violence and sexual assault to which they were exposed. Yet, as uneducated teens seeking this power and recognition away from home, their choices were perforce limited.

Bernice had a passion for education, training, and work, but the older man into whose arms she naïvely fled at age 14 was threatened by her quest for economic independence. He sabotaged her every effort through brutal violence that led to Bernice's drug addiction and her many years on welfare. Welfare further trapped her in poverty and so made escape from the violence even more difficult. When the system refused to allow her to retake her nursing exam, it reinforced her entrapment by her partner.

Determined to live without a man and to stand on her own two feet, Olivia was recruited into stripping where there was a demand for her 16-year-old body. Initially, stripping gave Olivia a strong sense of power over these thousands of inebriated men, but unable to perform so many sexual acts on strangers, she too became addicted to alcohol and drugs, further trapping her in the sex trade industry in which she was violently abused.

Tammy developed an aggressive personality early in response to childhood sexual assaults, and from a young age sought to be powerful and respected. Leaving home prematurely without education or training meant she was unable to achieve that authority in legitimate venues. Like Bernice and Olivia, she developed a drug habit that allowed her to continue to get through her days without being overwhelmed by her sense of powerlessness or thoughts of what might have been.

Already abused, the three young women could not figure out how to realize their intense desire for authority and respect. However, effective in masking their disappointments in the short run, narcotics ultimately exacerbated the women's disempowerment, causing a downward spiral into poverty, further violence, and failure of self-care. Their stories contain clues for necessary violence prevention and early intervention.

Second, the crimes the women committed should be seen as a response to their ultimate powerlessness.

Powerless to safely escape her violent situation, Bernice dreamt about killing her abuser, and it was these fantasies that convinced her she had to risk her own death by leaving him. Had Bernice not gone to shelter, it is altogether likely she would be behind bars today serving time for manslaughter or homicide.

Olivia was involved in many illegal acts, including prostitution and robbery of customers. She was arrested 66 times. Anger fueled the robberies, an aggressive and dangerous attempt to wreak revenge on the men who were abusing her and taking away all her power.

Tammy's felony conviction represented her attempt to control a fast-deteriorating abusive environment that was sapping her of her money and possessions.

Understanding the origins of women's crime and recognizing that the women's offenses do not stem from antisocial motives suggest drastically different responses from the criminal justice system than are currently employed.

Third, societal institutions with which the women interacted made their situations worse, reinforcing their entrapment in abuse, addiction, and low self-esteem.

The institutions to which the women turned for help turned a blind eye and failed to respond. When the police and courts refused to take Bernice's complaints seriously, they made her life even more dangerous and violent. The hospitals to which Olivia turned in her distress were unresponsive. These institutional failures raise fundamental questions about equity, justice, and sense of commitment to the most needy in society. The institutional net in which they were caught was more dangerous than "safe."

Because it does not offer enough financial support to enable battered women to leave their abusers, the U.S. welfare system contributes to women's entrapment in abusive relationships. With their young children and slim financial resources, women on welfare become magnets for abusers who are seeking easily controlled partners. If adequately funded and accompanied by meaningful job training that is sensitive to the complex realities of abuse, welfare can play an important role in providing temporary resources, skill building, and opportunities for poor battered women and their children to escape abusive situations. Since the welfare department office is also one of the few places that the abuser lets his partner visit, it could be a good place for providing information about domestic violence and needed support services to these severely isolated women.

Exploiting their need for money and a sense of power, the sex trade industry attracts girls who have been dually victimized by poverty and childhood sexual assault. But the conditions in the industry, along with the alcohol and drugs without which the girls cannot continue, trap them in additional violence and abuse. Despite these realities, the sex trade industry continues to be viewed as paid, consensual sex between two adults, obscuring the exploitation and abuse of young and needy girls. Educating customers and cutting off demand through arrests of customers would be more effective responses than arresting and incarcerating women and girls in prostitution.

With its reliance on jails and prisons, the criminal justice system constitutes another problematic response to abused women who commit nonviolent crimes related to drug use. We punish and stigmatize women drug users, further aggravating their proclivities for disassociation, hence for the use of illicit substances. We do not offer adequate help for the drug abuse, nor provide therapy to assist in recovery from violence. Incarceration mires the women even further in violence and poverty. Clearly, drug treatment and help escaping and recovering from sexual abuse and partner violence are inextricable parts of the recovery process.

These women made their choices under restricted circumstances and as teens who were already victims of violence. Yet, our society continues to blame women who become trapped in violence and drug addiction. We label their dependencies as personal failures, and we stigmatize and punish them for being trapped. Typically, those who have injured these young women go unrecognized and unpunished.

The institutional responses to poverty and drug addiction further entrapped these female victims of violence. Bernice felt like a second-class citizen because of her welfare receipt, and it was this sense of shame and powerlessness that her abuser exploited. Once on welfare, who would take her abuse seriously? And how could she be expected to complete job training, let alone pass her exam or get a decent job, so long as she was being abused by a man who saw her economic independence as a threat to his control?

Many view women in prostitution like Olivia as deviants, sex addicts, junkies, or abnormal women and girls different from the rest of us. By contrast, we assume their customers are merely normal red-blooded males. When this stigma is combined with the lengthy rap sheets these women accumulate, it becomes nearly impossible for them to enter the labor market or even to ask for assistance and support to leave prostitution. Traditional helping institutions also stigmatize these women, often excluding them from available supports, if only unofficially.

We also stigmatize women like Tammy who have served time for felonies. Finding a job with a felony record is difficult at best, and women drug offenders are doubly stigmatized as bad mothers whose hedonistic pursuit of drug pleasure makes them immoral individuals who need to be punished into a greater sense of responsibility. For many of these women, the pain of punishment and the resulting stigmatization are difficult to overcome, closing off the ability to stay free of drugs and crime.

Stigmatization and shame prevent girls from seeking help early and from reporting childhood sexual assault, encouraging them instead to cope on their own, often through self-medicating the effects of violence. Were violence victims treated with dignity and respect rather than shamed and stigmatized, it is likely that fewer young needy women would find themselves trapped in lives marked by violence and poverty. As a result of stigmatization, we are unable to look beyond stereotypical images of women who have been abused to imagine new humane approaches and solutions.

Former President Jimmy Carter characterizes stigmatization as part of an unacceptable fundamentalism. True, compassionate Christians, he says, break through the barrier and reach out to embrace others unlike themselves,[18] a prescription that activist Jane Addams wrote about as early as 1902 as the foundation and guarantee of democracy. "We have learned as common knowledge that much of the insensibility and hardness of the world is due to the lack of imagination which prevents a realization of the experiences of other people," she wrote at the time.[19]

Poor women know full well that they are already considered second-class citizens, and when they are abused they believe they sink even lower in society's estimation. Negative stereotypes hamper caring responses from our institutions. The stories of Bernice, Olivia, and Tammy compel us to take a hard look at ourselves and our own attitudes.

With all of the challenges they faced, these women were finally able to contribute to society, although they paid a terrible price along the way. All three of the women serve others today. But if these women have become what the historian Linda Gordon calls "heroes of their own lives," they were forced to do so against odds no one should have to face and continue to experience residues of abuse, stigma, and their lives as drug abusers that will be with them always. And these are the "success" stories. For every Bernice, Olivia, and Tammy, there are thousands of abused, poor women whose lives will continue on a downward trajectory until, with our help, things change.

NOTES

1. The three books are Jody Raphael, *Saving Bernice: Battered Women, Welfare, and Poverty* (Boston: Northeastern University Press, 2000); Jody Raphael, *Listening to Olivia: Violence, Poverty, and Prostitution* (Boston: Northeastern University Press, 2004); and Jody Raphael, *Freeing Tammy: Women, Drugs, and Incarceration* (Hanover, NH: University Press of New England, 2007). Courtesy of University Press of New England on behalf of Northeastern University Press.

2. Raphael, *Saving Bernice*, 23–28.

3. S. Naylor Goodwin, D. Chandler, and J. Meisel, *Violence against Women: The Role of Welfare Reform, Summary Report* (Washington, D.C.: National Institute of Justice, 2003), http://www.ncjrs.org/pdffiles1/nij/grants/205791.pdf.

4. E. A. Lown, L. A. Schmidt, and J. Wiley, "Interpersonal Violence among Women Seeking Welfare: Unraveling Lives," *American Journal of Public Health* 96, no. 8 (2006): 1413.

5. S. Riger and S. L. Staggs, "Welfare Reform, Domestic Violence, and Employment: What Do We Know, and What Do We Need to Know," *Violence against Women* 10, no. 9 (2004): 11.

6. "Teen Girls Report Abusive Boyfriends Try to Get Them Pregnant," 2007, http://www.eurekalert.org/pub_releases/2007-09/uoc—tgr092007.php.

7. Raphael, *Listening to Olivia*, 24–28.

8. Ibid., 33–37.

9. C. O'Leary and O. Howard, *The Prostitution of Women and Girls in Metropolitan Chicago: A Preliminary Prevalence Report* (Chicago: Center for Impact Research, 2001), http://www.impactresearch.org/documents/prostitutionexecutive.pdf.

10. Raphael, *Freeing Tammy*, 158.

11. Ibid., 37.

12. W. J. Sabol, T. D. Minton, and P. M. Harrison, "Prison and Jail Inmates at Midyear 2006," *Bureau of Justice Statistics Bulletin* (June 2007).

13. Raphael, *Freeing Tammy*, 38.

14. Ibid., 38.

15. Ibid., 72.

16. Ibid., 72.

17. Ibid., 41.

18. Ibid., 165.

19. Ibid., 165.

Chapter 7

Domestic Violence and the Postindustrial Household

Deborah M. Weissman

DOMESTIC VIOLENCE PARADIGMS: PATRIARCHY, LEGAL PARITY, AND CRIMINAL JUSTICE INTERVENTION

All social movements that engage matters of law and intimate relationships confront the challenge of sustaining theoretical coherence. Time passes; circumstances change. Theory developed in the context of one set of objective conditions, at a discrete historical moment, must possess the capacity to adapt to different conditions at later historical moments. This is particularly true when theory serves to inform interventions that affect the lives of real people. The domestic violence movement is no exception.

Much of domestic violence advocacy and scholarship has developed around the demand for state intervention. Domestic violence has been framed primarily as criminal conduct, largely as acts committed by men against women, which then requires efforts to ensure that such acts would be treated on par with other crimes. The reasons for this are compelling. Violence against women has been understood as a social problem that often takes the form of patriarchy and misogyny practiced by men for the purpose of subordinating women and to which the state was historically complicit. Advocates turned to the criminal justice system to guarantee the safety of women. They insisted that the failure of the legal system to respond to domestic violence was itself symptomatic of the public apathy and political indifference that tolerated women's inequality and vulnerability to violence. The demands made of the criminal justice system reflected feminist desires to shift cultural norms concerning the legal rights of women.

Thus, the principal theoretical framework that developed for thinking about domestic violence focused on two concepts: challenging patriarchy and demanding legal parity within the criminal justice system. The ensuing legal polices that developed focused primarily on police arrest practices and prosecutorial "no-drop" protocols. New teams of legal practitioners convened to move the problem of domestic violence from the margins of social concerns into the mainstream of criminal justice policy. Indeed, such reforms emerged as a new legal field that was wholly dependent on the state's criminal justice system.

Sufficient time has passed to permit scholars to evaluate the outcomes of these legal reforms. A body of critical domestic violence scholarship and activism has emerged to challenge the prevailing domestic violence/criminal justice paradigm. The first critiques of the model, written from the vantage of women of color and women in nontraditional sexual relationships, questioned whether its claims to universality masked its reliance only on the experiences of white, heterosexual women. This scholarship suggested that the convergence of interests between the domestic violence movement and the criminal justice system has been largely illusory. Some advocates who have criticized the criminal justice system have either denounced mandatory arrest protocols or proposed alternative policies and practices to improve their outcomes, such as better training for police, or relying on evidence-based prosecution to avoid coercing testimony of battered women.

In the ensuing dialogue, critics have raised new questions. Have domestic violence advocates relied unduly on the state? Is it possible to alter the relationship with police and prosecutors? Do racism, bias against the poor, and authoritarianism constitute immutable characteristics of the criminal justice system, and hence preclude all reasonable expectation of remedy for battered women?

These questions are fully relevant to the critique of the domestic violence/criminal justice paradigm, and they are necessary to improving the conditions for battered women. But the current critique must do more than debate the strengths and weaknesses of law-and-order responses. Instead, a paradigm shift is required, one that considers the multifaceted circumstances that contribute to domestic violence and examines economic hardship and the demise of community resources as social conditions by which domestic violence is both cause and effect. The demand for state intervention remains key, although a very different sort of state intervention than what the criminal justice system offers.

LINKING DOMESTIC VIOLENCE TO THE GLOBAL POLITICAL ECONOMY

To reinvigorate the debate surrounding the proper relationship of policy, law, and domestic violence, analysts must expand their range of vision beyond patriarchal determinants and criminal justice interventions to contextualize domestic violence within the political economy. The research agenda for domestic violence must include the implications of socioeconomic transformations in communities and households. To consider the relationship between global developments and domestic violence does not, of course, reduce the importance of existing theories related to patriarchy. Nor does it minimize the role of individual agency in criminal behaviors. Rather, it provides a more nuanced understanding of the relationship between those socioeconomic forces that insinuate themselves into neighborhoods and households, there to produce chronic stress, instability, and fear—all circumstances associated with domestic violence.

There have been significant economic transformations beginning in the second half of the twentieth century that have occurred in communities throughout the United States and that have resulted in plant closings and a loss of work opportunities. Entire towns have been affected, and families who reside there suffer chronic unemployment and economic strain. Economic loss devastates neighborhoods and creates community characteristics associated with increased violence and rising crime rates. These same characteristics permeate households, affect individuals, and produce a range of symptoms, syndromes, and behaviors, including domestic violence.

POLITICAL ECONOMIES IN TRANSITION

A brief examination of the global economy is necessary to provide the context for the relationship between domestic violence and market forces. Globalization has been experienced largely as an economic process facilitated by technological advances and deregulation that has transformed the "spatial organization of social relations and transactions."[1] Americans have experienced globalization as a structural transformation whereby the once industry-based economy has evolved into a post-industrial and service-dominated market. Though this transformation has had far-reaching repercussions for American workers and their families, it has been especially onerous for entire communities that have suffered the loss of manufacturing employment that once sustained households over successive generations. What had been prevailing episodic unemployment in many communities has developed into a chronic condition.

Even for those who have remained employed, job security is uncertain, wages have declined, and health and pension benefits, once considered the mainstay of the waged economy, have been sacrificed in the face of threats of plant closings and relocations.

Feminist scholars have contributed to the debate by identifying the relationship between the global economy and the circumstances in which women live their lives. Rejecting the notion that globalization is a gender-neutral phenomenon, researchers have demonstrated that women have disproportionately suffered bleak working conditions, forced migration, sex and labor trafficking, changes to family structures, and violence. Women's responsibilities have, by necessity, expanded beyond the realm of domestic care and into the workplace in response to both the need for low-cost laborers and the material needs of households. Economic shifts have rearranged traditional household norms, and modifications to time-honored gender roles have overtaken the process of cultural adaptation.

The literature that examines the impact of global economics on gender relations focuses principally on women as subordinated workers in export zones and transnational factories. Scholars have paid less attention to the effects of economic globalization policies on family relationships at the household level. To appreciate how current economic shifts in the United States serve as a source of gender-based violence, it is necessary to examine the dynamics of wage labor and the consequences of its loss on communities and individuals.

UNCERTAINTY IN THE WORKPLACE: IMPLICATIONS FOR VIOLENCE IN THE HOUSEHOLD

Work as Social Stability

Values of self-sufficiency, initiative, and liberty associated with the ideal of productive labor are deeply ingrained in the American ethos. Indeed, the dominant cultural norm of work pervades systems of national morality. This norm privileges people with paying jobs and recognizes them as individuals who possess sufficient discipline, determination, and worth to claim the fruits and benefits of the market and the state. Unemployed Americans, especially unemployed American men, are often considered failures or otherwise defective for their inability or unwillingness to support themselves and their families through productive economic means.

The opportunity to work makes possible an expansive set of benefits, both material and moral. Gainful employment provides the wage, the basis of daily life, and the structure by which men and women order their world. Waged labor promises a sense of self-worth, a feeling of well-being, and the opportunity to establish social networks. Workers develop contacts and information channels as a form of social capital; they have opportunities to exercise social skills by which a range of needs both within and outside of the workplace are met.

Although the workplace remains a potential site for worker exploitation and subordination, as a general matter, people need work "for the rewards it brings, both tangible and intangible."[2] These work-based networks, referred to as social capital, also benefit communities, contributing to the leveraging of resources, improved economic development, reduced unemployment and crime rates, and increased civic and political engagement.

Communities without Work

The social cost to communities of chronic unemployment has been the subject of increasing concern and research. Scholars report profound consequences indicating that "work is embedded in relationships and structures that transcend formal economic processes, as it is set in communities with their own histories, geographies, and social relations."[3] Sociologist William Julius Wilson chronicles the gradual decline of neighborhoods that experienced industrial restructuring during the latter part of the twentieth century as a "cumulative process of economic and social dislocation."[4] He describes a well-recognized pattern that follows the closing of a large factory: increased joblessness and a succession of business closings as a consequence of deindustrialization.

Municipal infrastructures that previously served as the context by which daily life was experienced have deteriorated in the wake of plant closings. Social services have also diminished as tax revenues have declined, while needs have increased. Deindustrialization has contributed to the loss of affordable housing, high rates of foreclosures, and the deterioration of neighborhoods as property values decline. Cities and towns throughout the United States have suffered declining populations and a disappearing tax base because they are no longer capable of providing opportunities for economic well-being.

Economic insecurity has also had a corrosive effect on community identity. The humiliation, despair, and hopelessness that follow loss of work can be devastating to a downwardly mobile populace, causing a collective diminution of self-worth. Even in communities where jobs are replaced, a sense of security and community identity is lost. Commentators who have studied the aftermath of deindustrialization have noted the desperation that often seizes hold of entire communities. Cities that have experienced plant closings often suffer a type of moral stigmatization not dissimilar to that experienced by unemployed individuals.

Such economic instability produces a cultural shift that often results in social disorganization attended by uprootedness and weakened social controls. As social capital deteriorates, vulnerable groups are especially susceptible to the harms of downward turns of the economy. As wage inequality increases, intergroup polarization deepens. Trade assistance programs that differentiate between categories of dislocated workers who are eligible for benefits have created resentment among the unemployed who do not qualify for such programs. The combined effect of the intergroup polarization and the resentment is to weaken social solidarity networks.

As social solidarity networks erode, so too does their prophylactic effect on community crime rates. The effects of this erosion, such as abandoned neighborhoods, vacant commercial centers, and the lack of opportunities to engage in productive endeavors, often result in increased vandalism, theft, robberies, and drug abuse in communities that previously avoided noticeable crime rates. Indeed, as social networks disintegrate, the risk of violent crime, including domestic violence, appreciates considerably.

Community Characteristics and Domestic Violence

The consequences of deindustrialization—economic disadvantage, social fragmentation and disorganization, high residential mobility, and neighborhood instability—are also conditions associated with increased domestic violence. Decreased opportunities for neighbors and coworkers to provide social support, reduced police presence, and diminished social services have been linked to community crime generally and especially to family dysfunction, including an increased risk of intimate partner violence. The demise of social capital, which, as Jeffrey Fagan notes, functions as an "intervening process between social structures and domestic violence," has resulted in a loss of community controls on behavior generally, including established relationships between intimate partners.[5] The social isolation attending the collapse of occupational networks has been recognized as a risk factor for domestic violence.

Recent studies suggest that these community characteristics have been linked to a rise in domestic violence. Increased rates of domestic violence are associated with community decline even after controlling for factors such as prior violence and drug abuse. Community characteristics have also been shown to correlate with more serious domestic violence injuries. Moreover, neighborhood disadvantage has a direct effect on the rates of domestic violence even for couples not considered economically vulnerable.

Although community poverty and social disorganization existed prior to current forms of economic globalization, the heightened contradiction between the promises and expectations of the social contract and the consequences of its breach distinguishes between current socioeconomic developments and conditions in the past. As time-honored conventions about work and self-sufficiency clash with the material reality of deindustrialization, the subjective experience of injustice takes hold, resulting in anger, frustration, and self-destructive behavior. The collapse of communities delegitimizes behavioral norms and creates a "cynicism regarding the conventional social system and a weakened attachment to it."[6] Indeed, the collective experience of downward mobility accompanied by a sense of hopelessness has produced measurable levels of crime, generally, including domestic violence in families previously not considered at risk.

Studies of the impact of changing regional economies have emphasized the demoralization and stress experienced by workers. Workers interviewed during the course of these studies described the loss of work as triggering depression, stress, and a mental nightmare and their resulting state of mind as desperate, insecure, discouraged, irritable, and mad.[7] For many workers who face the bleak prospect of irreversible downward mobility and economic insecurity, life loses its meaning. Suicide and attempted suicide rates increase, as do incidents of crime and homicide rates. The repercussion of these economic shifts has produced a values crisis that reverberates in households, with disturbing consequences for families.

THE RELATIONSHIP BETWEEN THE GENDER ROLES, WORK, AND DOMESTIC VIOLENCE

Empirical studies demonstrate that the consequences of economic uncertainty correlate to domestic violence. An understanding of gender roles and identity associated with work and family further illuminates this relationship and provides insights into how economic strain contributes to domestic violence. Social problems such as domestic violence are often outcomes of both material structures and ideological influences by which people make sense of their lives.

An examination of the gendered dimensions of work and economics serves as a conceptual framework by which to consider domestic violence. Gender roles and the notion of the ideal worker assign to men primary responsibility in the workplace. There are consequences to the gendered dimension of work, particularly the way in which gender prescriptive roles contribute to the different ways men and women react to unemployment and economic uncertainty. As a result of these assigned roles, workplace tensions increase and are reproduced within households, and contribute to increased rates of domestic violence.

THE SOCIAL CONSTRUCTION OF GENDER IN WAGE-LABOR AND SELF-SUFFICIENCY

An examination of gender as a function of economic and market conditions provides insight into domestic violence as one response to downward economic mobility. Men and women are socialized to assume gender roles and thereupon to discharge those duties and responsibilities deemed appropriate to their sex. Such prescriptive roles

are transmitted through a vast array of cultural formulations and con-
secrated through social practice, and also communicated as conventional and legal wisdom and accepted as self-evident truths. In this
regard, traditional norms regarding male and female roles in the realm
of work tend to prevail.

The assignment of gender roles has long functioned to signify men's
place in wage labor and women's place in unpaid work. Based on the
nineteenth-century notions of a "family wage," the ideal husband earned
wages sufficient to maintain a safe and comfortable environment in the
home for his wife and family. This norm was reinforced by employer
efforts to control labor and reduce employee turnover, such as the Ford
Motor Company's historic Five Dollar Day, which offered increased
wages mostly to men who were married and supporting their families.

For men, these developments acted to reinforce culturally determined responsibilities associated with manhood. They gave rise to
long-standing normative assumptions that have shaped popular understanding associated with the maintenance of the family household,
even when those assumptions failed to meet the needs of either men or
women, or of men and women equally. Men understand their primary
role to be that of the ideal worker whose responsibilities to the workplace take precedence over home and family.

Although the male identity has assumed different forms at different
historical periods and within different cultural and social groupings,
the male identity in the United States remains bound principally with
paid work. Indeed, the very understanding of masculinity is linked
with a man's ability to provide for his family. Fulfillment of this role
continues to be transmitted as an imperative for men, idealized as the
convention of manliness and particularly critical to the male sense of
self-worth. Economic insecurity within the family is equated with a
man's failure and is perceived as a threat to masculinity.

These constructs hold constant despite the fact that wage labor has
been transformed by women workers who are employed full-time outside of the home. The notion of the male ideal worker may seem less
persuasive, if not obsolete, given the reality of dual-earning families,
but work continues to function as a gendered activity. The processes
by which these norms are enforced operate simultaneously as external
and internal pressures.

Employers frequently demonstrate hostility toward men who want
to take family leave. Men forfeit their family leave rights because they
have accepted the belief that they should prioritize work over family.
Women also face similar pressures. Women with children who perform
as the ideal worker are often disparaged as bad mothers. On the other
hand, they may decline to use family leave rights and quit their jobs altogether because of their concerns that work outside of the home conflicts with the proper fulfillment of the role of a good mother.

This is not to suggest that men and women necessarily achieve a sense of well-being and fulfillment in the discharge of their prescribed gender roles. Nor does it suggest that such norms are static. Cultural norms related to gender have varied effects on individuals. The entry of increasing numbers of women into the wage-labor force has certainly gained normative endorsement. But it is also true that these gains have been subject to countervailing pressure by long-held attitudes about the proper place of men and women in society. Although the distribution of responsibility for household work and child care has expanded, women remain disproportionately responsible for house work. The number of women entering the full-time workforce in recent years has declined, a trend attributed both to the weakening job market and the burdens that women bear as homemakers. Although women experience anxiety related to their own job security, studies demonstrate that they tend to suffer more distress and exhibit greater concern over their spouse's job security. The new economy has in fact created new gender concerns.

SOCIALLY CONSTRUCTED REACTIONS
TO ECONOMIC UNCERTAINTY

Not surprisingly, intrafamily problems, including domestic violence, are related to the efficacy with which gender roles can be fulfilled. As Rayna Rapp has noted, "It is through families that people enter into productive, reproductive, and consumption relations"; however, as she notes, "The two genders enter them differently."[8] Gender identity not only functions as an important determinant of the responsibilities men and women discharge in the economy, but also affects the psychosocial consequences related to how well they perform their obligations. Gender is also a significant factor in differentiating between men's and women's psychological reactions to unemployment. When norms associated with gender-appropriate work categories are transgressed, there are repercussions for the transgressor as well as for those with whom he interacts. The failure by a man to fulfill his role as breadwinner, the predominant means by which men obtain self-esteem and self-worth within the household, implies a failure to fulfill family roles. Tensions often develop as men struggle to maintain their assigned place in and outside of the home. Patriarchal hierarchies that may no longer be transacted through performance of socially constructed roles in the economic realm may be exercised in self-destructive behaviors and abusive conduct in the home.

Job insecurity often translates into increased psychological aggression. Some men resort to physical violence as an alternative, socially inscribed facet of manhood. Men who are precluded from fulfilling the dominant model of masculinity as a result of their subordinated role in the workplace often resort to personal aggression in an attempt to gain social status. Violence becomes an equalizing force as traditional gender roles are unfulfilled and the prescribed order of household obligations is destabilized. Indeed, violence against women becomes the proxy for male economic dominance in the family as serves as the means by which men can reestablish their authority in the household. In contrast, women, as a general principle, are not conditioned to respond with physical violence. Not all women react the same to economic decline, of course, but studies suggest that they are more likely to seek support from friends and relatives, a strategy that may further exacerbate a man's self-esteem and call further attention to his failure in fulfilling his role as breadwinner.

Given the relationship between masculinity and violence, as well as the centrality of paid labor to male identity, the impact of economic uncertainty produces a demonstrably greater reaction among men than among women that often includes antisocial behavior. When gender norms cannot be fulfilled, men are likely to experience the stress, anxiety, and heightened states of anger and frustration that contribute to those conditions that often produce domestic violence. In an ironic use of terminology, some have described men's lack of control in their responses to the loss of identity that arises out of events such as a plant closing as a socially constructed type of "learned helplessness," the very concept used to describe battered women's inability to exit from abusive relationships.

POWER DIFFERENTIALS IN THE WORKPLACE AND IN THE HOME

Domestic violence is not only a product of the absence of work. It is also a consequence of the uncertainty at work during periods of economic dislocation. Unstable work conditions act to erode the benefits of employment. Those who remain employed experience high levels of stress and anxiety and endure the heightened tension of unequal power relations between employers and employees. Worker acquiescence to pay cuts, the growing prerogative of employers to reassign and redeploy employees without constraints, and the loss of benefits are often achieved by operation of modalities of power that enact patriarchal hierarchies. Employers require heightened productivity from male workers who must successfully compete with other men—and even more so with women—in order to maintain their male identities at work. Stress related to workplace tensions and shifting cultural norms is likely to find outlet in households, where established patriarchal norms afford men greater power and authority over women.

As a result, workplace tensions have increasingly given way to physical violence on the job and eventually in the home. Violence at work has been described as a staggering problem: each year, there are approximately 1,000 murders of coworkers and at least 2 million reported aggravated assaults at the workplace. The International Labor Organization reports that workplace violence is considered to be "not just an episodic, individual problem, but a structural, strategic issue rooted in wider social, economic, organizational, and cultural factors" and one that moves on a continuum affecting households as well.[9] This workplace violence is disproportionately suffered by women. International Labor Organization statistics demonstrate that homicide in the United States has become the second leading cause of occupational death overall and the leading cause of occupational death for women.[10] The gender dimension to workplace violence adds yet another consequence for domestic violence as these experiences are reproduced in households; norms established in one venue carry over to the other.

Employment practices that discriminate against women also contribute to domestic violence in the home. These behaviors, which enact the hierarchies within the realm of the labor market and are increasingly visited on women workers during periods of economic decline, are often the result of efforts to perpetrate male norms and render women powerless as a way to demonstrate that they are not welcomed in the workplace. Short of violence, these practices are often enacted through overt hostility and contribute to perceptions of women's powerlessness in the home. Indeed, states of inequality produced through gender animus at work are often associated with violence against women in the home.

Women are vulnerable to domestic violence in part because they are vulnerable to the economic uncertainties of their male partners and also because of conditions experienced by both men and women in the workplace. The sum total of these consequences of downward economic transitions indicates that domestic violence must be understood as implicating more than the individual behaviors and characteristics of individuals and couples.

NEW MODES OF INTERVENTION AND NEW ALLIES

A paradigm shift from the criminal justice system—which relocates domestic violence from a single site of human interaction—to the multiple realms of political economy would offer a number of promising analytical possibilities. First, this shift would recast the obstacles that prevent women from leaving abusive relationships as difficulties that transcend issues of individual victim agency and the exercise of power by individual perpetrators. This approach offers the possibility of a better understanding of the interaction between gender violence and social class. Second, the use of a different analytical framework also suggests a change in tactics and strategies by which to respond to domestic violence. Finally, a revised framework in which domestic violence prevention is linked to activism critical of globalization improves the conditions for collaboration between the two movements. Establishing these links sets in relief the structural nature of domestic violence and reveals the gendered social costs of market forces.

TRANSCENDING THE INDIVIDUAL FRAMEWORK

Domestic violence scholars have long pondered the factors that prevent battered women from leaving violent relationships. Researchers contend that many victims remain in abusive relationships as a matter of need, principally a financial dependency on their abusers. They have established that the difficulty a victim faces in achieving economic self sufficiency is often related to the abuser's exercise of power to deny her freedom of movement or to physically impair her work-related capabilities. These observations usually focus on a woman's financial constraints in the context of her individual situation and in regard to her immediate circumstances.

However, more than gender-based power keeps a woman economically dependent. Women are also constrained by limited economic opportunities. Studies tracking the unemployment effect of plant closings note that women are disproportionately affected. Women laid off from their jobs are "twice as likely as men to remain unemployed for longer than a year."[11] The U.S. unemployment rate for women has grown at a faster rate than for men. Because many women are also contingent workers, they are often ineligible for unemployment benefits. As unemployment becomes a chronic condition and safety net programs are eviscerated, households have become the site where survival strategies and coping mechanisms are developed with other household members. The importance of household economies may discourage women from reporting domestic violence to public authorities for fear that such disclosure might affect future job prospects for themselves or for their abusive partners. They may also be reluctant to initiate court processes, which may be expensive, may be time consuming, and may exacerbate economic stress. Unfortunately, battered women who do not exit violent relationships often are characterized as individuals who fail to take responsibility for their plight. The conflation of battered women as powerless victims unable to leave, and as individuals unable to achieve economic self sufficiency, results in their representation as persons inherently unworthy of assistance.

To think about domestic violence as a phenomenon related to market forces is to examine the structural context of the household. This acknowledges the political aspects of battered women's coping abilities that can be viewed as both resistance and survival strategies in the context of the larger social and economic issues, as well as within the context of their relationships. Such a shift in the discourse restores agency to women and allows victims of domestic violence to be seen as having strength and power. This shatters the stereotypical image of a battered woman as a helpless victim entrapped in a personal relationship gone bad.

An examination of the links between market conditions and domestic violence also requires a more textured consideration of the relationship between poverty and domestic violence. This relationship has been undertheorized due to fear that domestic violence would receive less attention as just one more problem emanating from a culture of poverty. To focus on economic forces, however, is not to disparage the men and women who live with economic uncertainty. Rather, it serves to illustrate the ways in which current global economic restructuring often contributes to despair and violence. This paradigm shift emphasizes the importance of structural forces in the lives of families who experience domestic violence.

ENHANCING AND EXPANDING DOMESTIC VIOLENCE INTERVENTION STRATEGIES

Although some domestic violence programs provide job counseling for victims, most services focus on emergency shelter, transitional housing, trauma counseling, and safety planning. Domestic violence agencies have taken on the characteristics of service providers rather than struggling for sustainable social change. A paradigm shift that connects domestic violence to global economics sets in relief the need for strategies that extend beyond the customary offerings of domestic violence programs.

Public/Private Dichotomy Redux

An understanding that the new economy creates conditions that contribute to intimate violence suggests that the domestic violence movement might think about interventions that focus on the new economy. For example, few demands have been made for greater government intervention and public accountability in decisions affecting plant closings and deindustrialization. These matters are customarily considered to be wholly within the province of the private sector and beyond the reach of government, a construct with which domestic violence specialists are familiar. Domestic violence scholars have sought to demonstrate the public nature of private acts and the accompanying need for public intervention in these realms traditionally considered "private." Indeed, the battered women's movement has long demanded state intervention in family violence, a matter once considered a private issue. Given the relationship between chronic unemployment and battering, it is not unreasonable to call upon domestic violence advocates to challenge the public/private dichotomy in the realm of the market as they have challenged violence in the realm of the family.

The domestic violence movement may be mismatched against market forces. However, undertaking such an initiative would nonetheless frame the issue that progressive groups might aspire to address and invite a larger coalition with whom to address the issue. The arguments invoked by feminists in an earlier period to demand public intervention against domestic violence bring a historically relevant critique of laissez-faire policies in the market and in their demands for public accountability and regulation of private determinations in plant closings. Domestic violence analysts are well situated to identify the structural economic determinants of domestic violence as private matters with public repercussions to justify economic regulation for the protection of women and families.

IMPROVING TRADE ADJUSTMENT ASSISTANCE PROGRAMS

Domestic violence advocates possess the analytical framework to identify ways to improve Trade Adjustment Assistance (TAA) and Workforce Investment Act (WIA) programs designed to assist dislocated workers. TAA and WIA programs are often housed in the same government centers with welfare offices whose caseworkers are charged with implementing the Family Violence Option (FVO) to assist domestic violence victims who rely on welfare benefits to achieve economic independence. Many of the obstacles to implementing the FVO are similar to those that exist in TAA and WIA programs. These programs suffer from similar bureaucratic cultures and untrained and underpaid program staff. TAA, WIA, and FVO programs are subject to, and limited by, the pressures of program performance and outcome measures. These constraints deny comprehensive assistance to hard-to-place clients deemed unlikely to succeed, and instead emphasize short term services rather than meeting the challenges of both battered women and dislocated workers.

Domestic violence policy activists who have studied the implementation of the FVO are familiar with the structural, cultural, and programmatic deficiencies associated with programs that offer work and training assistance to the unemployed. As a result of their efforts to improve the effectiveness of the FVO, they have identified elements relevant to improving TAA and WIA programs, including the requirement of confidential office space in which to disclose domestic violence and other sensitive issues, and trained caseworkers with whom such problems can be discussed. They have also identified the importance of case management skills in order to bridge the goals between work assistance programs and domestic violence prevention. These programmatic components should be incorporated into TAA and WIA programs to improve outcomes in job assistance efforts, particularly for battered women who are seeking training and work relocation assistance.

Domestic violence and workers rights advocates could join together to lobby for funding for such programs. They could establish help centers to guide clients through the burdensome and bureaucratic process of applying for TAA benefits and provide comprehensive information about the FVO. They could also demand an expanded range of TAA and FVO services, including transportation and child care. As a coalition of activists focused on related agendas, they are more likely to change the culture of these programs to address the rights of both battered women and workers.

Developing Progressive Criminal Justice Responses to Domestic Violence

Scholars and advocates face a difficult predicament when considering the relationship between domestic violence and the criminal justice system. It is inconceivable to return to a time when acts of domestic violence were not criminalized. Responses to domestic violence will always depend on a range of strategies, including the criminal justice system. However, to reduce troubling choices when resorting to the criminal justice system, advocates could analyze crime to take into account social context and community characteristics. Responses to crimes of domestic violence could consider the ways individual actions are constrained by various social, political, and economic structures that diminish choice. The few progressive initiatives that exist with regard to crime and deterrence generally should be incorporated into the disposition of domestic violence cases. Poverty and joblessness should be a focus of sentencing, abuser treatment, probation, and reentry services in order to improve outcomes for batterers and victims alike.

Restorative justice models that emphasize repairing the harm caused by criminal acts more than emphasizing punishment also offer potentially useful intervention strategies in domestic violence cases. Progressive community policing designed to assist individuals in accessing services such as housing, treatment programs, employment training and placement, and education opportunities as means of crime prevention have been found to be meaningful interventions. These model programs focus on underlying causes of crime rather than simply punishing the offender and include the ways in which criminal behavior arises from a complex set of facts and circumstances.

These practices and sentencing models are suitable for batterers' treatment programs. Currently, such programs rely on group counseling methods that incorporate a psychoeducational approach. Such programs generally require defendants to abide by program rules, which include counseling, random substance abuse tests, payment of program fees, and completion of home assignments. While such programmatic components may be an integral part of changing the behavior of abusive men, as one researcher has noted, they lack a social justice framework within which to consider the effects and causes of domestic violence.

Focusing on the perpetrator's economic circumstances as a factor in batterers' intervention programs and as an outcome of criminal justice intervention serves a number of purposes. The elimination of male poverty is a critical part of domestic violence prevention strategy. In other words, class is a category that must be central to all discussions on domestic violence. Police replication studies measuring the effects of arrest on domestic violence perpetrators have demonstrated the weakness of such an approach when dealing with unemployed men. Court services, including diversion and probation that focus on assisting batterers with employment and job training, might be a better approach to lower recidivism rates. After studying risk factors associated with intimate femicide, Jacquelyn Campbell has concluded that increasing employment opportunities for abusers may reduce the rate of domestic violence homicides.[12]

Guided by a political economic analysis of domestic violence, advocates are also more likely to avoid tactics and strategies within the criminal justice system that have an adverse impact on women of color and poor women. By addressing the relationship between domestic violence and social class, advocates could resist wholesale affiliation with the criminal justice system that has previously undermined their ability to be effective advocates for social change. A more constructive criminal justice approach might promise the possibility of comprehensive social changes required to end gender-based violence. These contributions would not only inure to the benefit of domestic violence outcomes, but would also contribute to the development of criminological theory and practice in the realm of social justice.

Reframing the domestic violence discussion reveals the ways in which market forces reach into households and transform the daily lives of working women and men. It demonstrates to workers and unions concerned with plant closings and job protection that the consequences associated with job loss pervade the private spaces of family. Such a shift establishes the context for connecting work productivity to gender violence with a wide range of issues related to the depletion of the social capital of poor neighborhoods and communities of color. This would advance the best practices of the early battered women's movement that successfully challenged the public/private dichotomy— a bifurcation that feminists have long held has marginalized the condition of women. This ideology underscores the fact that the personal is indeed political and economic. It would demonstrate how issues of gender, described by Martha Fineman as "theoretically relevant to almost all human endeavors," are specifically "relevant beyond the sexual, the violent, and the familial."[13] Nor does it purport to explain the long history of violence against women, but identifying the nexus makes space for a broader approach that considers a fuller panoply of hierarchical influences than patriarchy alone. Furthermore, it is a project rooted in feminist traditions that reconfigure the relationships between the public and the private and the personal and the political, while seeking to find common ground with activists whose primary concerns involve race and social class. Families, and the individual members of which they are comprised, are shaped by the political and economic world in which they live. While the goal to eliminate domestic violence has been sufficiently articulated, the need to eradicate its political economic determinants has yet to be fully grasped. Connecting these issues draws political life out of the household and emphasizes the experiences, needs, and interests of women. The fusion of global economics and domestic violence enhances the opportunity for creative advocacy while marking the urgency to shift the course.

AUTHOR'S NOTE

Courtesy of Deborah M. Weissman.

NOTES

1. D. Held et al., *Global Transformations: Politics, Economics, and Culture* (Stanford, CA: Stanford University Press, 1999), 16.

2. K. L. Karst, "The Coming Crisis of Work in Constitutional Perspective," *Cornell Law Review* 82 (1997): 523, 531.

3. W. W. Falk et al., "Introduction" in *Communities of Work*, ed. W. W. Falk et al. (Athens: Ohio University Press, 2003), xv.

4. W. J. Wilson, *When Work Disappears* (New York: Knopf, 1996), 34.

5. J. Fagan et al., "Social and Ecological Risks of Domestic and Non Domestic Violence against Women in New York City," Final Report, Grant 1999 WTVW 0005 (Washington, D.C.: National Institute of Justice, U.S. Department of Justice, 2003), 5.

6. E. S. Shihadeh and D. J. Steffensmeier, "The Effects of Economic Inequality and Family Disruption on Urban Black Violence: Cities as Units of Stratification and Social Control," *Social Forces* 73 (1994): 729, 734.

7. J. Gaventa, *From the Mountains to the Maquiladoras: A Case Study of Capital Flight and Its Impact on Workers* (New Market, TN: Highlander Research and Education Center, 1989), 49, available from the Highlander Research and Education Center, Route 3, Box 370, New Market, TN 37820.

8. R. Rapp, "Family and Class in Contemporary America: Notes towards an Understanding of Ideology" in *Family, Household, and Gender Relations in Latin America*, ed. E. Jelin (London and Paris: Kegan Paul International/ UNESCO, 1991), 199.

9. International Labor Organization, "Safework: Introduction to Violence at Work," http://www.ilo.org/public/english/protection/safework/violence/intro.htm (accessed September 28, 2008).

10. Ibid.

11. B. Phillips, *Global Production and Domestic Decay* (New York: Garland, 1998), 80.

12. J. Campbell et al., "Risk Factors for Femicide in Abusive Relationships: Results from a Multi-site Case Control Study," 93 *Am. J. Pub. Health* 1089, 1092 (2003).

13. M. A. Fineman, "Feminist Legal Theory," *American University Journal of Gender, Social Policy and the Law.* 13 (2005): 14, 20.

BIBLIOGRAPHY

Broman, C. L. et al. *Stress and Distress among the Unemployed.* New York: Kluwer Academic/Plenum, 2001.

Harris, A. P. "Gender, Violence, Race, and Criminal Justice." *Stanford Law Review* 52 (2000): 777.

Litton Fox, G. and D. Chancey. "Sources of Economic Distress: Individual and Family Outcomes." *Journal of Family Issues* 19 (1998): 725.

McCorquodale, R. and R. Fairbrothersee. "Globalization and Human Rights." *Human Rights Quarterly* 21 (1999): 735.

Ms. Foundation for Women. "Safety and Justice for All: Examining the Relationship between the Women's Anti Violence Movement and the Criminal Legal System" (2003), available at http://www.ms.foundation.org/user assets/PDF/Program/safety_justice.pdf.

Selmi, M. "Sex Discrimination in the Nineties, Seventies Style: Case Studies in the Preservation of Male Workplace Norms." *Employee Rights and Employer Policy Journal* 9 (2005): 1.

Stark, E. "Insults, Injury, and Injustice: Rethinking State Intervention in Domestic Violence Cases." *Violence against Women* 10 (2004): 1302.

Warren, E. "The New Economics of the American Family." *American Banker Institute Law Review* 12 (2004): 1, 21.

Williams, J. *Unbending Gender: Why Family and Work Conflict and What to Do about It.* New York: Oxford University Press, 2000.

Chapter 8

Understanding Violence in Lesbian Relationships

Janice Ristock

*It was my first relationship. First long-term relationship. But you know I was—
I was head over heels madly in love and I thought this is the relationship for life.
And it started out really good. This woman was nine years older than myself. It
was verbally abusive to start off with and then physically, I was, quite often had
black eyes and she tried—she almost killed me once. Strangled me and then this
went on for three years. . . . I was too young and insecure about the whole relationship—gay relationships, whatever. Anybody could have walked all over me.
(Ellen)*

*I feel like I can't talk about it, I mean, how many therapists/social service providers
are going to understand queer, s/m, abuse, intersexed, interracial—It's too complicated, there is too much explaining that I'd have to do. (Natalie)*

The opening quotations are from participants in an interview project
I conducted with lesbians who had experienced violence in their intimate relationships with other women.[1] Their words reveal some of the
challenges to understanding and addressing same-sex relationship violence. Ellen describes the violence she experienced in the context of the
isolation and vulnerability she faced as a young gay woman in her first
relationship. Her story dispels the misconception that violence between
female partners is not as bad as violence in heterosexual relationships
or that it typically involves "mutual battering." Natalie is reluctant to
seek supportive services because she fears that mainstream services for
domestic violence victims will find the marginalized features of her
relationship "too complicated" to understand. Her story points to an
important theme in this chapter. Despite the important work done by

feminists to address male violence against women, when they adapt the largely gender-exclusive framework that focuses on the roots of violence within sexism, patriarchy, and male domination, they often ignore or misunderstand relationship violence in lesbian, gay, bisexual, and transgender people's lives. Understanding violence in lesbian relationships requires appreciating how violence is connected to larger contexts of prejudice and oppression. These contexts include (but are not limited to) homophobia; the negative attitudes, stereotypes, and prejudices that still exist in society about individuals who are not heterosexual; and heterosexism, the assumption that everyone is heterosexual and that heterosexual relationships are the only relationships that are natural, normal, and worthy of support.

In 1986, Kerry Lobel edited the first anthology on abuse in lesbian relationships. It contained personal testimonies, poetry, chapters on community organizing, ways to improve shelters, and strategies for combatting homophobia. In her introduction, Lobel wrote,

> *Publicly addressing the issue of lesbian battering, while necessary, is done with the recognition that we live in increasingly repressive times. The hard-won gains of the civil rights movement, women's movement, and gay and lesbian rights movement over the past twenty-five years have been met by increasing resistance and setbacks. Many lesbians are understandably reluctant to air issues related to lesbian battering, for fear of triggering homophobic attacks on our communities. In a society where there has been no acceptance of lesbian relationships, the fears are legitimate. By discussing these issues openly we risk further repression. Yet our only alternative is one of silence, a silence that traps battered lesbians into believing that they are alone and that there are no resources available to them.*[2]

We have moved beyond the silence and secretiveness that faced the few brave lesbians who raised the issue of lesbian battering within the domestic violence movement in the early 1980s. Cities throughout the United States, Canada, the United Kingdom, and Australia now host public education campaigns designed to raise awareness of same-sex domestic violence. Programs to respond to partner abuse have also been established within gay and lesbian and women's organizations. And yet, as continuing debate about same-sex marriage, adoption rights for same-sex couples, and bans on discrimination against gay and transgender persons suggests, Kerry Lobel's assessment that "we risk further repression" in openly discussing lesbian battering remains pertinent. Resistance to fully examining abuse in lesbian relationships also continues within the domestic violence movement. Apart from the general lack of knowledge about violence in same-sex relationships, this resistance stems from a fear that abandoning the singular focus on male violence against women in heterosexual relationships will mean replacing the prevailing feminist gender-based framework and compromising support for holding "men" accountable. This resistance continues despite growing recognition that policies and interventions designed to protect women from male partners fail to adequately address women's violence against women, or against people whose lives and identities do not fit the binary gender categories of male and female. Violence in same-sex relationships remains an albatross for the domestic violence movement.

In addition, research on same-sex domestic violence lags behind the studies on heterosexual domestic violence. We cannot say with certainty what the prevalence rate is for same-sex domestic violence since studies that have been conducted most often rely on small, nonrandom samples of gay, lesbian, and bisexual respondents. A marked exception is the National Violence Against Women Survey (NVAWS). Of the women who identified themselves as lesbians to the NVAWS, 11.4 percent reported abuse by female partners over their lifetime, a little more than half the proportion of heterosexual women who did so (20.3 percent). Interestingly, however, the women who identified as lesbian were also half again *more* likely than heterosexual women to report abuse by a man (30.4 versus 20.3 percent) and three times as likely to be abused by a male than a female partner (30.4 versus 11.4 percent).[3] While the contexts for this abuse are not spelled out in the NVAWS, it is likely that some proportion of these women were assaulted by men *because* they were lesbians. We know that not only do the same range and forms of violence exist (physical, sexual, emotional, verbal abuse) in lesbian and heterosexual relationships, but also lesbians face an added risk because of homophobia (hatred of someone because of their sexual orientation). Moreover, the prevalence of homophobia creates a unique weapon of control in same-sex relationships: the threat of "outing," revealing a partner's sexual identity at work or in another hostile environment where retaliation or humiliation is likely.

This chapter gives voice to lesbians who have experienced violence in their intimate relationships based on interviews with 102 lesbians. The range and diversity of experiences presented illustrate the need to incorporate new understandings and response frameworks into domestic violence work that better reflect the specific and often complex contexts in which violence occurs.

THE MANY CONTEXTS OF LESBIAN RELATIONSHIP VIOLENCE

The interview research was conducted in six Canadian cities: Vancouver, Calgary, Winnipeg, Toronto, London, and Halifax. In each city, notices about the research were placed in gay and lesbian community newspapers, women's bookstores, and women's bars and in a variety of LGBTQ (lesbian, gay, bisexual, transgendered, and queer), ethno-cultural, and feminist organizations. Women who volunteered for the study self-identified as having experienced abuse in an intimate relationship with another woman. The interviews lasted from one-and-a-half to two hours on average. They were semistructured and included the following topics: information about the relationship (length of time, commitment, dynamics); when the abuse started; the types of abuse experienced; patterns in relationship dynamics; the responses of friends, family, coworkers, and professionals (e.g., police, shelters, counselors, and doctors); the impact of the violence (long-term and short-term effects); and the background of the participant and their partner, including previous histories of abuse and use of drugs and alcohol.

The women I interviewed reported a range of abusive experiences. These included physical assaults such as slapping, hitting, punching, restraining, shoving, and using weapons; threats and intimidation, extending from threats to reveal sexual identity to threats to kill; emotional abuse, extending from psychological manipulation to chronic putdowns; and sexual abuse. The latter included sexually coercive behaviors, rape and sexual assault, and emotional sexual abuse, illustrated by partners who act in sexually controlling ways that are not consensual, such as making demeaning comments about their partner's sexual behavior or body parts. Understandably, the women often found it particularly difficult to talk about the sexual violence that they had experienced and commonly expressed shame that another woman could have abused them in this manner. Some felt that the term "sexual assault" did not apply to their experiences even though their partner had sexually violated them, because they associated that language with the behavior of male perpetrators. One woman described how her partner would come home and wake her up to assault her:

> She'd come home, wake me up and say, "I want to do this or that" and it's like "no," you know. And she used to give me bruises all over my arms when she'd come on the waterbed and hold my arms down . . . and stuff like that.
>
> [Would she be forcing you to have sex?]
>
> Yeah, now there's something new, I hadn't really saw that. (Wanda)

Wanda had not considered this to be forced sex until describing her experiences in the interview.

In addition to experiencing different types of abuse, women's accounts also highlighted different patterns of intimate violence stemming from distinctive societal roots, indicating that not all violence in lesbian relationships is the same. To better understand the interpersonal dynamics implicated in abuse, I found it more useful to look at the specific contextual features they spoke about than to create typologies or identify empirical correlates of lesbian partner violence. Ignoring these contexts can leave the misimpression that all cases of relationship violence are equivalent. Some social contexts contribute to violence by isolating lesbians or by rendering them invisible. Examples include first relationships; geographical dislocation, such as through migration or immigration; exposure to homophobia, racism, or poverty; and keeping one's sexual orientation or identity "in the closet." The following sections illustrate how women interpreted the meaning of these varied contexts for their experiences of relationship violence. Exploring these contexts shows that many structural factors in addition to patriarchy contribute to violence in intimate relationships.

INVISIBILITY AND ISOLATION: A CONTEXT OF FIRST RELATIONSHIPS

The opening quote from Ellen points to an important pattern that emerged from these interviews: abuse in a woman's first relationship with another woman. More than half of the participants described their first relationship as abusive. In the following quotation, Melissa describes her vulnerability as a young, "impressionable," socially marginalized lesbian with seemingly few options for relationships:

> I lived with two gay men and I always knew that I was a lesbian, but there was no community that I was aware of. Gay men, boy there seemed like there was lots of them, but I didn't know any women, and one of these guys knew this lesbian from another city. I didn't get a good impression when I met her the first time, but then she kind of won me over and I guess I was impressionable because I hadn't really met, you know, a real live lesbian. She was about four years older, a former school teacher. . . . I was really taken by her, you know this was sort of the first affection that I'd gotten from a woman, which I had longed for. (Melissa)

She remained involved with this woman for several years and endured physical and emotional abuse.

In many ways this pattern is not surprising given the additional barriers that lesbians (particularly young lesbians) face when initially coming out. Lesbian women enter into a first relationship as outsiders to lesbian communities and are often not plugged in to any support systems. It suggests that violence is part of the cost of a heterosexist context in which lesbians may be isolated, unable to access meeting places, and often dependent on their first lover for information about living as a lesbian.

DISLOCATION

Consistent with the isolating context of first relationships being abusive, some participants described how moving to a new city, moving from another country, or speaking English as a second language increased their social vulnerability. One woman described the extra pressure that she and her partner felt as recent immigrants who were dislocated, which she believes contributed to the abuse:

> *I was around 24, I guess, when I met her and we were both immigrants. She had just been in Canada for about 6 months. It was a really big thing for her and for me to find a lesbian who was Latina. That was a big thing for us. I could understand what she was going through in terms of learning the language and family. . . . She considered herself lesbian, but she couldn't really handle the fact that her family was here. She didn't know how to come out to them. The family was starting to pressure her—why was she spending so much time with me? Why was she sleeping over at my place? And I put pressure on her too, it's like we don't see each other as much and I would like to see you more. . . . The dynamics in our relationship were very weird. I think they were not healthy. At the time we were also best friends, we didn't have no supports whatsoever and we didn't know any other lesbians either. (Rita)*

Rita is not excusing her abusive partner's behavior but describing the isolating context in which they found themselves.

HOMOPHOBIA AND THE CLOSET

Gays, lesbians, and transgender people have all experienced the impact of living in a homophobic culture. Even though considerable gains have been made in human rights and in visibility, many lesbians remain at least partially closeted, feeling that they must hide their sexuality from some of those with whom they regularly associate, at work or in their friendship network for instance, even when they are "out" to others. Because of homophobia or fear of homophobic reactions, abusers can use a threat of "outing" to exert power and maintain control in the relationship, which they often do.[4] For many of the women I interviewed, the specific power of these threats was often connected to the context in which they felt they had to hide their sexual orientation. Thus, outing was most often effective in small, rural, or northern locations where the dangers of being openly identified as a lesbian added to a victim's isolation and invisibility, often leaving them unable to speak with anyone about what they were going through. A college teacher in a rural town talked about how her partner used her past history of losing a job because she was gay to keep her in their relationship:

> *I'm living in this small town, population five, six thousand. I was very concerned about people knowing that I'm gay because I just don't want the harassment. I meet this woman with two children . . . and within two weeks I realize that there is something seriously wrong with this woman. She's got a mean streak. And I was like, I'm outta there, this isn't good. She goes, "If you even think about leaving or breaking up this relationship, I will ruin your life." Meanwhile, I have the memory of this other harassment when I was an elementary school teacher and I don't want to have to leave this small town because it takes a particularly long time, in education, to get your career on track again. (Kelly)*

Although this relationship became progressively more abusive, Kelly remained for 18 months. Another woman and her abusive partner lived in a small, rural town and worked in the same place, where they were thought to be roommates rather than partners:

> I would go to work, of course, with bizarre excuses for why I had a black eye or this that or the other thing. And we weren't out—we worked together—we weren't out at work. So we were always just like buddies and "Ha, ha, this happened." You know? Whatever . . . and she was a Baptist minister's daughter. (Mary Ann)

The social context of homophobia, heterosexism, and the closet continues to affect abused lesbians both within and outside of their relationships.

Other social contexts contribute to the normalization of violence, in which victims endure abuse because it seems like a normal part of life. These contexts include the use of drugs and alcohol, a history of previous abuse, and experiencing a lifetime of abuse in a context of poverty and racism. Each of these contextual factors may increase one's risk of experiencing violence; however, this does not suggest that they caused the violence.

A LIFETIME OF VIOLENCE: RACISM AND POVERTY

A recurrent feature of women's accounts was a lifetime of violence that occurred on many levels. One woman spoke about her abuse in the context of colonization. She identified as Metis, and her partner as Aboriginal. Each had experienced sexual violence and racial violence, as had their families:

> My mother is Cree, and her parents were really devastated by residential schools and my mother grew up in an extremely violent, abusive, alcoholic home. And I remember thinking that I was living out that legacy. I recall thinking . . . it was like two opposites. At one hand it was like this is the legacy that we carry. It is to be expected, I mean what do you expect from an Indian? Right? Just because we are so inundated with violence, we become normalized to it. And on the other hand, I also knew this is not normal, this is not acceptable. (Ruth)

Ruth also explained how racism caused her partner to feel powerless and contributed to her abusiveness. This did not affect her as much because she could pass as white.

The impact of racism and colonization demonstrates how personal stories are inextricably linked to the historical contexts that root people's lives. Racism, sexism, and homophobia do not cause abuse, but they often intersect to shape the context in which sexual abuse, child abuse, and domestic violence are initiated and continue. Social structures that create and sustain inequalities and disadvantages frame how abusive partners and their victims interpret their experience, normalizing abusiveness in some circumstances and justifying it in others,

helping to make lesbians "appropriate victims" by reinforcing their isolation and marginalization. To grasp lesbian abuse, it is necessary to
recognize the diverse sociohistorical spaces in which it occurs.

RELATIONSHIP DYNAMICS: SHIFTING POWER
AND FIGHTING BACK

A popular model of the dynamics in abusive relationships is the "cycle
of violence" introduced by psychologist Lenore Walker to describe heterosexual relationships. In Walker's view, relationship violence involves a period of tension buildup, an "explosion" of violence, and a period of calm,
reconciliation, or apology, what she terms "the honeymoon phase." Over
time, violence may escalate in severity and the honeymoon phase diminish
in importance or disappear.[5] Many of the women described relationship
dynamics that resemble Walker's "cycle of violence" model. In this relationship dynamic there is a clear perpetrator and a victim. Perpetrators are
seen as using abusive tactics as a way to gain and maintain power and
control over their partner throughout the relationship. Several women also
mentioned the status of their partner that contributed to their power over
them. For example, women's abusive partners included their therapists,
professors, and bosses. In one case, the abuser was a police officer, meaning that the respondent could not call the police for support. In another
case, the abuser worked at a battered women's shelter, thus limiting the
interviewee's options for support.

However, other women spoke not of a cycle but of a constant pattern
of abuse, often daily emotional abuse that had existed throughout their
relationship. Some told me that the physical violence increased whenever
they tried to leave the relationship or resist the abuser's control, and two
women described the violence increasing when they were pregnant.
These are more familiar stories of what has come to be understood as
abusive relationship dynamics. Other women spoke of less predictable
and even fluctuating power dynamics within their relationships. In their
accounts, power was relational rather than being exercised solely by one
partner. This is illustrated in the following quotations:

> The imbalance of power between a man and a woman is constant just because a man
> has privilege in society. And so there's always going to be that, whether he's going to
> choose to work on it or not. Different factors may change some aspects of power but
> that power will remain constant. Whereas with two women, I think that the power
> fluctuates more ... there's more variables involved that can change. I know with my
> relationship with S. at certain times she was so weak I had the power. I remember at
> certain times I would say things and I would go, "Oh my God, I can't believe I said
> that." And I think I was verbally abusive to her in several ways. (Rhonda)

> I don't like getting beat up and so you defend yourself physically. And your adrena-
> line runs. You get an energy, no matter what size you are, you have more power

and strength. I would say to her, you know, "Take your arm off me or whatever, the hair pulling or whatever was going on, or I will break your arm." And I knew I would; I was ready to break her arm. But what that does to you basically is it makes you taste—and it is a literal taste in the mouth—the adrenaline of your own violence. And it doesn't go away the next day. It's a really amazing, bitterish, aftertaste thing. It's a horror and I resent the fact that another human being would bring me to a place where I would do that. (Michaela)

These excerpts suggest that we must explore the meaning of "power and control" in same-sex couples as well as its distribution relative to the distribution of violence in ways that take us beyond the gendered assumptions (male/perpetrator; female/victim) that dominate the current understanding of domestic violence. Moreover, the complex, shifting power dynamics within same-sex abusive relationships have implications for how we understand the categories of victim and perpetrator themselves. For Michaela, the "rush" of adrenaline that she resists is both an expression of her power and "control" in the relationship and a negative consequence of her partner's assault. The image of a victim as pure, innocent, and helpless looms large in dominant culture and makes it difficult to speak about agency, strength, resiliency, and even a "taste" for revenge as other features of being a victim.[6]

FIGHTING BACK

Many of the women with whom I spoke were not passive victims and described physically fighting back within their abusive relationships. There may be more opportunities for both partners to use violence in lesbian relationships because of their relatively similar physical sizes and strengths and because of the construction of femininity (unlike masculinity) as something not to be feared. Perhaps it is this particular gendered dynamic of two women that leads to different relations of power. Some women I interviewed described fighting back with the intent to hurt their partner and to retaliate, while others spoke of fighting back in self-defense throughout the relationship, and, of those, a few indicated that their efforts at self-defense evolved into a desire to hurt their partner.

Some women spoke of fighting back once or twice, often toward the end of the relationship, in episodes that reached a point where they had had enough. Others fought back to stop the violence but stopped because it did not work. Some women commented that they were abused in one relationship and then became controlling in the next. Women's reasons for fighting back included fighting back as a coping strategy, a form of resistance, an intentional act to cause harm, and/or a self-defense reaction. A similar diversity and complexity characterized how they fought back.

Kirstie, a 25-year-old woman whose mother had just died when she became involved in a relationship, provided the following account: "I was very attracted to her and I was also trying to fill a void with my mom not being there. I just put all of my energy into this person." She described her partner as very jealous and always phoning to check up on her at work. The relationship began as emotionally and verbally abusive and then became physically abusive:

> We would be okay as long as we didn't drink. We both started drinking heavily. She was dealing with stuff from her past and I was dealing with my grief and now my grief was shut off because I was just so involved with my relationship and just trying to appease her. I stopped grieving totally and the unfortunate thing is I stopped it in an angry period and I guess my anger took over. We started out getting destructive. We just started cursing each other out, throwing things around, destroying things. The turning point for me was when I couldn't take it any more. I started becoming, I guess aggressive with her when she had taken a picture of my mom and she tried to burn it. I couldn't believe that she did that. (Kirstie)

Their relationship worsened with further episodes of physical violence and with each partner upping the ante of intensity. Kirstie's partner then left her and became involved with another woman. Kirstie began stalking her, punctured her car tires, and also threatened to kill her or commit suicide. In her interview she attributed the shift in her behavior to her partner attacking her core of vulnerability at that moment—a picture of her dead mother.

Another woman described how her defensive use of violence evolved into proactive retaliation when she knew what was going to happen next and thought she needed to defend herself in order to not be further victimized. Barb had experienced so much violence in her life, she said, "I had victim written all over my forehead." This is how she explained the fighting back:

> And the third time, I knew it was going to happen again, I beat her up. And I couldn't stop—I'm not that kind of person at all. I've never done anything like that before or since. I did it on the street and I think that's why I did it, because I knew there were people around in case. And I was angry. (Barb)

In her story, Barb both hurts her partner and protects her by staging the violence where someone was likely to intervene.

Each woman's story reflects different reasons for the shifting power dynamics. Yet, all suggest a resistance to being controlled. These complex dynamics in violent lesbian relationships have too often been labeled mutual abuse. Like "innocent victim," "mutual abuse" is a problematic term because it implies that the power, motivation, and intent to harm are identical in both partners, though this is not what interviewees described. Grappling with these complexities in abusive relationship dynamics is necessary not only for theorizing and researching lesbian partner violence but also for developing effective responses.

INTERVENTION AND SUPPORT

The range and diversity of the violence women in same-sex couples recounted are not reflected in the responses that have been developed to domestic violence. More often, the assumption is that there is only one type of relationship violence and that the violence is a unidirectional expression of power and control exercised in a patriarchal context. Interventions are predicated on the belief that the behavioral, motivational, and contextual factors in lesbian abuse are *the same* as in heterosexual abuse. But too often, the women that I interviewed felt that they had few options to turn to, as they did not see themselves reflected in the existing domestic violence services.

Getting Support: Friends and Family

Some women abused in same-sex relationships did not tell anyone what was happening because of a combination of shame, isolation, fear of homophobic responses, not being out, and fear of retaliation from an abusive partner. But most women I interviewed reached outside their abusive relationships to other people to get support. They turned to friends and family members as a primary source of support. While some women reached out to friends throughout the relationship, this happened more frequently when it was ending or over. Friends played an important role by making comments to women about the inappropriateness of their abusive partner's behaviors or even by being the first to name a relationship abusive. Women spoke of how they might not have been able to listen to the advice of friends at the time but they remembered their words later, which helped them to see they were not imagining the abuse or exaggerating it. Some friends were helpful by directly intervening. One woman described the way her friends protected her from her lover whom she had just left but who was stalking her and following her to university classes:

> I stayed with two friends of mine (in a communal house). I stayed in their room for about a week. And I did go to class but the people in the class took turns going with me everywhere. She tried to find me and track me down. They spent time with her on the phone constantly—I wouldn't talk to her on the phone. They did crisis management on the phone with her. It was only recently when I saw someone from the house that they reminded me how awful it all was. Like I blocked a lot of that out over the years and the woman was just reminding me how scared they were of her, which I didn't know. (Sandi)

In some cases, friends were not helpful and claimed they did not want to get involved or choose sides in the relationship and would often minimize the abuse. This seemed more likely to occur when the abuse was primarily emotional and when friends didn't see evidence of physically abusive behavior. Denial and minimizing by friends are also related to the ongoing reluctance to acknowledge partner violence within lesbian communities because of concerns that this will contribute to societal oppression of gay and lesbian people. In a couple of instances, women that I interviewed described friends joining in on the verbal abuse being launched against them, often in a context where drugs and alcohol were involved. Further, because some abusers told friends that it was their partner who was being abusive, the response of friends could be hostile and contribute to their isolation. As Ramona said about her friends' responses, "They said, 'We don't know who to believe, someone is lying' and then I was left to deal with it." Finally, many women commented on the charming public personality of their Jekyll and Hyde abuser, making it difficult for them to be believed by friends. Overall, their accounts suggest that although lesbians are most likely to turn to friends, they cannot be sure that they will receive positive responses because of lack of evidence of abuse, manipulative tactics used by perpetrators who claim to be victims, and incorrect assumptions about violent relationships that friends use to determine whether or not they are truly "victims" of relationship violence.

Some lesbians also turned to family members for support. This was often a very difficult step, particularly when having to tell a parent that your first lesbian relationship is an abusive one. Many family members did come through in supportive ways, even though women may not have had any contact with them for a few months or years because of their isolation within the abusive relationship. Family members, like many friends, assisted women by offering places to stay, giving them money, or talking supportively on the phone. Yet, many women simply did not reach out to family members because they expected a negative homophobic reaction. Sometimes women also found support from unexpected places like neighbors, coworkers, or strangers who intervened and helped them out in ways that they wouldn't have anticipated. One woman explained that she and her partner were the only lesbians living in a housing cooperative and that she was worried that people in the community would no longer want her once their already marginalized status was tainted by abuse. She explained,

I really felt weirded out—I thought, how are co-op members going to feel about me? I'm very committed to the garden committee and I really worried whether anyone would stay on the committee. But everybody came back onto the committee and I was really taken aback by how much support I had. (Trudy)

Although several friends, family members, and acquaintances did respond in helpful ways, many women still felt they needed to turn to formal support services in order to receive more consistent responses.

Getting Support: Formal Services

Many recent studies on same-sex domestic violence include discussions about a lack of social services available to lesbians and gay men. They report on the barriers gays and lesbians experience when accessing services, such as perceived or actual homophobia and racism; and they comment on the inability of most services to respond fully to same-sex partner violence because of mainstream heterosexual approaches and assumptions.[7] In my study, very few women reported going to shelters for battered women. Some women told stories that involved the police, whereas more than half reported going to counselors. There are many regional disparities in the level of helpful resources available for lesbian partner abuse. Urban areas are more likely to have gay and lesbian resource centers, organizations for women who are victims of violence, and more and more agencies with programs or individuals who do specific work on same-sex domestic violence. This is not the case for smaller cities or rural areas. Further, a lack of knowledge about same-sex partner abuse is commonplace in formal service systems as a result of both lesbian invisibility and heterosexism. Several women reported going to the hospital because of their injuries. Yet in none of these instances did health care providers ask them about how they got their injuries, even though most hospitals now have screening questions regarding domestic violence as part of their routine intakes. Another woman told me how she wrote a counselor since there were none for her to see in the northern, rural area in which she lived but got a response that ignored the issue of lesbian partner violence:

> I started writing to feminist therapists because there aren't any nearby. And so I wrote to this one woman who was advertising in (a feminist newspaper). And I remember it must have been an awful letter (laughs). I poured everything out on just how awful I was feeling, and I was suicidal, and I was smoking too much, and drinking too much, and my mother had just died, and my best friend had just died and I was in this abusive relationship. That was the first time I named it, used that word. And this woman wrote back to me and addressed every single one of those things, with all she could offer, except the abuse. She went on for pages and pages about the alcohol abuse and about grief counseling and you know all the stuff she could help me with and didn't mention it. And I thought, you know, this was sort of the first time that I kinda twigged that there may be some resistance out there to believing this sort of thing. (Lindsay)

Smaller cities, rural towns and isolated areas present specific barriers for lesbians trying to reach out: few or no services, and great concerns about confidentiality and homophobia. A few women turned to books, printed resources, and the Internet as ways of finding helpful information to validate their experiences. Others called crisis lines, sometimes paying long distance fees, in order to talk with someone who could understand their situation. These barriers are not limited to certain geographic regions since they are also related to firmly rooted assumptions that everyone is heterosexual and to the smallness of lesbian communities in general. Thus, many interrelated layers of complexity arise when lesbians seek formal services. For example, many women felt that the services set up to respond to domestic violence, like shelters, were only for heterosexuals and therefore they do not think of or risk going there. In other research that I have done where I surveyed shelter workers about their accessibility to lesbians, they had a different perception. They felt that shelters were open to serving all women. Yet this open and supposedly nondiscriminatory view most often did not extend to explicitly stating that lesbians were welcome in their service brochures and mandates,[8] which is why many lesbians get the message that they cannot qualify for services. Further, in small communities or within gay and lesbian or women's services, many women did not trust that there would be confidentiality, given another sometimes well-founded reason not to seek them out. In fact, several women reported breaches in confidentiality within different services. For example, one woman with a physical disability that made it difficult for her to go to an organization in person explained her experience of the insularity of communities when calling a crisis line:

> I had a very negative experience when I called a crisis line for battered women. When I phoned there it turned out to be a former friend and colleague of my partner's and she didn't believe that I was involved in an abusive relationship with her. She started yelling at me on the phone. (Gio)

This lack of confidentiality and anonymity is often compounded for lesbians of color seeking services in women-of-color organizations and for lesbians who are themselves service providers and who may not be out. As one service provider who was very closeted and living in a community of just 100,000 people said,

> Because it is such a small area, I was trying to find someone for myself to go to. And it took me eight months. Eight months of me asking people that know me quite well, and that I am even willing to talk to about what happened. I finally found someone. . . . But it is a safety thing. I know at my agency [workplace], it doesn't feel safe for them to know [about her sexuality]. Yet, if I can't talk about domestic abuse, where the hell am I? It's tough. (Donna)

Another woman described the difficult interconnections within a smaller city, for example when she attended a meeting for service providers:

> I was sitting beside the woman who counseled me and across from the woman was her [her abusive ex-partner's] therapist . . . and there was another individual in the room who was her girlfriend after me . . . and I just don't know, what did she tell them? (Heather)

A further complication for responding to lesbian relationship violence is who gets to the service first. Because of an assumption that women are always victims, a few women described how their abusive partners were able to identify as victims and use victim services, which meant that they could not themselves access that service. Just as friends and family members may have trouble believing whether or not a woman has really been victimized, services that are set up to respond to the needs of women who are victims of violence often end up being unable to discern who is being abused and who is being abusive and may rely on certain assumptions or stereotypes of "victims," of masculinity and femininity and of lesbians. The responses of services, like those of friends, can end up reinforcing certain constructions of the "good, innocent" victim as they judge whether or not a woman has been victimized. Many lesbians who have been abused may not fit their assumptions, in particular if they are angry, have used substances, have used violence themselves, or are larger or less feminine looking in appearance than their partner. This of course is a double bind for lesbians who are already seen as falling outside dominant constructions of femininity and battering. Several women gave examples of how they were judged negatively by the police.

Police and Criminal Justice System Responses

Responses from the police reveal a continued belief in stereotypes. Police reportedly assessed lesbian partner abuse as a mutual fight rather than as domestic violence and often dismissed the seriousness of the abuse because two women were involved. Some of the women that I interviewed reported that the police were called to intervene at different times. It is not surprising that so few women called the police given the history of police harassment of gay and lesbian communities, poor people, and people of color. In fact, research on hate crimes[9] has reported that police are often perpetrators of anti-lesbian and anti-gay violence. Yet the heterosexual battered women's movement has been successful in advocating for changes in law and policy so that domestic violence is seen as a crime not to be tolerated, and in some American states, like California, campaigns on the crime of domestic violence have included the example of same-sex partner abuse. What is difficult for lesbians is not knowing how police and the criminal justice system will respond. In some cases women called 911 directly for help (they were less interested in pressing charges), sometimes a neighbor called, and, in a few cases, abusive partners tried to have the victim charged. The following extracts speak to the negative encounters that women had:

> M: And of course who do the cops believe? They were making comments about having to use leather gloves with the situation, all that kind of thing. They did lay charges against her but they took it as kind of a joke. They called us the UDS.
> JR: What's that?
> M: Ugly, domestic situation ... between two women, you know. They made jokes about it. [Meryl, describing an incident in which the police were called by a friend because her ex-partner arrived threatening her and their daughter with a gun.]

So my neighbor came over and I walked out the door with him and my kids and went to his house and called the cops. I put my kids in the car and drove to my girlfriend's, and I phoned my place about an hour later and the cops are there and they said, "You better get back here or else." So I go back and she had basically packed up three-fourths of my stuff and said it was her stuff and she told them that I had tried to kill her. They took her home and charged me! (Sharon; the charges were later dropped.)

We were having an argument and she cracked a glass over my head. By the time the police got there, she was acting as if I was crazy—the one who did it. And they just totally ignored me, they were laughing it off and everything. I had glass in my hair and they didn't even want to look, they could care less. They basically said, "Whose house is this?" At the time I was staying with her and they told me to leave. (Vanessa).

Most often women were hoping the police could defuse the situation and offer some protection. Those few who had more positive encounters with police, in which they accurately assessed the situation, tended to be in larger cities with more sizable gay and lesbian communities in which police might have had antihomophobia training.

A few women were successful in getting restraining orders, which offered them some temporary security. Very few women wanted to press charges against their abusive partner, and only three women spoke of these court cases. One case involved a woman trying to charge her partner with sexual assault but the police refusing to lay that charge because it was another woman, thereby denying the possibility of sex and sexual assault between women; in another case, a butch woman was countercharged by her abusive femme partner, which then resulted in each of them having to take a peace bond out on the other (implying they were equally at fault); the third case is still pending. Thus, individuals at many levels of the criminal justice system (police, sergeants, lawyers, and judges) fail lesbians who have been abused, which reinforces a reluctance to interact with these systems.

Counselors

More than half the women that I interviewed sought the help of a counselor. Lesbians may feel they have a greater chance to receive positive support in a one-on-one setting where you can pay for and choose the person that you will talk to. In most urban areas there are also lesbian and feminist counselors who may be more likely to be understanding and nonhomophobic. Women in this study went to counselors or therapists who worked in social service agencies or in private practice. A few women covered by insurance at work reported seeing psychiatrists, although this was not an option for women who were not out at work regardless of whether they had insurance. As a woman in the armed forces said when I asked her if she thought of going to the army's psychiatrist when she was suicidal, "They'd kick me out—send me to a psychiatrist, then kick me out" (Robyn).

Several women who had emigrated to the United States from other countries explained that they didn't seek counseling because they felt these services were based on North American, white, middle-class values. Women from Australia, South Africa, and Nicaragua, for instance, felt individual counseling was not a strong part of their culture and that these services would likely be unable to understand all the components of their identity (i.e., cultural and sexual). A few poor women whose lives had been overly controlled by social services like welfare and child and family services also felt uncomfortable about the option of counseling. For women living on the streets, the most realistic options often are to try and minimize violence in their lives and get safety where they can rather than go to counseling sessions. Finally, a few women saw counseling as something you turn to only if you are really "crazy."

Women who did seek counseling commented on the great expense. Free services often have long waiting lists, limits on the number of sessions you can have, and strict criteria for who qualifies. Some women were very creative when trying to get access to counseling services. One woman spoke of being desperate and going to a drug crisis center where she knew they offered free services:

I didn't have a drug problem but because it was a crisis center they let me in. And actually it was a guy and I wasn't sure I would be okay with a guy and I told him. But he said, "Why don't we just go with this and see if we can do it." And actually he was one of the best therapists I've ever had. (Judy)

Most women went to individual counseling near the end of the relationship or after it was over, although several had started out in couples counseling hoping that they could salvage their relationships. Several women described troubling, ineffective responses, seeing therapists who did not seem to understand or explore their lesbian relationships, and in one extreme case a psychiatrist who responded by asking if the woman wanted to change gender, a comment she found to be both insensitive to her particular concerns and homophobic. Another woman described how her abusive partner killed herself and how full of guilt, anger, and self-blame she was. She went to a straight therapist who was insensitive to her loss and to the horrific abuse that she had endured:

Like she'd say things to me, "I want you to think of five things you like about yourself." And I'm like, "You've got to be fucking kidding? Like I'm dying here, I'm bleeding on your nice leather chair and you want me to think of five things I like about myself?" So I think I had two or three more sessions with her and I just decided, "OK. I can't do therapy now." (Sherri)

Unfortunately, many counselors are simply not knowledgeable about lesbian relationships or partner violence. What stands out in women's descriptions of counseling as effective is that therapists named their relationships as abusive. Often women themselves struggle with whether or not to call a relationship abusive. As we have seen, responses from friends or the police can add confusion to their feelings by questioning their status as "victims." Understandably, many women sought out counseling for depression or anxiety attacks or for help getting through the break-up rather than specifically identifying relationship violence as the issue they needed to address. Anita went to a therapist because of anxiety attacks, and after describing a recent episode her therapist named the relationship as abusive:

A: She said that it was very abusive.
JR: Did that change things, hearing your therapist say something like that, so strongly?
A: Yeah, she named it and so did a friend of mine. And I didn't want to get caught up in that because my previous relationship had been abusive, like not as much, not to the same extent, but it was hurtful. And I new it would be really hard and gut-wrenching to do this [counseling work] but it was something that I needed to do. And I was having anxiety attacks all the time. (Anita)

A few women spoke of being in support groups specifically for abused lesbians, although these groups were mainly available in larger cities and were not offered frequently. Women who went to them consistently commented on how helpful they were because of the validation of their experiences. For example, one woman said,

I didn't want to get into the group. I'd have to sit and talk with other people and hash it all over again, um, it was just too much. But I decided it might be the only thing that would get me through. As it turned out it was excellent. . . . Sharing with other people, just hearing their stories and relating to it . . . not just that but dealing with anger and self-esteem and it just covers so much stuff. And we've all remained friends, which is really nice. (Margo)

Another woman said,

I guess it was six months after she died that I started doing this group. And then I really started embracing and naming things and the denial was falling away. I heard other women's relationships and heard how similar they were. And you know, I started to realize that they use the same lines and they say the same things. I thought there was "abuse college" because it's like they learned these same tactics . . . it would blow me away—the exact same words. (Sherri)

Women found giving a name to their abuse and seeing that they were not alone the most helpful aspects of individual and group counseling. Still, what was most marked about women's accounts are the difficulties many lesbians encounter in finding and receiving help, and the extent to which social services, health care, and the criminal justice system view violence in same-sex relationships through the prism of the dominant understanding of domestic violence as involving a male perpetrator and female victim. What is lacking is a capacity to appreciate or respond to the range of women's experiences in a variety of contexts. Lesbians are forced to figure out ways of coping on their own while negotiating within a heterosexist and homophobic culture that marginalizes and misrecognizes them.

INNOVATIVE APPROACHES

Despite the barriers lesbians face in accessing services in the mainstream domestic violence movement, there are examples of innovative programs that work outside the box of established heterosexual domestic violence protocols. Many of these programs are being developed by and within LGBTQ communities. For instance, some programs broaden victim-only mandates by serving perpetrators as well as survivors, but in ways that still prioritize safety concerns. Some are offering court-mandated batterer intervention programs for LGBTQ abusers as well as advocacy programs to help LGBTQ people better access the legal and criminal justice system.

The Queer Asian Women's Shelter has documented their approach to understanding the needs of queer Asian women and made several recommendations on how to better respond to relationship violence and address the complexities of being part of a small marginalized community.[10] Another project uncovered the particular needs of queer Asian and Pacific Islander women and developed strategies for addressing those needs since they found that very few Asian Pacific Islander women were turning to service providers and shelters for help. A significant theme that emerged in their meetings was "the need to build friendship networks and community ties in order to empower community members to support their friends who struggle with domestic violence."[11] The handbook they published includes a description of two community projects that use community building as a way to address partner violence.

Other community-based outreach initiatives involve holding workshops and forums to address healthy relationships. One group of service providers offered a support group for survivors of lesbian relationship violence, but found that very few women joined. This, they learned, reflected concerns about confidentiality given the small size of the lesbian community in that city. They were much more successful when they hosted an evening discussion on building healthy relationships that included abuse among other topics. Rather than identifying who in the room had experienced abuse, the discussion explored expectations in relationships, negotiating differences, power issues, warning signs of abuse, and the lack of institutional and social supports surrounding lesbian relationships. The forum offered an important shift in strategy from organizational intervention to a community-based prevention and educational initiative that supported healthy relationships.

Another example of a community-based response is the use of popular theater to provide education and information to lesbian communities. A play called *Bruised* developed by lesbians in a smaller urban center presents four different scenes of lesbian relationship violence.[12] A discussion after the play with the actors and writers includes members of the lesbian community with knowledge of lesbian partner violence. The play has traveled to different cities and has been performed in bars and community centers, reaching different parts of the LGBTQ communities. These programs illustrate how the domestic violence movement can embrace the challenges that addressing same-sex relationships violence raises.

CONCLUSIONS

This chapter has featured the voices and experiences of lesbians who have experienced violence in their intimate relationships. The key finding is that only responses based on the range and diversity of the experiences women recounted and the complexity of their social contexts can be accountable to all women. As Beth E. Richie reminds us,

> *Despite the progress in bringing mainstream attention to the issue of violence against women, we might ask how much of the work has focused on providing individual social services at the expense of addressing structures that leave women vulnerable to abuse. For instance, is partner abuse different for lesbians when those relationships are not even recognized by the state? How does federalism leave Native women vulnerable to abuse on reservations in this country? What is the relationship between U.S.-sponsored war in developing countries and violence against women abroad as well as in the United States.... And yet by not even raising complex issues, we seriously threaten the authenticity, the legitimacy, and relevance of the anti-violence movement and the success we ascribe to it.[13]*

Richie reminds us that violence in lesbian relationships is a political issue. Our challenge is this: we must target our responses to the nuanced dynamics involved in lesbian abuse and the complex social factors and contexts without forgetting how a focus on lesbian violence can be turned to support the homophobic view that same-sex relationships are deviant and unhealthy.

NOTES

1. This chapter draws heavily on, *No More Secrets: Violence in Lesbian Relationships* by Janice Ristock. Copyright © 2002 by Routledge. Reprinted by permission of Routledge via the Copyright Clearance Center. (New York: Routledge, 2002); and J. Ristock, "Relationship Violence in Lesbian/Gay/Bisexual/

Transgender/Queer [LGBTQ] Communities: Moving beyond a Gender-Based Framework," Violence against Women On-Line Resources, 2005, http://www.mincava.umn.edu/documents/lgbtqviolence/lgbtqviolence.html.

The names and initials used in this chapter are all pseudonyms. The term "lesbian relationship" is used to include women who are involved in an intimate relationship with another woman. However, not all women in relationships with other women identify as lesbians and might prefer terms such as "bisexual," "male identified," "butch," "femme," "gay," "two-spirited," "dyke," or "queer." Further, other women may more strongly identify with their ethnic or cultural background rather than with their sexual identity.

2. K. Lobel, ed., *Naming the Violence: Speaking Out about Lesbian Battering* (Seattle, WA: Seal Press, 1986), 7.

3. P. Tjaden, N. Thoennes, and C. Allison, "Comparing Violence Over the Life-Span in Samples of Same Sex and Opposite Sex Cohabitants." *Violence and Victims* 14 (1999): 413–25.

4. See, for example, C. Renzetti, *Violent Betrayal: Partner Abuse in Lesbian Relationships* (Newbury Park, CA: Sage, 2002); and Carol Tully, *Lesbians, Gays and the Empowerment Perspective* (New York: Columbia University Press, 2000).

5. L. Walker, *The Battered Woman* (New York: Harper & Row, 1979).

6. S. Lamb, "Constructing the Victim: Popular Images and Lasting Labels," in *New Versions of Victims: Feminists Struggle with the Concept* (New York: New York University Press, 1999), 108–38.

7. See A. Russo, *Taking Back Our Lives: A Call to Action for the Feminist Movement* (New York: Routledge, 2001); and E. Simpson and C. Helfirch, "Lesbian Survivors of Intimate Partner Violence: Providers Perspectives on Barriers to Accessing Services," *Journal of Gay and Lesbian Social Services* 18 (2005): 45.

8. J. Ristock, "Decentering Heterosexuality: Responses of Feminist Service Counselors to Abuse in Lesbian Relationships," *Women and Therapy* 23, no. 3 (2001): 59–72.

9. G. Herek, R. Gillis, J.C. Cogan, and E.K. Glunt, "Hate Crime Victimization among Lesbian, Gay, and Bisexual Adults: Prevalence, Psychological Correlates, and Methodological Issues," *Journal of Interpersonal Violence* 1, no. 2 (1997): 195–215.

10. C. Chung and S. Lee, *Raising Our Voices: Queer Asian Women's Response to Relationship Violence* (San Francisco: Family Violence Prevention Fund, 1999).

11. S. Lee and H. Utarti, *Creating Community, Hope and Change* (San Francisco: Family Violence Prevention Fund, 2003), 5.

12. L. Allen-Agostini and Jesekah, *Bruised*, performed June 12–13, 1996, Winnipeg, Manitoba.

13. B. Richie, "Foreword," in *Domestic Violence at the Margins: Readings on Race, Class, Gender and Culture*, ed. Natalie Sokoloff with Christina Pratt (New Brunswick, NJ: Rutgers University Press, 2005), xvi.

Chapter 9

Domestic Violence and the African American Community

Katherine E. Morrison

Society has become increasingly aware of the devastating effects of male-to-female intimate partner violence (IPV). Recent estimates indicate that approximately one in three women are assaulted by their male intimate partner each year. Although research has been conducted in this area for decades, only relatively recently have researchers and practitioners assessed the unique experiences of African American women with regard to IPV. The studies that have been conducted within the past decade indicate that African American women are at greater risk for experiencing violence at the hands of a male intimate partner than are women from other racial and/or ethnic groups.[1] The evidence also suggests that African American women are susceptible to both physical and psychological sequela as a result of this abuse.

The purpose of this chapter is to critically examine what the current literature tells us about IPV within the African American community. Included is information about the incidence and prevalence of IPV in African American communities, the consequences for the health of African American women, theories that explain the occurrence and dynamics of IPV within this community, a glimpse at current culturally sensitive prevention-related activities, and recommendations for intervention and further research.

INCIDENCE AND PREVALENCE

Research has indicated that IPV is a serious issue within the African American population. Using a clinical sample of African American women, Barnes found that almost 16 percent of the participants experienced physical abuse and approximately 12 percent experienced psychological abuse.[2] In a convenience sample of more than 800 African American women, Amar reported that approximately 48 percent of her participants reported having experienced some form of dating violence.[3] In a longitudinal study, Raiford found at baseline that 28 percent of adolescent females ages 14 to 18 years of age had experienced dating violence.[4]

There is also evidence that African American women are at increased risk for experiencing IPV when compared with white women. For instance, the Office of Justice Programs found that the rates of IPV among African American women were half-again as high as among white women (12 per 1,000 versus 8 per 1,000, respectively).[5] Using data from the 1998 National Crime Victimization Survey, Rennison and Welchans found that African American women experienced IPV at a rate that was nearly 35 percent higher than that of white women.[6] Finally, using data from a nationally representative study, Tjaden and Thoennes reported that approximately 26.3 percent of African American women had been physically assaulted by a male partner during their lifetime, compared with 21.3 percent of white women.[7]

CONSEQUENCES TO HEALTH

Physical

Just as with women of other races and ethnicities, African American women may be more likely to be physically injured as a result of IPV. Compared with other women, they are more likely to experience severe IPV-related attacks, more likely to have a weapon used against them, and six times more likely to have been hospitalized because of injuries caused by partner violence. In a study of injuries sustained by African American women residing in an inner city, Grisso found that of all the injuries caused by interpersonal violence, approximately 60 percent were caused by a male intimate partner (husband or boyfriend).[8]

In part because African American women are more susceptible to severe attacks, they are at greater risk than other women of suffering brain trauma as a result of IPV, as well as of being killed by a male intimate partner. Homicide at the hands of an intimate partner is a leading cause of death for African American women between the ages of 15 and 24. According to data collected by the Federal Bureau of Investigation, between 1981 and 1998, African American women were almost three times as likely to be killed by a male intimate partner than were white women.[9] In 2001, African American women were murdered by their male intimate partners at a rate of 3.34 per 100,000. In the same year, white women were murdered at a rate of 1.05 per 100,000.

Psychological Consequences

Despite the current onslaught of research surrounding African American victims, our understanding of the psychological impact of IPV is limited. However, the research that does exist on the topic reports that African American women suffer similar psychological consequences of IPV as women of other races and ethnicities. Among these mental health issues, the most prominent are depression, anxiety, alcohol abuse, and posttraumatic stress disorder.

In general, both African American and white women demonstrate higher levels of depression and anxiety if they are the victim of IPV than women who are not. Among black women, those reporting IPV were nine times more likely to report having some type of mental health issue than were nonabused black women. Depression and alcohol abuse are particularly significant outcomes of IPV among black women. In a study of 445 African American women, it was found that a history of IPV was associated with depression as well as an increased chance that a woman would need treatment for a sexually transmitted disease.[10]

THEORIES

Provided with the evidence that African American women are experiencing high rates of IPV and that their health and well-being is in jeopardy, what are some of the reasons underpinning the severity of this phenomenon within this particular community? Feminist theory is only one of a number of conceptual frameworks that has been used to explain the etiology of IPV in general. But few of these theories have been applied specifically to the African American population and among those, none have been empirically validated. The following section outlines few of these theories.

Institutionalized Racism

Institutionalized racism may be defined as the use of American systems, governances, and other practices to discriminate, subjugate, and oppress persons belonging to racially marginalized groups. This discrimination often comes in various forms of discrimination including the denial of employment or ensuring equality of education. In fact, there is substantial evidence that institutionalized racism influences the overall quality of life of those who are subject to it. As a result of this phenomenon, groups such as African Americans are denied access to adequate and affordable housing, have limited resources available to them in their neighborhoods, have limited access to health care, and are subjected to an intergenerational transmission cycle of poverty.

Although IPV occurs across all economic strata, poverty has been established as a predictor of male violence against female intimate partners (see the chapters by Renzetti and by Raphael in this volume). This may be due to the psychological and emotional stress caused by poverty as well as the scarcity of reliable community resources available to those who are impoverished. In effect, the cycle of institutionalized racism and poverty leads to the high rates of IPV witnessed in this community.

Black Male Masculinity

The introduction of Africans to the United States in 1619 was followed by centuries during which concerted efforts were made to manipulate, control, dominate, and oppress those of African descent. Chattel slavery was a business institution where, in order to "secure investments," cruel methods of discipline, not the least of which was torture, were used to maintain power over the enslaved population. While these punitive forms of discipline were used on both African women and men alike, men were often treated more severely than the women because they posed the most direct threat to the power establishment.

The view that men of African descent directly threatened the Eurocentric power structure endured through the Civil War, Reconstruction, Jim Crow, and the civil rights movement and is still in existence today. Continued racism is evident in a number of contemporary realities including but not limited to the overrepresentation of African American males in the prison system and on death row, the number of undereducated and unemployed black males, and the extent to which African American males are harassed, beaten, and killed by law enforcement agencies.

To be a part of a racial group where the men are routinely ostracized and kept from becoming fully integrated into mainstream society through institutionalized racism and discrimination is not only excessively stressful but overwhelmingly dehumanizing. It can be argued that in every society, men and women have distinctive gender roles and along with those gender roles are behavioral expectations and other responsibilities. In American society, these expectations include emotional resiliency as well as the ability to provide for family through employment. African American men are not only treated as second-class citizens but also denied resources they need in order to be providers for their families as well as productive members of American society.

Despite their capacity and willingness to participate as full citizens, the United States has established a strong legacy of denying African American men the ability and the right to fulfill their gender role expectations. African American men experience how little they are valued both directly, by experiencing discrimination in their everyday encounters outside the African American community, and indirectly, by watching others suffer the consequences of racism. The lessons from these experiences have been integrated into the social fabric of this community. As a result, it may be argued that many African American men feel emasculated, stripped of their manhood and their ability to exercise their right to be a "man"—that is, they feel dehumanized.

Some scholars have argued that one result of this process of dehumanization and emasculation is that many black males have responded to their caustic environment by adopting a "tough guy" persona that provides a psychological buffer to the influences of institutionalized racism. Integrated with the ideal of being the "tough guy" is a tendency toward violence that may play out through violence against women.

Alongside the "tough guy" image, the black male may become a "playa," a male who acts out sexually through promiscuity. As Oliver observes, "[M]any lower-class black males see themselves as 'users of women' and are overtly concerned with presenting themselves as exploiters of women and expect other men to do the same."[11] Coupled with the image of the playa is the need for African American males to dominate and control women. Thus, imagery that has developed as an adaptive mechanism to safeguard against racism may be directly linked to male-to-female violence in the African American community.

The "Strong Black Woman"

Romero calls the image of the "Strong Black Woman" "the substance around which folklore and legends, fact and fiction, have been written." The "Strong Black Woman," she writes, "is a mantra so much a part of the U.S. culture that it is seldom realized how great a toll it has taken on the emotional well-being of the African American woman. As much as it may give her the illusion of control, it keeps her from identifying what she needs and reaching out for help."[12] This culturally based construct Romero describes is gaining some recognition within the scientific community because of how it influences the overall health of African American women.

According to this construct, a woman finds a strong sense of racial identity only if she portrays herself as autonomous, self-sufficient, and emotionally resilient in times of unrest or turmoil. Although there is only limited research on this issue, there is some evidence that women who strive to become the "Strong Black Woman" are at increased risk for negative health outcomes. This is because adapting this role hinders help seeking: women who adopt this self-image believe they can take care of all problem situations on their own. This socialization process makes it less likely that black women will seek outside assistance when they need it.[13]

This theory may be applied to women who are involved in abusive relationships, particularly those in abusive relationships with African American men. An African American woman who adheres to this ideology will be reluctant to not only ask for help with the abusive relationship but also leave the perpetrator because of the idea that the real Strong Black Woman stays with her African American partner regardless of how unhealthy or destructive the relationship.

Additionally, some African American women may feel that reporting IPV to the authorities is a form of racial disloyalty and that by calling police, for example, they are not only betraying their African American partner but also, by turning him over to an unjust legal system, undermining the African American community as a whole. These views enhance the risk of black women involved in IPV.

RESPONSES TO IPV IN THE AFRICAN AMERICAN COMMUNITY

The development, implementation, and evaluation of culturally sensitive methods to prevent IPV in the African American community have been almost as sparse as research studies of this problem. However, that is starting to change.

Popular Culture Interventions

There are popular culture methods of influencing attitudes, thoughts, and behaviors with regard to IPV that have been tailored specifically to African Americans. Prominent among these is the "It's Your Business" campaign that has been designed by the Family Prevention Fund and is being implemented in a number of communities across the United States.[14] This is a broad-based health communication campaign that uses different popular culture venues to distribute anti-IPV messages. Designed from data gleaned from focus groups, this campaign has developed educational print media such as posters and brochures to be used by community leaders and groups concerned about the level of IPV within their neighborhoods.

In addition to the print media, the Family Violence Prevention Fund also developed a series of 12 ninety-second public service announcements (PSAs) for the radio-listening audience. This method is viewed as being particularly effective with African Americans because of a strong oral tradition within the culture rooted in West African traditions. Using a method of education that is readily recognizable to the target audience makes the messages more palatable since they are parallel to certain cultural practices of the community. Each of the PSAs is part of a dramatic story line about representative IPV situations occurring among African American couples. The PSAs use engaging methods of storytelling, relationship building, and dramatization. Preliminary indications are that these PSAs have had some success in increasing the awareness of IPV among the target population.

The popular music industry offered another method of prevention. A song titled "How Come, How Long" written and performed by African American R&B artists Babyface and Stevie Wonder was released in 1996 and is still used as an educational tool. The song tells the story of a young woman who was involved in an abusive relationship with a male partner, describes the abuse she suffered, and describes the ultimate outcome, that the woman was killed by her boyfriend.

Research and Sharing of Ideas

An increasing number of scholars and practitioners are investing their energies in preventing IPV within the African American community. In 1993, the Institute on Domestic Violence in the African American Community (IDVAAC) was established to recognize the needs and concerns of this growing cadre of professionals and is today a nationally recognized source of institutional support for research and practice. The IDVAAC addresses several components of domestic violence, including IPV, elder abuse, and child maltreatment.

The board of IDVAAC is composed of well-established experts in the field of African American violence. Among its most notable accomplishments is an annual conference with a changing overarching theme. Past themes have included the influence of rap and hip-hop on IPV, women as victims of IPV, ending the silence surrounding IPV within the culture, and the role of black male masculinity.

Activism

INCITE! Women of Color against Violence is a nationally recognized organization with chapters in major cities across the United States. Through grassroots activism, INCITE! members combat IPV through direct action, education, and community organizing. Among their most notable activities are influencing social norms through media advocacy, political activism, direct education in communities, and hosting political conferences.[15]

RECOMMENDATIONS

Although there is much activity and research dedicated to preventing IPV within the African American community, to reduce the currently alarming rates of lethal and nonlethal violence, a more sophisticated coordinated response to this issue is needed. To accomplish this requires a new convergence of research, practice, and policy on the issue.

Practice

Much more needs to be accomplished with regard to building awareness about IPV within the African American community. Other research with this community has found that a narrow understanding prevails of what domestic violence is and how destructive it can be for the victim and the community. Conversely, it has been found that individuals within the community have a very limited set of skills bearing on how to help victims of domestic violence. Others have also observed how little sympathy or support there is for African American women who are abused in intimate relationships and a reluctance to support victims.

Only by sharpening our commitment to all levels of prevention will we be able to adequately address the need for culturally sensitive IPV education. Battered women shelters are among the most important examples of tertiary prevention, where the aim is helping persons who are in the throes of serious abuse. Routine questioning of all medical patients is a good example of secondary prevention. Here the aim is early identification and stopping the progression of the problem before it becomes severe. But there is a paucity of primary prevention programs to stop domestic violence from occurring in the first place and even fewer programs that have been designed to be culturally specific for African American audiences. Unfortunately, there are far too few educational outreach activities to raise the awareness of IPV in the African American communities. The precedent-setting "It's Your Business" campaign should be replicated nationwide. This will require institutions such as hospitals and social service agencies to combine resources and expertise to create a climate conducive to social change in attitudes, values, and beliefs.

Another essential ingredient of successful prevention is enlisting as partners organizations that are skilled at working with African Americans, such as the church. The black church has historically been a sanctuary where the African American community is able to congregate, discuss critical issues in the community, and identify a course of action to address them. As a result, the church provides fertile ground for providing health education programs, including those programs that are related to violence within the African American community.

Research

If interventions to decrease IPV within the African American community have been largely ineffective, this is because more often than not professionals adopt initiatives based on what has been successful among other groups rather than by building upon the unique viewpoints and experiences of African Americans. Such initiatives fail to effectively engage the community or communicate the advantage of healthy relationships. While research on the unique dynamics of problems among African Americans is growing, there is still much that we do not know or fully understand about the occurrence of IPV within this community.

In essence, the task now becomes to gain a better understanding of IPV through the lens of African Americans. Research with this aim should have at least two dimensions. First, there needs to be a more in-depth exploration of the structural and cultural variables that influence IPV in African American communities. The theoretical perspectives sketched above offer some insight into why IPV occurs in this community at such high rates, but there is little phenomenological or empirical evidence to support these theories. At the same time, the empirical work that is conducted on IPV among African Americans should be theoretically grounded or theory driven so that findings can be linked to explanations, hence to interventions.

A second essential for developing effective prevention programs is to garner much more evidence on the attitudes held by African American men and women toward IPV, including teens. We also need a much better understanding of how attitudes held by other groups toward IPV are mediated by cultural values, traditions, and beliefs specific to African Americans. If aspects of the African American culture present obstacles to the prevention of IPV, what are these elements? Mixed-methods research (i.e., a coupling of qualitative and quantitative methods) may be most beneficial in unearthing the community's general understanding of and reaction to women as victims of IPV.

CONCLUSIONS

Because of its physical, psychological, and social consequences, IPV is a tremendous threat to the health and well-being of all women. The experience of IPV transcends race, culture, ethnicity, and socioeconomic status. Nevertheless, evidence suggests that African American women are at increased risk for experiencing IPV. A range of structural and cultural theories has been proposed to explain this elevated risk. Most notable are theories that emphasize the role of racism in shaping the self-esteem of African American men in particular; attitudes toward gender roles, including masculinity; and help seeking by victims.

It is clear that an appropriate response requires a concerted and coordinated response that is both rooted in the unique facets of African American culture and based in institutions such as the black church to which African Americans have turned for help in times of trouble and in the emerging community of professionals who are dedicated to researching and lowering rates of IPV in African American communities. A first step toward limiting the particular vulnerability of African

American women, but by no means the last, is to explore this group's understanding of and reaction to IPV within the context of institution-alized racism and to develop and target culturally appropriate mes-sages of change accordingly.

NOTES

1. L. A. Greenfield, M. R. Rand, D. Craven, P. A. Klaus, C.A. Perkins, C. Ringel, et al., *Violence by Intimates: Analysis of Data on Crimes by Current or Former Spouses, Boyfriends, and Girlfriends*, no. NCJ-167237 (Washington, D.C.: U.S. Department of Justice, Bureau of Justice Statistics, 1998).

2. S. Y. Barnes, "Physical and Psychological Abuse among a Predominately African-American Sample," Association of Black Nursing Faculty (2001): 36–41.

3. A. F. Amar, "Dating Violence in College Women: Associated Physical Injury, Healthcare Usage, and Mental Health Symptoms," *Nursing Research* 54, no. 4 (2005): 235–42.

4. J. L. Raiford, G.M. Wingood, and R. J. DiClemente, "Prevalence, Incidence, and Predictors of Dating Violence: A Longitudinal Study of African American Female Adolescents," *Journal of Women's Health* 16, no. 6 (2007): 822–32.

5. Greenfield et al., *Violence by Intimates*.

6. C. M. Rennison and S. Welchans, *Intimate Partner Violence*, no. NCJ 178247 (Washington, D.C.: United States Department of Justice, Office of Justice Programs, Bureau of Justice Statistics, 2000).

7. P. Tjaden and N. Thoennes, *Extent, Nature, and Consequences of Intimate Partner Violence: Findings from the National Violence against Women Survey*, no. NCJ-181867 (Washington, D.C.: Department of Justice, Office of Justice Pro-grams, 2000).

8. J. A. Grisso, D.F. Schwarz, C. G. Miles, and J. H. Holmes, "Injuries among Inner-City Minority Women: A Population-Based Longitudinal Study," *American Journal of Public Health* 86, no. 1 (2006): 67–70.

9. L. J. Paulozzi, L. E. Saltzman, M. P. Thompson, and P. Holmgreen, "Sur-veillance for Homicide among Intimate Partners—United States—1981–1998," *Surveillance Summaries* 50, no. SS03 (2001): 1–16.

10. K. Laughon, A. C. Gielen, J. C. Campbell, J. Burke, K. McDonnell, and P. O'Campo, "The Relationships among Sexually Transmitted Infection, Depression, and Lifetime Violence in a Sample of Predominantly African American Women," *Research in Nursing & Health* 30, no. 4 (2007): 413–28.

11. W. Oliver, "Black Males and Social Problems: Prevention through Afro-centric Socialization," *Journal of Black Studies* 20, no. 1 (1989): 22.

12. R. E. Romero, "The Icon of the Strong Black Woman: The Paradox of Strength" in *Psychotherapy with African-American Women: Innovations in Psycho-dynamic Perspectives and Practice*, ed L.C. Jackson and B. Greene (New York: Guilford, 2000), 225.

13. V. L. De Francisco and C. A. Chatham, "Self in Community: African American Women's Views of Self-Esteem," *Howard Journal of Communications* 11, no. 2 (2000): 73–92.

14. W. Oliver, "Sexual Conquest and Black-on-Black Violence: A Structural-Cultural Perspective," *Violence and Victims* 4, no. 4 (1989): 257–73; and

R. J. Wray and R. M. Hornik, "Preventing Domestic Violence in the African-American Community: Assessing the Impact of a Dramatic Radio Serial," *Journal of Health Communication* 9 (2004): 31–52.

15. INCITE! Women of Color against Violence, 2008, http://www.incite-national.org (accessed May 4, 2008).

BIBLIOGRAPHY

Amankwaa, L. C. "Postpartum Depression among African-American Women." *Issues in Mental Health Nursing* 24 (2003): 297–316.

American Medical Association. *Diagnostic and Treatment Guidelines on Domestic Violence*, Pamphlet no. AA 22-92-406 20M. Chicago: Author, 1992.

Banks, M. and R. Ackerman. "Head and Brain Injuries Experienced by African-American Women Victims of Intimate Partner Violence," in *Violence in the Lives of Black Women: Battered, Black, and Blue*, ed. C. M. West. New York: Haworth Press, 2002, 133–43.

Benson, M. L., G. L. Fox, A. DeMaris, and J. Van Wyk. "Violence in Families: The Intersection of Race, Poverty, and Community Context," in *Families, Crime and Criminal Justice*, ed. G. L. Fox and M.L. Benson. New York: JAI, 2000, 2:91–109.

Bent-Goodley, T. B. "Eradicating Domestic Violence in the African-American Community: A Literature Review and Action Agenda." *Trauma, Violence, and Abuse* 2, no. 4 (2001): 316–30.

Coker, A. L. "Primary Prevention of Intimate Partner Violence for Women's Health." *Journal of Interpersonal Violence* 19, no. 11 (2004): 1325–34.

Hammond, W. P. and J. S. Mattis. "Being a Man about It: Manhood Meaning among African American Men." *Psychology of Men and Masculinity* 6 (2005): 114–26.

Hampton, R., W. Oliver, and L. Magarian. "Domestic Violence in the African American Community: An Analysis of Social and Structural Factors." *Violence against Women* 9, no. 5 (2003): 533–57.

Hampton, R. L. and B. R. Yung. "Violence in Communities of Color: Where We Were, Where We Are, and Where We Need to Be" in *Preventing Violence in America*, ed. R. L. Hampton, P. Jenkins, and T. P. Gullotta. Thousand Oaks, CA: Sage, 1996.

Harris-Lacewell, M. "No Place to Rest: African-American Political Attitudes and the Myth of Black Women's Strength." *Women and Politics* 23, no. 3 (2001): 1–33.

Institute on Domestic Violence in the African-American Community. http://www.dvinstitute.org (accessed May 4, 2008).

Jenkins, E. J. "Black Women and Community Violence: Trauma, Grief, and Coping." *Women & Therapy* 25, nos. 3–4 (2002): 29–44.

Jenkins, S. Y. "Psychotherapy and Black Female Identity Conflicts." *Women and Therapy* 18, no. 1 (1996): 59–71.

Jordan, J. V., L. M. Hartling, and M. Walker. *The Complexity of Connection: Writings from the Stone Center's Jean Baker Miller Training Institute*. New York: Guilford, 2004.

Joseph, J. "Woman Battering: A Comparative Analysis of Black and White Women." In *Out of Darkness*, ed. G. Kaufman-Kantor and J. Jasinski. Thousand Oaks, CA: Sage, 1997, 161–69.

King, A. E. O. "Understanding Violence among Young African-American Males: An Afrocentric Perspective." *Journal of Black Studies* 28, no. 1 (1997): 79–96.

Morrison, K. E. "Voices from the Margins: Advantages of Using Qualitative Methodology to Explore the Experiences of African-American Survivors of Intimate Partner Violence," in *Intimate Partner Violence*, ed. K. Kendall-Tackett and S. Giacomoni. Kingston, NJ: Civic Research Institute, 2007.

Morrison, K. E. (unpublished). *Beliefs Surrounding Intimate Partner Violence within the African-American Community: An Exploratory Study.*

National Center for Injury Prevention and Control. *Leading Causes of Death by Age Group, Black Females, United States 2004.* Fact Sheet. Retrieved from http://www.cdc.gov/Women/lcod04black.pdf database (accessed May 5, 2008).

Oliver, W. "Preventing Domestic Violence in the African-American Community: The Rationale for Popular Culture Interventions." *Violence against Women* 6, no. 5 (2000): 533–49.

Paranjape, A., S. Heron, S. and N. Kaslow. "Utilization of Services by Abused, Low-Income African-Americans." *Journal of General Internal Medicine* 17, no. 1 (2007): 189–92.

Ramos, B. M., B. E. Carlson, and L.-A. McNutt. "Lifetime Abuse, Mental Health, and African American Women." *Journal of Family Violence* 19, no. 3 (2004): 153–64.

Riggs, M. Y. "Plenty Good Room: Women versus Male Power," in *The Black Church*. Cleveland, OH: Pilgrim, 2006.

See, L. A., W. Oliver, and O.J. Williams. "Domestic Violence in African-American Families," in *Handbook of Violence*, ed. L. A. Rapp-Paglicci, A. R. Roberts, and J. S. Wodarski. New York: John Wiley, 2002, 67–105.

Sullivan, C. M. and M. H. Rumptz. "Adjustment and Needs of African-American Women Who Utilized a Domestic Violence Shelter," *Violence and Victims* 9, no. 3 (1994): 275–86.

Thompson, M. P., N. Kaslow, L. Short, and S. Wyckoff, S. "The Mediating Roles of Perceived Social Support and Resources in the Self-Efficacy Suicide Attempts Relation among African-American Abused Women." *Journal of Consulting and Clinical Psychology* 70, no. 4 (2002): 942–49.

Violence Policy Center. *When Men Murder Women: An Analysis of 2001 Homicide Data.* Washington, D.C.: Violence Policy Center, 2003.

West, C. *Race Matters.* New York: Vintage, 1993.

Williams, O. and L. Becker. Focus Groups of African-American Men: Perspectives on Addressing Domestic Violence. Minnesota Center Against Violence and Abuse. July 25, 1998. Report retrieved from http://www.mincava.umn.edu/documents/2oliver/2oliver.pdf.

Williams, O. J. and R. L. Becker. "Domestic Partner Abuse Treatment Programs and Cultural Competence: The Results of a National Survey." *Violence and Victims* 9, no. 3 (1994): 287–96.

Chapter 10

The Health System Response to Domestic Violence

Emma Williamson

This chapter critically examines recent developments in medical and health responses to domestic violence in the United States and England. Advances in the provision of health services to women who experience abuse pose a challenge: how to highlight the limits of research and services in this area without being insensitive to the very real progress that has occurred. I am fortunate to be a part of a dynamic research group with members from around the globe, many of whom are concerned with the wider psychological and spiritual well-being of those who experience domestic violence. From this experience comes an underlying concern that, as the medical profession moves to identify and quantify domestic violence, it not lose sight of the broad array of health needs of victims, survivors, and perpetrators.

In previous work on this topic,[1] it was suggested that health practitioners should receive training about domestic violence and that screening for domestic violence should occur systematically within medical settings. These recommendations relate directly to practice yet take place within wider debates in medicine about professionalism and notions of knowledge and power. This chapter will consider how debates about intimate terrorism and coercive control have relevance for the definitions of domestic violence that are used both within health but also within the criminal justice system. This is important because the use of definitions in relation to health and crime shape how practice and knowledge of practice develop. Finally, this chapter will examine specific tensions that characterize the delivery of health care in the context of domestic violence in four areas primarily—knowledge and research, training, screening, and mental health.

DOMESTIC VIOLENCE AND HEALTH: HISTORICAL DEVELOPMENTS IN RESEARCH

Domestic violence is a health issue because of the physical and non-physical consequences of abuse. Research has shown that domestic violence–related harms are diverse and include abrasions, lacerations, contusions, sprains, strains, alterations in nutrition, sleep disturbances, agoraphobia, panic attacks, drug overdose, suicide attempts, depression, substance misuse, fatigue, miscarriage, early labor, anxiety, depression, facial injuries (particularly to the lips, eyes, and teeth), hair loss and perforated tympanic membrane, posttraumatic stress and posttraumatic stress disorder (PTSD), abdominal or pelvic pain, headaches, gastrointestinal disorders, low birth rate, hematomas, fractures, inflammation, and penetrating puncture wounds. In addition to this comprehensive list, domestic violence regularly includes rape and often ends in a fatality.

In addition to the wide range of physical and psychological harms caused by domestic violence—an issue that programs for perpetrators rarely emphasize—researchers have also documented the prevalence of such injuries. Among a group of 25 women who identified domestic violence as the source of their injuries in a medical setting, it was found that 24 percent suffered abrasions or lacerations; more than half (52 percent) suffered contusions such as soft tissue injury; 16 percent had fractures, sprain, or strains; and 8 percent had puncture or rupture wounds. Importantly, the site of injuries suggests the sexual nature of domestic violence: 16 percent of the injuries occurred to extremities, like the hands or feet; fully 36 percent occurred to the face, head, and neck area; 8 percent affected the genitalia; and 4 percent of injuries were directed toward the chest and abdomen, and back and buttocks.[2]

Domestic violence also impacts others in the victim's social world, including children, immediate and extended family members, friends, work colleagues and acquaintances, professionals, as well as society as a whole. Most people would agree that being harmed in intimate relationships on the basis of one's gender, race, sexual identity, or culture is incompatible with a healthy society and that our working definition of harm should be broad enough to encompass the fear, anxiety, guilt, disappointment, and loss of trust and love that abuse victims experience (see, for example, the chapter by Platt and her colleagues in this volume). It is this broad understanding of health that directs our discussion of domestic violence.

THE HEALTH SYSTEM RESPONSE

Within the United States, health practitioners have been addressing the issue of domestic violence since the late 1970s. The first interventions in medical settings were built on the earlier response to rape victims and were implemented largely by volunteer nurses and social workers. But the responses quickly extended to the American Medical Association (AMA), the American Nursing Association, and the American Public Health Association; and to organizations representing army medics, emergency medical personnel, psychiatrists, dentists, pediatricians, pharmacists, and even surgeons working with traumatic brain injury.

Initially focused on the importance of domestic violence as a source of adult injury and on the emergency service as the point at which injuries were most likely to be presented, this early work quickly broadened to encompass the range of health outcomes associated with abuse as well as to nonemergent settings such as the obstetrical service and the community clinic. The emphasis in this early period was on developing and implementing domestic violence policies and protocols within specific institutions, mainly hospitals and medical departments, providing "guidelines" for intervention to private practitioners through their professional associations, and training practitioners in all health settings to respond more appropriately. In 1985, after an unprecedented national workshop he had convened, U.S. Surgeon General C. Everett Koop publicly identified violence as a major public health problem, rather than merely a criminal justice concern—a relatively new idea—and targeted violence against women and children in particular. Importantly, his declaration acknowledged the economic and social costs of domestic violence as well as the toll it takes on victims.

Social scientists in the United States also addressed the issue of domestic violence and health. Based on a review of more than 3,500 medical records of women who had come to Yale–New Haven Hospital complaining of injury, sociologist Evan Stark and Anne Flitcraft, MD, concluded that domestic violence was the leading cause of injuries for which women sought medical attention, far more common than auto accidents, then thought to be the most common source of adult injuries.[3] In addition to further documenting the significance of domestic violence as a source of women's health problems, this body of work raised a number of concerns about the medical response, which was often described as harmful as well as inadequate. One important issue was that domestic violence injuries were treated symptomatically rather than as the consequence of abuse. This led to a related problem, the extent to which clinicians applied pseudo-psychiatric labels to abused women, suggesting that their repeat visits were the consequence of their personality traits or behavioral problems rather than a reflection of their partner's assaults. As women developed the secondary consequences of abuse or attempted to medicate their stressful situation with alcohol, drugs, or pain pills, clinicians took these consequences of abuse and inverted them as its cause, concluding that if a woman was beaten, it was because she was alcoholic or was unable to deal with conflict because of her depression, for instance. This process discredited women's claim to care by implicitly defining them as "unworthy," and reinforced the message they were often getting from their partner that *they* were crazy and required psychiatric care or clinical management.

Even as the labels applied to women isolated them within the health care system from the care they needed, focusing on some perceived flaw in their character individualized the problem and highlighted their "dependence" or "passivity" rather than the power that was being exercised over them in the relationship. This approach also minimized the extent to which abused women resisted the abuse. In addition to documenting the disproportionate use of psychiatric labels with abused women, social scientists identified a pattern of harmful clinical responses that included overprescriptions of pain pills and antidepressant medication. These prescriptions were particularly harmful to abused women because they are more prone to cope with their situations by attempting suicide. Even when hospitals developed a specialized response to domestic violence, clinicians only rarely used the suggested referrals, regardless of whether they had been trained to do so and there were sufficient resources in place. Finally, practitioners raised concerns about asking about domestic abuse. They feared they would open the emotional flood gates without adequate training or knowledge about how to respond. In England, where the government bears direct responsibility for the delivery of most health care, researchers relied more heavily on survivors' accounts of their help-seeking experiences to address domestic violence in health settings. Alongside and stimulated by this work were interagency initiatives that specifically identified the role and responsibilities of health authorities in engaging with other practitioners to address this issue.

One result of these efforts was that the Department of Health produced a domestic violence resource manual for health care practitioners in 2000, which was updated in 2007. The original manual drew guidance from a number of professional bodies and was warmly received by those working in the field. Still, despite the publication of the resource manual and other research in the field, a study conducted by Women's Aid, the national organization of refuges for victims, concluded that "mental health professionals had a generally low awareness of domestic violence."[4]

Those conducting training with interagency groups that included health practitioners drew similar conclusions, noting that the majority of participants either had not heard of the manual or had never seen a copy. Further work within England focused on the role of psychological intervention and of health visitors, midwives, dentists, general practitioners, and health policy makers.

DEFINITIONS: THE MUNDANE

Back in 1995, shortly after the British government released an interagency circular that provided explicit guidance for health commissioners on how to address domestic violence, many local health authorities, in conjunction with local multiagency forums, took up the challenge of defining the problem. Interagency forums would meet regularly at a community level to discuss local provisions for abused women. Similar bodies of service providers, called coordinating councils, also began meeting in the United States at the time.

Interagency collaboration was difficult to sustain. Frustration and conflict often hampered the process because agencies brought differing and in some cases competing definitions of abuse to the table. For example, groups from the voluntary sector defined domestic violence in its broadest sense, whereas the police were more concerned with acts that fell within the boundaries of criminal law. Despite these differences, and for the sake of pragmatism, most authorities developed a working definition of domestic violence that (1) included physical, psychological, sexual, and emotional abuse; (2) recognized that financial abuse and controls could be part of this pattern; (3) identified the majority of victims as female; and (4) emphasized the criminal and unacceptable nature of any domestic violence. Although a consensus emerged on these points, at the root of many of the ideological differences between agencies about how to define domestic violence was the contrast between the emphasis placed on discrete incidents by the criminal justice system and on outcomes or impact, as in health.

GLOBAL CONCERNS

In 1997, the World Health Organization acknowledged violence against women as a preventable public health problem. Importantly, its global definition identified the gender-specific nature of the problem and included psychological alongside physical abuse. Too frequently, rape, domestic violence, child abuse, forced marriage, sexual abuse, and related forms of violence whose victims are overwhelmingly female are described as if they were gender neutral, masking the roots of many of these problems in the different social and cultural contexts in which men and women experience violence. An illustration from the policy arena is the English government's domestic violence strategy.

Though it recognized that women are the predominant victims of domestic violence, it defined it in gender-neutral terms, as consisting of

> *[a]ny incident of threatening behavior, violence or abuse (psychological, physical, sexual, financial, or emotional) between adults, aged 18 or over, who are or have been intimate partners or family members, regardless of gender and sexuality. Family members are defined as mother, father, son, daughter, brother, sister, and grandparents, whether directly or indirectly related, in-laws or step-family.*[5]

This definition sharply contrasted with the experience of most service providers, whose help was sought by female victims of male violence almost exclusively. As importantly, it made it impossible to draw a single gendered policy that linked strategies to combat domestic violence to interventions to stem the diverse range of violence committed against women. The definition of domestic violence that is adopted is clearly important. In a criminal justice context, domestic violence is defined in terms of incidents that can be recorded, investigated, and ultimately prosecuted. Within a medical context there is more choice about whether to look at discrete incidents, long-term patterns (as in a "chronic" health problem), and/or impact or outcomes. The investigation of impact allows health care providers to employ a much broader understanding of which facets of domestic violence should be considered when trying to sustain health and well-being.

Like the definition adopted in England, the U.S. Violence Against Women Act (VAWA) first passed in 1994 defines domestic violence as gender neutral and focuses on its criminal justice dimensions rather than on a wider pattern of abuse. The thrust of the act stands in marked contrast to its progressive title, which locates all forms of domestic violence within a wider concept of violence against women, including harassment and sexual violence.

In England, local refuges get little funding for direct services from the government beyond basic housing provision. By contrast, VAWA enshrines within legislation the provision of funds for victim services and requires a response from a range of statutory and voluntary agencies. Moreover, in its 2005 iteration, VAWA specifically recognizes the important role of health providers. The act recognizes that, "Because almost all women see a health care provider at least once a year, the health care system is uniquely positioned to proactively reach out to women who are or have been victims of domestic or sexual violence. Health care providers, if trained and educated, can be the first-responders to a woman experiencing violence and can help her find safety long before she might turn to a shelter or call the police."[6] Moreover, Title V strengthens the health care system's response to family violence with programs to train and educate health care professionals about domestic and sexual violence, foster family violence screening for patients, and more studies on the health ramifications of family violence.

Definitions matter. In a subsequent section, I cite specific examples of how the differences in the definition of domestic violence used in the United States and England have played out in the health care response.

COST

As most readers are undoubtedly aware, the United States and England differ markedly in how they finance health care. In the United States, medical care is accessed through private contractual relationships and financed through an eclectic mix of private payment, work-based insurance, and government funds. By contrast, the health services in the United Kingdom are provided as part of the National Health Service (NHS), a state-managed welfare system. The NHS, which began in 1948, had at its core three guiding principles: (1) to meet the needs of everyone, (2) to be free at the point of delivery, and (3) to be based on clinical need, not ability to pay. Since its inception, technological advances, the aging of the population, and the increased prevalence of chronic ailments have led to the rationing of resources across the NHS. Whatever the differences between health care in the United States and the United Kingdom, however, the economic health costs of domestic violence are significant in both countries.

Above and beyond the human cost of domestic violence, research has shown that the financial cost of addressing the issue of domestic violence is huge. In the United States, the Centers for Disease Control and Prevention (CDC) reported in 2003 that health costs of domestic violence against women exceeded $5.8 billion a year.[7] In 1998, Elizabeth Stanko looked at the costs of domestic violence for a range of statutory agencies within England and found that the health costs of providing services in Greater London alone were £19 million a year (approx. US$40 million).[8] Further study in England found that the health costs to the NHS for physical injuries from abuse is around £1.2 billion, including general practice doctors and hospital costs. Mental health care related to domestic violence costs an estimated additional £176 million.[9] Victims of domestic violence also disproportionately experience a range of physical, behavioral, and psychosocial problems that are not typically identified with abuse. As a result, their overall utilization of health services is significantly greater than the comparable utilization by nonvictims. Thus, U.S. research has found that the annual total health care costs were 19 percent higher for women with a history of domestic violence compared with women without such a history.[10]

PREVALENCE AND IMPACT

To design and target health services most effectively, it is critical to know the likely number of new cases (incidence) practitioners will see in a given period, the total number of cases in the community at a given time (prevalence), and the general nature of these cases. Without accurate information on prevalence, it is impossible to determine the quantity or nature of services required or to know whether intervention is making a significant difference.

During the past 10 years, a number of population studies have reported that violence between intimate partners is gender symmetrical or even in some cases that women are more abusive and violent than their male partners. Critics of these claims argue that women often use violence in response to violence or other forms of coercion by their partners; that women experience more severe abuse than their male partners; that women experience more frequent violence than their partners; that women are more likely to identify their own use of violence as abusive than are men; and that women experience more types of abuse than men during their lifetime. While there is extensive literature documenting the prevalence of female domestic violence victims at service sites, there are few comparable studies of male victims and even fewer that have studied the impact of partner abuse on males who identify themselves as victims in random population samples. One such study conducted on behalf of the Scottish Executive compared the impact of domestic violence on male and female victims using a sample identified from the Scottish Crime Survey. The study found that male victims of domestic violence reported better health and higher incomes than female victims and were less likely to live in rented accommodations. They also found that repeat physical violence was comparatively rare among male victims.[11]

The British Crime Survey (BCS) is the other source of information about prevalence that also considers impact. The most recent version of the BCS interpersonal violence module found that 28 percent of women and 18 percent of men had experienced nonsexual partner abuse since the age of 16; 8 percent of women and 7 percent of men reported experiencing stalking; and 3 percent of women and 1 percent of men had experienced an attempted sexual assault in the last year. In terms of impact, women were more likely (58 percent) than men (48 percent) to have experienced injuries or emotional effects as a result of the abuse. Women were also more likely than men to report minor bruising or a black eye (21 versus 16 percent) and mental or emotional problems (33 versus 14 percent), and to have stopped trusting people (15 versus 9 percent). In relation to health, the survey found that women were more likely than men to seek medical help, an important finding in relation to the provision of services.[12]

The significance of these studies lies in their consideration of impact as part of their understanding of domestic violence. Female victims have suffered more than 60 percent of the partner abuse occurring since age 16 in the crime survey population and 75 percent of the sexual assaults, for instance. As a result, female victims of male partner violence are more than twice as likely as male victims to experience "mental or emotional" problems, accounting for more than 70 percent of these problems in this population, as well as for more than 60 percent of the minor bruising or black eyes. Even if the incidence of physical violence by male and female partners is roughly equivalent, therefore including impact in the definition dispels the belief that domestic violence can be usefully understood as gender neutral or that it can be limited to physical violence or injurious assaults. Incorporating impact in the definition does something more. Once we appreciate that women's experiences of partner abuse are different than men's, we can consider how these differences are shaped by the wider social and cultural contexts in which these experiences occur. Studies of the impact of "stop and search" strategies by the police, which ignore the context of racism, are not going to provide accurate information, particularly with respect to ethnic minority groups. In the same way, an accurate understanding of domestic violence entails linking the differential impact on women to differences in the power dynamics when male or female partners initiate abuse.

DEFINITIONS: INTIMATE TERRORISM AND COERCIVE CONTROL

A growing realization that population data do not match the reality of police, health providers, and refuge or shelters workers has prompted a major reconsideration of what we mean by domestic violence in policy and practice. If men and women hit one another in similar numbers, why are the outcomes so much more serious for women?

To explain why women's experience of abuse is so different than men's, sociologist Michael Johnson has identified a type of violence he calls "intimate terrorism," in which an individual is violent and controlling to their nonabusing partner.[13] In Johnson's schema, intimate terrorism is one of four types of abuse, which also includes "violent resistance" in which an individual is violent but not controlling, in response to a controlling violent partner; "situational couple violence" in which an individual is violent but neither is controlling; and, finally, "mutual violent control" in which both partners are both violent and controlling. Johnson argues that in relation to policy and practice, we need to be clear about the types of abuse we are referring too. He believes that general surveys that examine prevalence are measuring "situational couple violence" and not these other types of abuse, which are more common in clinical samples from agencies. He also argues that, while men and women may engage in situational couple violence in similar numbers and with similar motives, intimate terrorism is committed largely by male partners, a fact not picked up by population surveys, which typically ask only about the use of force. Violent resistance mainly involves women responding with force to control by male partners, and "mutual violent control" is relatively rare. If this typology proves valid, it could explain differences in impact as well as offer useful information on which to base service provision and need.

Johnson's typology helps explain why prevalence studies do not reflect practice. But it also raises a more fundamental question about what is and is not abusive within intimate relationships. This question is fundamental if we are to address the wider impact, and thus health implications, of domestic violence. For instance, if the typical forms of partner abuse by men—but not by women—include a range of control tactics in addition to assault, the consequences of these tactics might well be missed by narrow definition focused only on violent incidents or injurious outcomes.

Johnson's notion of a more complex definition of abuse is linked to a growing body of work on the dynamics of coercion and control in partner relationships, including researchers who looked at these dynamics in lesbian relationships. This body of work defines the experience and significance of abuse in terms of its impact on an individual and/or group as well as the behaviors of the abusive partner.

The idea that the measures of prevalence used in population studies largely identify behaviors that are neither as serious nor as far-reaching in their effects of what most people consider domestic violence challenges us to reconsider prevailing definitions. Sociologist Evan Stark argues that failure to reach a consensus on a definition of abuse that corresponds to victim experience has confounded attempts to accurately measure or understand the problem as it is seen by practitioners. He writes,

> Researchers have yet to provide satisfactory answers to such basic questions as to whether abuse by male and female partners is similar, how many victims require assistance, why abusive relationships last as long as they do, or why so many battered women—but not men assaulted by female partners—develop medical, psychosocial, and behavioral problems that compromise their physical and mental health.[14]

Returning to definitional issues in the domestic violence field can sometimes seem like a backward step, particularly for those who may have spent years arguing for the definitions we now have. But it may be necessary because defining behavior as abusive has significant legal, moral, cultural, and individual consequences. Moreover, if we limit our purview to incidents of physical violence, as do the prevalence studies, rather than weigh the meaning of behavior on the basis of its context and impact, we risk missing whole classes of victims and so precluding forms of service intervention that bear on the experience of these victims.

For Stark, the primary "harm" caused by coercive control is a violation of women's "liberty rights" to full personhood. This has obvious implications for our understanding of the health impact of domestic violence as legal and criminal implications.

"Control" is more difficult to measure or "see" than physical violence and undoubtedly exists as a motive, tactic, or outcome in all intimate partnerships to some extent. Similarly, it is easy to confuse the voluntary compromise of our autonomy in intimate relationships with the subordination characteristic of abusive relationships. Still, if Johnson, Stark, and others who write about the significance of coercive control are correct, an array of control tactics not only distinguish men and women's experiences of abuse but go a long way toward explaining the very different health outcomes and presentations of abuse by men and women.

THE MEDICAL RESPONSE TO ABUSE IN ENGLAND AND THE UNITED STATES

Much of the early research on domestic violence and health focused on documenting the extent to which abused women utilized medical services for injuries caused by partner violence and the secondary health consequences of this violence. Researchers in the United States focused on emergency medical services, the most frequent site for injury-related visits, and on the significance of abuse-related injuries in obstetrical sites as well as in community clinics. This work also showed that abused women used emergency services more frequently than did their nonabused counterparts and were also more likely to present a range of medical, behavioral, and mental health problems, although a majority did not evidence these problems. Since these problems only became disproportionate after the onset of domestic violence, it was concluded that abuse was their cause rather than their consequence. Conversely, abused women were shown to comprise a significant proportion of women who carried a primary diagnosis of alcoholism, depression, or whose children were identified as having been abused or neglected. Given the relatively unobstructed access women have to medical care in the United Kingdom, the emphasis in British research was on the significance of abuse in general practice rather than in emergency services.

Having demonstrated the importance of domestic violence as a health issue, the emphasis shifted to preparing medical practitioners to meet the need by adopting appropriate methods to identify, assess, and refer abuse victims. In the United States, advocates for domestic violence intervention by medical practitioners received widespread support from the professional medical associations as well as from federal and state government. As we've seen, this work highlighted the importance of devising hospital-based "protocols" and enhanced training regimes for established physicians and nurses.

The development of medical interventions occurred more slowly in England and, apart from some specific areas of practice such as antenatal practice and health visiting, for instance, relied heavily on the work already done in the United States. Much of the emphasis was on routine questioning in general practice (GP) offices and within prenatal midwifery services and on the identification of the issue and policy-related concerns rather than looking at what services individual survivors need. For example, women who have experienced domestic violence will request ongoing support, advocacy, and counseling to enable them to move on from an abusive relationship. Such advocacy services are also increasingly linked to criminal justice advocacy whereby advocates accompany victims to give evidence and see convictions through to conclusion. Yet funding for such services has increasingly been removed in favor of more short-term and generically focused advocacy services.

Their different modes of finance help explain why domestic violence intervention developed more slowly in the United Kingdom than in the United States and the greater support medical intervention received in the United States. In the U.S. system where medical income is a function of the quantity of services delivered and most reimbursement comes from third parties (private insurers or the government), there is an incentive to expand the range of problems defined as medical, a process termed "medicalization." By contrast, when physicians are largely salaried and financing comes from the government, as in the United Kingdom, increased "demand" creates a greater cost burden. Here, public pressure provides the major incentive to expand the scope of service. Thus, whereas health providers in both countries rely on the same basic medical paradigm, a model that marginalizes health problems that are not biophysiologically based, the propensity to "look beyond" such a model is greater where there are associated financial incentives to do so.

SCREENING

As the domestic violence movement shifted its focus from initial crisis housing to other statutory and voluntary service needs of women and children, health became an obvious area of concern. Research that looked at the interaction between patients and practitioners found that women were often embarrassed to inform practitioners about the nature of their injuries. If domestic violence was mentioned at all, then, it appeared as part of the background information in a patient's charts rather than as a primary diagnosis. One of the suggested solutions was to pressure practitioners to routinely screen for domestic violence in order to offer interventions (health or otherwise) that might prevent subsequent adverse health consequences as a result of abuse. Women's testimony about the difficulty of discussing abuse in the medical context suggested this was a useful step forward. But attempts to implement routine screening resulted in a stand-off between the medical establishment and those working directly with domestic violence.

In the United States, practitioners and advocates first broached the need to implement routine screening for domestic violence in the context of training initiatives designed to elicit a uniform response from the health care system. From the start, this required addressing professional and personal resistance to asking patients about abuse, an issue they often referred to as "opening a Pandora's box," or "opening a can of worms." The U.S. literature referred to this process as "screening," hoping to "normalize" questioning by evoking the common practice of assessing a patient's risk by asking them about a range of other behavioral problems in their lives, such as smoking or unsafe sex.

In England, the screening debate took a very different route. The screening criteria used by the UK National Screening Committee precluded the inclusion of domestic violence because (1) it is not a disease per se, (2) the risk factors are complex (excluding gender), (3) there is not an identifiable effective treatment with recognized evidence, and (4) currently there are no randomized control trials (RCTs) that prove that screening is effective in reducing mortality or morbidity.[15] Some health researchers have looked at providing RCT evidence to fulfill the final criteria, but most researchers acknowledge that applying randomization in the provision of services to domestic violence victims and perpetrators is potentially unethical. The conclusion to this debate in England has been the introduction of the term "routine enquiry" as opposed to screening.

Following the screening debate in England, a similar debate emerged in the United States. In the face of calls for universal screening from advocates, the U.S. Preventive Task Force (a panel of clinical experts charged with evaluating scientific evidence of various conditions) decided not to recommend universal screening for domestic violence. Critics of this decision pointed to the existence of numerous validated screening tools as well as evidence that suggested that patients (abused and nonabused) supported screening. Additional criticism emerged from various professional organizations that supported screening in the clinical setting. The research committee of the Family Violence Prevention Fund, a leading health advocacy group based in San Francisco, also responded to the Preventive Task Force recommendation by challenging whether the "narrow" criteria for screening applied to IPV. To maneuver around the medical criteria required, they suggested that "[t]he task force view IPV identification as a behavioral assessment as opposed to a medical screen and evaluate its potential for risk reduction and public health benefit within the context behavioral health assessment and counseling."[16] As we've seen, this was the original intent of advocates.

The result of these debates was the use of similar approaches to identification of abuse within England and the United States. What is interesting in both contexts is that the debate was couched as a controversy over what sorts of knowledge can be legitimately considered "medical." No one denies the importance of domestic violence as a health issue. Rather, the focus seems to be on reframing political pressure for medicine to acknowledge the extent to which women's health problems are rooted in their social position rather than in their behavioral missteps or physiological vulnerability.

The screening debate served as a smokescreen for the frustration that many feel about the reception of domestic violence by a range of institutions. In a process familiar to those who work in the criminal justice system, advocates and health researchers are increasingly finding their specialist work in health undermined, discounted, depoliticized, and neutralized, as the health impacts of gendered violence are repackaged in a format that is compatible with generic, gender-neutral, and short-term health interventions. A recent example of this in England is a trend for the government to shift funding from rape crisis services to more generic services. A narrow medical model of abuse, meanwhile, is unlikely to protect or provide for those most in need of help, including those who experience mental health, alcohol, or drug consequences secondary to being exposed to coercive control. This problem is more than academic, since the health context is one of the few places in which the broad consequences of ongoing abuse can be recognized and managed as opposed to the effects of isolated partner assaults, for example. This merely reinforces the earlier point—that definitions matter—and illustrates how the power to define what abuse is and how we measure it shapes how and when we intervene and with whom. In addition, this raises issues about the extent to which our services confront the secondary consequence of sexual inequality, particularly when it is enforced with coercion and control. Narrow definitions often serve medicine by narrowing the scope of intervention to specific symptoms or problems that broader assessments might miss. But they do not serve us well with domestic violence, where the harms are cumulative and wide-ranging.

TRAINING

There is a long-standing belief that domestic violence training for clinicians offers the best way out of the thicket of definitions and missed opportunities in health care. But is this so?

There is a body of literature, predominately in the United States, that has evaluated the impact of training on practitioners' responses to domestic violence. This includes training conducted during medical education as well as with practicing clinicians. Both types of training are included here because in England there is still a reluctance to include issues such as domestic violence within the general medical curriculum. This means that the only information physicians in England get about domestic violence is provided "on the job," so to speak.

A 2006 study assessed the extent of domestic violence education at 16 U.S. medical schools at three different time periods. Although 91 percent of the students reported at least some discussion of IPV by their fourth year, only one-fifth described that it was "extensive." Seventy-three percent of students entering hospital wards thought that IPV was highly relevant to their practice. But only 55 percent of the fourth-year students reported talking with patients at least sometimes about IPV. The authors raise concerns that this situation is likely to have an impact on screening and prevention.[17]

In terms of practitioners, training appears to yield real benefits for victims. A research team in the United States tested whether a three-hour training program would produce (1) increased self-efficacy to identify and help victims, (2) increased endorsement of the role of health care practitioners and settings to help victims, and (3) increased comfort in making referrals, and whether (4) the effects would be moderated by prior helping experience. They found that gains were made in the first three areas and that prior experience of helping did indeed have an impact. They also found that these benefits continued six months after the training had taken place.[18]

A similar study was conducted in the UK context, in this case to evaluate the effectiveness of a training program intended to introduce routine antenatal enquiry for domestic violence. This UK-based study found that the training program was "positively received by participants, particularly in relation to an increased awareness and confidence."[19] During posttest evaluation, the researchers found improvements in knowledge, attitudes, and efficacy, changes that declined over time but were still above pretest results at the six-month follow-up. Perhaps more significant in terms of the debate about routine enquiry, this study found that midwives routinely asked about domestic violence only 50 percent of the time after the program had been introduced. The key barrier identified was the presence of a male partner.

In *Domestic Violence and Health*, the provision of training for health care practitioners and specifically for undergraduate medical students was advocated. The book was published in 2000, around the same time that I began working as a researcher within a medical faculty where students were taught about a range of social issues, though domestic violence and health was not among them. I was also volunteering on the National Domestic Violence Helpline (England) on behalf of Women's Aid.

I mention these experiences because they changed my views on domestic violence training for medical students. My first realization was that many medical students were more preoccupied with areas of the curriculum on which they would be examined than with the impact of their learning on future patients. My second realization came during the course of interviewing potential medical students. It became clear that while a majority of prospective students had excellent social skills, a sizable number of them lacked the requisite skills to offer a nonjudgmental and supportive response to domestic violence victims. Thirdly, as I came to appreciate the scope of medical responsibilities, I realized that practitioners would rarely be able to keep abreast of available services in their communities and so could not make appropriate referrals. These realizations led me to conclude that rather than train all health practitioners to respond to domestic violence, it would be more beneficial if they could simply refer victims to agencies with the expertise and knowledge to deal with the issues. Telling medical students that they should be nonjudgmental and refer patients to the experts via a single national telephone line was a relief to us both.

A similar stratified training model is incorporated in the Department of Health 2006 version of their *Domestic Violence Resource Manual for Health Care Practitioners*. Here, too, it is recognized that not all practitioners need in-depth training on the issue if they know how to refer appropriately. Asking practitioners to make appropriate referrals when they identify a case of domestic violence does not change the ongoing responsibility for practitioners to address the medical needs of patients, albeit in the context of the violence they have experienced, particularly where those needs are psychological as well as physical. The last section addresses this issue in more detail.

MENTAL HEALTH AND LIVING WITH ABUSE

Despite widespread acknowledgment of the significance of domestic violence for health and mental health in particular and the massive utilization of health and mental health services by victims and survivors, a stunning naïveté prevails about the importance of gender for psychology. The CDC estimates that mental health services are provided to 26.4 percent of victims of partner violence, 43.6 percent of stalking victims, and 33 percent of rape victims. The BCS module on interpersonal violence found that 15 percent of those experiencing some form of IPV sought assistance from a specialist mental health service, particularly impressive given the relative paucity of mental health services in the United Kingdom as compared with that in the United States.

Clinical studies have also found that abused women have significantly greater rates of depression, suicide, alcohol abuse, and drug abuse than women who have not been abused.

In both my research, which included talking to women who had experienced domestic violence, and in my experiences working with abused women, they repeatedly described how control by abusive partners impacted their everyday lives. For example, expectations of a controlling partner would influence how women shopped, cooked, and kept the house, resulting in an undermining of the woman's own skills, self-esteem, and ability to make decisions. Of particular relevance to this chapter is the way in which this type of psychological harm is identified and treated in the context of domestic violence.

Two examples must suffice. On the hotline, a call was received from a woman whose washing machine had broken. Her anxiety bordered on panic. When asked whether calling a repairman was an option, she explained that the previous time she had called a repairman her partner had accused her of sleeping with the man, and an abusive incident followed. Asked, "What about just waiting until her partner returned?" she replied that when she had taken this course of action in the past, he called her lazy and had abused her. While I hope my comments were supportive, we both recognized there was nothing she could do that was "right"—her only options were to do things that were "wrong," and this left her feeling unsafe and anxious.

During earlier research, a woman who had had an anxiety attack in the supermarket was interviewed. When asked to describe the incident, she explained that the shop only had a piece of meat her partner would define as "the wrong shape." She became increasingly anxious because, once again, she knew she would be criticized and probably abused whatever choice she made. Her partner had died several years earlier, but she explained and then showed me that she continued to place tinned food within the cupboard in a certain way, wiped the surfaces a specific way, and never left anything on the draining board. While I was there, she washed my cup at least twice.

Both of these women suffered classic panic attacks. Importantly, though, the etiology of these problems is only intelligible in the context of their partners' coercion and control and taking from them the autonomy in decision making without which our sense of self is significantly diminished. These examples involve ordinary events—a household repair and shopping for a piece of meat—which the abused women must approach not as problems in everyday living but as existential threats to their personal safety. In both cases, reality is not circumscribed by what they perceive in front of them but by the projected standards set by the perpetrator for how they are to behave. Tragically, however, there is no way to bring their behavior in conformity with their abusers' expectations. As a result, these women are simultaneously conditioned to think of the standards set for them and paralyzed because the perpetrators left no room for them to enact these standards without fearing for their safety. Neither man is physically present—in the second case, he is not even alive. His control is effective because his partner carries a level of fear of *not* meeting his expectations that pervades all aspects of her life.

Because of incidents like these, all of the women I interviewed had had some contact with mental health services. In addition to anxiety disorders and panic attacks, the nonphysical injuries and/or symptoms these women experienced included self-harm; eating disorders; sleep disturbance; parasuicidal activity; depression; PTSD; low self-esteem; low self-confidence; erosion of social skills; and, finally, a lack of confidence in their own perceptions and thought processes, a condition that is termed "perspecticide" in the hostage literature.

Researchers as well as practitioners have offered various theoretical models to explain the mental health issues arising from domestic violence. This work includes, most prominently, psychiatrist Judith Herman's description of "complex posttraumatic stress disorder" and psychologist Lenore Walker's model of "battered woman syndrome" with its emphasis on learned helplessness. These theories were useful in explaining the psychological processes in play when abuse victims negotiated the unreality of an abuser's world. Too frequently, however, they represented the victim as weak and passive. This becomes problematic when we consider how many women resist control by their abusers (including the "violent resistance" identified by Johnson) and are consequently vilified for not conforming to social notions of femininity. In many cases, they subsequently become the "unworthy" victims or patients who fail to receive adequate service from a range of practitioners, as was alluded to earlier.

Advocates in England and in the United States have been reluctant to address the psychological impact of domestic violence. This is primarily because this focus has been used historically to depict abused women as flawed and responsible for "choosing" abusive partners. An important exception is the work of Hilary Abrahams on the long-term emotional needs of women fleeing violent partners (see the chapter by Abrahams in this volume).

Recent work in England and the United States also highlights the very real mental health consequences of domestic violence without resorting to a victim-blaming vocabulary. However, workers still find that accessing counseling or other mental health services can be used against women, particularly in cases in which they are disputing child custody with their abusive partners. Additionally, in criminal cases, women's testimony about abuse can be discredited if they are thought to have a mental disease. Helpline workers regularly encountered cases in which the mere history of attending counseling sessions was used, in court, to undermine a woman's credibility or to question her ability to care for her children. In some cases, the fact that she had sought mental health services was used to imply that she had a problem and was responsible for the abuse.

CONCLUSIONS

This chapter has looked at the interplay between emerging knowledge about the dynamics of domestic violence and the response to abuse victims and survivors by the health system. Our main point is that definitions matter and that adopting an incident-specific and gender-neutral definition has narrowed the scope of the health response in ways that discount the ongoing nature of most partner abuse, the unique impact of domestic violence on women due to their unequal social standing, and the dynamics that differentiate partner abuse by men and women.

It is impossible to look at health without considering the institution of law and how (gendered) experiences are mediated through both. It is critical that those providing health services recognize that certain aspects of domestic violence and coercive control will never fulfill the criteria required within a criminal justice system because that system is not suited to recognizing fundamental harms to the psychological well-being of those subjected to coercion and control. The health care system has made major progress in introducing domestic violence into the medical school curriculum and in training for physicians, in supporting routine questioning about abuse if not "screening" in the formal sense, and in recognizing that physicians can be expected to refer domestic violence to appropriate local specialists rather than to incorporate a full understanding of the problem into their clinical work. Still, the current danger is that the medical profession too is creating barriers to appropriate intervention by rejection of routine screening for domestic violence (in the United States) and by failing to recognize the psychological harms that follow when women are deprived of their liberty rights as well as harmed physically. Only by setting aside a narrow definition of what makes a problem "medical" can the profession comprehend the impact of coercive control on global well-being.

In previous work, a number of questions were raised about how adequately the health system has addressed the broad psychosocial and medical needs of victims. Achievements in this regard remain extremely limited. While most observers would accept that asking about the issue is helpful for patients and practitioners, debate about how best to do this continues. Despite originally opting for screening, the United States is increasingly following the English lead in questioning whether this approach to identification is appropriate. The compromise is that practitioners are expected to make "routine enquiries" about abuse. Unfortunately, most research suggests that only about half of all practitioners actually implement this policy.

Things have changed since domestic violence training for medical practitioners began in the United States in the late 1970s, but nowhere nearly as much as they have in the justice arena, for instance. In England, domestic violence victims receive better service where there are champions of the issue on site, but staff move on, become disillusioned, or become mired in debates about what constitutes "real" knowledge. While most medical students in the United States appear to be exposed to domestic violence, it is rarely a focus of clinical units. In England, medical students still do not find domestic violence on their undergraduate curriculum as a matter of course. Despite the introduction of domestic violence protocols in hundreds of hospitals in the United States, the dissemination of guidelines by the major medical and nursing associations, and the requirement that hospitals adopt such protocols as a condition of continued licensure, only 1 battered woman in 10 is appropriately identified, slightly better than the identification rates before these provisions but hardly sufficient to ensure quality service. Many of the financial incentives that initially included domestic violence screening as part of the large process of medicalizing social problems in the United States have now been eroded. Although there are no comparable figures from England, given the disincentive (financial and in terms of additional workload) to identify a new class of problem patients, it is likely that an even smaller proportion of victims is accurately identified by medical providers in the United Kingdom than in the United States. On the other hand, because emergency services in the United States remain the primary care of the poor, it is likely that services in England are more responsive to domestic violence injuries than they are in the United States.

Mental health or appropriate behavioral intervention is even less common than responsive medical care. While mental health is viewed more positively in the United States than in the United Kingdom, where it still carries a certain stigma, again largely because of cultural differences and financial incentives, in both countries women often acquire "labels" associated with victim blaming that can undermine their status in the legal system, particularly in family law cases. At the same time, there is no evidence that any substantial proportion of clinicians on either side of the Atlantic is identifying the multiple psychosocial consequences of coercive control or making appropriate referrals.

This chapter has considered how definitional changes might help us, particularly within the health sphere, to address the psychological well-being of victims of domestic violence. This is important in England as the government moves increasingly away from a reliance on specialist, community-based services toward a more generic and criminal justice-focused response strategy and toward replacing a holistic and primary care approach to victim populations with an approach that targets short-term solutions (such as emergency care for injury and acquiring court orders of protection). In this context, the gender-neutral, incident-focused approach of the criminal justice system is more attractive to government and other funders than the more broadly based concerns with confidentiality and safety raised when domestic violence is viewed through the prism of health. This means that collaboration between health services and specialized services for domestic violence is more important than ever.

Much of the debate in the coming years will involve the definition of the problem, whether to adopt a narrow, injury-based focus on discrete incidents or to recognize the negative health consequences when women's personhood and liberty are put at risk, as well as their physical integrity. In this debate, the medical profession needs to consider how its focus on technical knowledge can exclude from the discussion public health professionals and others who understand how domestic violence undermines one's ability to live a healthy and happy life. The health sphere can only improve its services to victims if it engages coercive control and if those who experience abuse are given the space, time, and resources to help us understand the dynamics of coercive control; how it affects physical, mental, and behavioral health as well as self-perception; and what we must do to prevent it.

NOTES

1. See E. Williamson, "Domestic Violence and the Response of the Medical Profession," PhD thesis (University of Derby, 1999); and E. Williamson, *Domestic Violence and Health* (Bristol, UK: Policy Press, 2000).

2. F. F. Varvaro and D. L. Lasko, "Physical Abuse as Cause of Injury in Women: Information for Orthopaedic Nurses," *Orthopedic Nursing* 12 (1993): 37–41.

3. See E. Stark and A. Flitcraft, *Women at Risk: Domestic Violence and Women's Health* (Thousand Oaks, CA: Sage, 1996).

4. J. Barron, *Struggle to Survive: Challenges for Delivering Services on Mental Health, Substance Misuse and Domestic Violence* (Bristol, UK: Women's Aid, 2004), 33, http://www.womensaid.org.uk.

5. See Home Office, *Domestic Violence: A National Report*. (London, UK, Home Office, 2005) Available from http://www.crimereduction.gov.uk/domesticviolence/domesticviolence51.htm.

6. See National Task Force to End Sexual and Domestic Violence Against Women, *The Violence Against Women Act of 2005* (National Task Force to End Sexual and Domestic Violence, 2005). Available from http://new.vawnet.org/Assoc_Files_VAWnet/VAWA2005-FieldSummary.pdf (accessed February, 2009).

7. See http://usgovinfo.about.com/gi/dynamic/offsite.htm?zi=1/XJ&sdn=us govinfo&cdn=newsissues&tm=5&gps=281_1327_1020_613&f=00&tt=2&bt=0&bts=0 &zu=http%3A//www.cdc.gov/ncipc/pub-res/ipv_cost/ipv.htm for a full copy of the report. Also note that figure of $5.8 billion annually relates to rape, physical assault, stalking, and homicide within the intimate domestic violence relationship.

8. E. A. Stanko, D. Crisp, C. Hale, and H. Lucraft, *Counting the Costs: Estimating the Impact of Domestic Violence in the London Borough of Hackney* (Swindon, UK: Crime Concern, 1998).

9. S. Walby, *Counting the Costs* (London: Equalities Unit, 2004); and see http://www.womenandequalityunit.gov.uk/research/cost_of_dv_Report_sept04.pdf.

10. F. Rivara, M. Anderson, P. Fishman, A. Bonomi, R. Reid, D. Carrell, R. Thompson, "Healthcare Utilization and Costs for Women with a History of Intimate Partner Violence" (*American Journal of Preventive Medicine*, 32, no. 2 (2007): 89–96.

11. D. Gadd et al., *Domestic Violence against Men in Scotland, for the Scottish Executive*, http://www.scotland.gov.uk/Publications/2002/09/15201/9609.

12. D. Povey, K. Coleman, P. Kaiza, J. Hoare, and K. Jansson, "British Crime Survey: Homicides, Firearm Offences and Intimate Violence 2006/07," suppl. vol. 2 to *Crime in England and Wales 2006/7*, 2008, http://www.homeoffice.gov.uk/rds/pdfs08/hosb0308.pdf.

13. M. Johnson, "Patriarchal Terrorism and Common Couple Violence: Two Forms of Violence against Women," *Journal of Marriage and the Family* 57 (1995): 283–94; and M. P. Johnson, "Violence Conflict and Control: Gender Symmetry and Asymmetry in Domestic," *Violence Against Women* 12 (2006): 1003.

14. E. Stark, *Coercive Control* (Oxford: Oxford University Press, 2007), 8.

15. See National Screening Committee, Second report of the UK National Screening Committee (London, UK, Department of Health, 2000). http://www.dh.gov.uk/en/Publicationsandstatistics/Publications/PublicationsPolicyAndGuidance/DH_4005942.

16. E. J. Alpert, R. D. Sege, and Y. S. Bradshaw, "Interpersonal violence and the education of physicians." *Academic Medicine* 72, Supplement 1 (1997): S41–50.

17. E. Frank, L. Elon, L. E. Saltzman, D. Houry, P. McMahon, and J. Doyle, "Clinical and Personal Intimate Partner Violence Training Experiences of U.S. Medical Students," *Journal of Women's Health* 15, no. 9 (2006): 1071–9.

18. L. Hamberger, K. Guse, C. Boerger, J. Minsky, D. Pape, C. Folsom, "Evaluation of a Health Care Provider Training Program to Identify and Help Partner Violence Victims," *Journal of Family Violence* 19, no. 1 (2004): 1–11.

19. D. Salmon, S. Murphy, S. K. Baird, and S. Price, "An Evaluation of the Effectiveness of an Educational Programme Promoting the Introduction of Routine Antenatal Enquiry for Domestic Violence," *Midwifery* 22, no. 1 (2006): 6–14.

Chapter 11

A Betrayal Trauma Perspective on Domestic Violence

Melissa Platt
Jocelyn Barton
Jennifer J. Freyd

I started going to the domestic violence shelter for counseling. But I was just, "Ehh. Why should I do this? I'm not going to sit here and tell you my business." I went to the shelter eight times. Eight! But there was always some reason that I went back to him. I wasn't ready. I was in denial. (Tanya M.)

Tanya shared her story with the Iowa Voices Project,[1] explaining that her partner beat her until she bled, set fire to her bed while she was sleeping, and used every weapon he could find to harm her. She did leave on several occasions, but returned again and again to the same person who hurt her so badly. At first glance, it is hard to imagine why a victim of domestic violence who is repeatedly beaten, degraded, and violated would voluntarily remain in the relationship with the abuser. Thinking about why it may sometimes actually be adaptive to ignore abuse by a trusted person can help make sense of why victims of domestic violence often do not report abuse, underreport the severity of ongoing violence, and return to or remain in abusive situations.

Domestic violence affects approximately one in five women worldwide and one in four women in the United States during their lifetime. It leaves physical scars from broken bones and increases the likelihood of developing illnesses from living in an intensely stressful environment for a prolonged period of time. It leaves psychological scars from anxiety due to living in ongoing danger, and a shaken world view from having been betrayed by a trusted person. Among those whose lives are directly affected by domestic violence, the majority of victims eventually leave the relationship. But the leaving process can involve years of cycling out of, then back into, the relationship. When a person is abused by an intimate partner, she experiences a devastating betrayal committed by someone she once may have viewed as her closest ally. She may be further betrayed when the institutions and communities she turns to for support fail to validate her experience and fail to provide access to necessary resources. To begin to understand how difficult it is for domestic violence victims to leave a relationship characterized by betrayal, it is imperative to listen to what victims and survivors have to say.

In this chapter we use the terms "victim" and "survivor" when referring to the person being abused. We use victim when discussing the situations of people who are still in the relationship with the perpetrator. Survivor is used when referring to those who were formerly victims of abuse but have since left the relationship. Many victims have been survivors in the past and will again be survivors in the future as they make several attempts to leave the relationship. Although we recognize that these two categories are rarely clear cut, we will rely on them to avoid confusion. In our examples of those affected by domestic violence, we frequently refer to the victim/survivor as *she* and the perpetrator as *he*. We do this to reflect the higher rates of domestic violence against women than against men and because the most severe outcomes of abuse have been documented in heterosexual relationships. Of course, men also are abused by their partners (both female and male) and abuse against lesbians or persons who identify as transgendered is also common. In any given case, these violations can be just as serious as violence against women by male partners.

Although the reasons victims stay in abusive relationships are complex, there is a simple, albeit often overlooked, way of approaching the question: one can ask the victims about their experience. The more people are able to set aside preconceived ideas about what makes victims stay, the better equipped society will be to understand and to help. Often people turn a deaf ear to issues of abuse, not because they don't care but because it is emotionally challenging to be aware of intimate partner violence. Domestic violence involves a betrayal of trust that can incite deep feelings of shame and anxiety in the victim. As individuals recognize that a family member or friend is being attacked on an ongoing basis by a partner who seems to be nice enough, committed enough, or loving enough, they must recognize that no one is immune to being deeply hurt by someone upon whom they depend. If it can happen to a sister, or a best friend, it can happen to anyone. It can happen to them. This realization can be a frightening prospect. In theory, listening to the stories of domestic violence victims is a simple task. But in reality, because of the emotional challenges it poses, it takes courage to start asking questions. Perhaps it takes even more courage to hear what is actually being said in response.

TELLING THEIR STORIES

In the 1960s, a small group of courageous women in Iowa began a dialogue about domestic violence. During the next two decades, the small group, echoed in similar efforts in other Iowa communities, evolved into the Iowa Coalition Against Domestic Violence, a state-level nonprofit organization comprised of 27 direct-service domestic violence programs. Working with the Coalition, Kathleen Thompson, an author who herself had been victimized, interviewed 31 female survivors of domestic violence about their experiences. In broaching this topic on a personal level, some of the things she heard gave her nightmares. With the women's permission, she published their stories in newspapers and on the Internet and so helped give voice to experiences that previously had been silenced by abuse. The pain embedded in these women's stories illustrates why asking—and answering—is so hard. However, the telling of the stories allows the women to connect with others who still are being abused, helping to empower victims to likewise become survivors. The voices from the Iowa Voices Project inform how we answer the question, "Why doesn't she leave?"

PHYSICAL IMPACT OF DOMESTIC VIOLENCE

Violence committed by an intimate partner has numerous and sometimes devastating consequences for the victim. In addition, children living in an abusive household are affected by violence, even if they are not directly attacked. The damage can occur insidiously; victims are only able to free themselves from abusive situations after they are able to recognize the problem. Verbal abuse often precedes physical abuse. This slow escalation in severity can facilitate the victim's ability to adjust to an ongoing intimate betrayal. Unfortunately, the victim is not always aware that her partner is betraying her and that the betrayal may cause her physical and psychological problems.

I was drained. I started calling in to work. I was using excessive sick leave. (Teama)

The doctor told me, "You have all of these physical conditions from the stress." It was killing me. Without a touch, it was killing me. (Kathy)

The association of domestic violence with women's increased risk of injury and of developing a broad range of medical, mental health, and behavioral problems has been widely documented. Long-term exposure to violence magnifies these consequences. Physical and psychological symptoms sometimes subside when the abuse ends, but without treatment many deleterious health effects can persist, and the medical, mental health, and behavioral effects of abuse can reinforce each other. Mental health problems such as depression, anxiety, and posttraumatic stress can weaken the immune system and increase the likelihood of physical illness. Compared with nonabused women, abuse victims and survivors disproportionately abuse alcohol, cigarettes, and other licit and illicit substances, particularly if they are already suffering the mental health effects of domestic violence. Much of this behavior involves attempts to self-medicate as a way to cope with the physical pain, depression, fear, anxiety, or otherwise distressing thoughts or memories associated with violence. Additionally, this behavior can further weaken the immune system, exacerbating health issues.

The hallmark of domestic violence assaults is the frequency and the duration of abuse rather than the severity of injuries caused. Somewhere between one-third and one-half of all domestic violence victims suffer serial abuse, many beaten once a week or more. Although most of these assaults involve pushes, shoves, hair pulling, or other acts that would be considered minor if taken in isolation, the cumulative effect is a level of vulnerability and fear that can be paralyzing.

Despite the fact that the typical domestic violence episode is noninjurious, domestic violence is the most common source of physical injury for which women seek medical attention, even more common than auto accidents. In contrast to muggings, where the main injuries are to extremities, the injuries resulting from domestic violence suggest its sexual nature and are disproportionately located in the face or other parts of the head, chest, and abdomen and frequently result from biting, choking, and/or sexual assault. Blows to the head and choking, when resulting in loss of consciousness, can have serious long-term neurological consequences. Repeated attacks may cause respiratory problems. But even women who experience broken bones may be afraid of angering the perpetrator by seeking treatment and may fail to report the injury to the doctor, thus making proper healing more difficult or impossible. The presence of numerous old wounds at various stages of healing is a classic presentation of domestic violence in medical settings.

> *I did have regrets that I never fought back. He smashed my nose a lot. I had a lot of bloody noses. A lot of black eyes. A lot of lumps on my head, fat lips, kicked, he lifted me off the ground with his cowboy boots, you know those pointed boots, he kicked me from behind and lifted me off the ground with that. (Kay)*

The frequency of abuse increases the risk of injuries and some chronic diseases, such as chronic pain, osteoarthritis, and severe headaches. In extreme situations, physical injuries from violence can be fatal.

In addition to the number of instances of abuse, the amount of time victims remain in relationships with their perpetrators also can contribute to negative health consequences. Those who remain in abusive relationships experience more physical ailments, including allergies, breathing problems, pain, fatigue, bowel problems, vaginal discharge, eyesight and hearing problems, low iron, asthma, bronchitis, emphysema, and cervical cancer.

Gynecological problems are the most consistent physical health difference between women who are abused and women who are not. Perpetrators of physical abuse frequently (but not always) force sex on their partners. Because women who are repeatedly threatened or assaulted are unlikely to resist a partner's sexual demands, many victims reported feeling like they were raped even when no force was used. Chronic urinary tract infections, pelvic pain, painful intercourse, fibroids, and other sexual problems arise from a combination of forced sex and the ensuing shame and depression that may further weaken the immune system. When perpetrators refuse to use condoms, intercourse increases the likelihood of acquiring a sexually transmitted disease or having an unwanted pregnancy. An enforced pregnancy also may be used to sabotage a woman's access to independent sources of support or income (such as school or work) or to increase her physical and emotional dependence.

IMPACT ON PREGNANCY AND CHILDREN

Physical, sexual, and emotional abuse do not necessarily stop if a woman suffering from intimate partner violence becomes pregnant.

When I became pregnant with his baby he became even worse, more abusive. (Kay)

During pregnancy, violence to the mother harms both her and the fetus, which may or may not survive the trauma. Babies exposed to an abusive environment before birth are more likely to be born prematurely and suffer a range of health problems. Exposure to abuse continues to have adverse consequences for children as they develop.

I thought my son was too young to remember that his father used to beat me. But he remembers. He goes, "Do you remember when daddy used to hit you?" I thought, at a year and a half that he was too young. At one point, he hated me. He hated his sister. He called his sister a bitch. He was five. He wasn't even a kindergartner. He would have anxiety attacks in front of school. He didn't want me close, but I couldn't leave the same room. He had nightmares. He wanted to die. (Elia)

Mothers who are being abused by their partners are often torn between protecting their children by keeping the family intact and protecting their children by removing them from the violent situation. If she leaves, she worries that she is breaking up the family and depriving her children of a father. Furthermore, in many cases the mother is financially dependent upon the father of her children and thus if she leaves, she risks poverty and homelessness for her children. If she stays, she must consider how they will be affected by ongoing exposure to violence between the people they depend on for love and protection. Children exposed to violence between their parents not only suffer the immediate fear and uncertainty of the situation, but also may be more likely to experience difficulty adjusting as they develop into adolescents and adults. Children who are taught to view violence in the household as normal or acceptable also may be more likely to enter into abusive relationships themselves when they get older, as either victim or perpetrator.

> If my kids end up not being abusive men, I will think I did a job well done. And I don't know if I have any hope of that because of what they saw in their dad. (Becky)

PSYCHOLOGICAL IMPACT

Victims often attempt to cope with violence by avoiding thoughts of the abuse or removing themselves psychologically while the abuse is happening. Psychologists refer to this phenomenon as "dissociation." When abuse becomes so severe that it is impossible to ignore, victims of domestic violence may turn to alcohol and other substances to push the thoughts and feelings away. Problems such as being chronically prepared for danger (hypervigilance), having difficulty concentrating, and reexperiencing moments of abuse through vivid memories are common experiences among people experiencing trauma. Cindy explains the enduring psychological consequences she struggles with even after she has left the relationship:

> I'm still scared to death of the dark. You'll never find my house completely dark. Ever. I have to be able to see. I have trouble being in crowds. I don't wear any jewelry because my brother choked me, along with the boyfriend, who choked me. I couldn't sleep in my bed. It took me eight months, I think. I slept on the couch for the longest time. I will not sit with my back to a door. It creeps me out, because I can't see who's coming in. (Cindy)

BETRAYAL TRAUMA THEORY

The widely documented harms caused by domestic violence make it even more imperative to explain the duration of abusive relationships and to ask the question, "Why does she stay?" or, equally common, "Why doesn't she just leave him?"

First and foremost, although domestic violence erodes the mutual trust and respect on which healthy partnerships rest and without which most relationships eventually dissolve, this erosion process is often slow and uneven and is often misunderstood by abuse victims. Although most victims can recall signs of abuse that occurred during dating, courtship, or in the first years of marriage, many did not recognize the behaviors as abusive at the time. This is particularly true in relationships in which the primary forms of abuse involve intimidation or control tactics rather than violence, or in which there are readily available rationalizations for a partner's abusive behavior, such as his drinking or "stress" at work. It may be months or even years of seemingly good times before things start to go awry. Jill and her husband spent more than a decade together establishing what seemed to Jill to be a loving, stable relationship before things became noticeably wrong:

> My husband, "X," and I have been married 14 years now. Everything was going fine. We had two careers, great stuff. Three boys ... then in 2002, something switched. I was always on eggshells. I would take the kids to the department store at night just to get out of the house until it was bedtime. But I had no idea why our marriage was falling apart. (Jill)

When partnerships erode slowly, the relatively minor instances of betrayal may not be enough to shake the victim's conception of the perpetrator as a good partner. Trust and respect also may erode slowly rather than all at once as a result of a single dramatic act of abuse or betrayal. Particularly for women in disadvantaged communities who may be facing any number of stressors and challenges in their lives, the abuse may not seem that serious or may be normalized as "just life." In these instances, victims may appear to be minimizing or even denying acts of violence that may seem quite serious to an outsider and, as a result of these defenses, decide not to report the assault to police or health providers.

Another important reason why victims are prone to denial and minimization is that domestic violence is one of the most devastating forms of betrayal a person can experience. Precisely because persons depend on intimate relationships to be safe and cared for, they are most vulnerable in these settings. When violence occurs within intimate relationships, victims may find their basic needs for solace, refuge, protection, and respect cannot be met. Furthermore, this intimate violence may undermine the victims' world view, and with it, their moorings in reality. Acts of violence by intimate partners throw into question what can truly be trusted.

According to Jennifer J. Freyd's[2] theory of betrayal trauma, abused children are able to separate the trauma from their consciousness in order to preserve the relationship with the needed caregiver. This may occur during the trauma (i.e., the child does not recognize that his parent is hurting him), after the trauma (i.e., the child is unable to remember what happened during the abuse), or both. This dissociation from the abuse facilitates the child's survival by helping him remain connected with the person who provides his food, clothing, and shelter as well as his social support. He is able to ignore the pain and betrayal to maintain this important relationship. If the betrayal were fully experienced, it would lead the child to withdraw from or confront the abuser, as these are the empowered responses to mistreatment and betrayal. But withdrawal and confrontation are likely to only make matters worse for the child by leading to an escalation of abuse and coercive control. Thus, by remaining fully or at least somewhat blind to the betrayal, the abused child is able to maintain behaviors that inspire attachment from the parent.

According to betrayal trauma theory, when an adult is abused by someone close to her, she is likewise prone to dissociate while the abuse is happening, or when she is reminded of it. She may also forget details or even forget the entire event and have trouble recalling it when questioned. The unawareness and forgetting are helpful to the victim who feels dependent on her abuser. These responses help her behave in ways that maintain the relationship rather than in ways that threaten it.

The next sections explore some of the ways in which numbing may help domestic violence victims. First, we turn to an example to illustrate the idea of a person disconnecting from pain in order to survive.

IGNORING PAIN

Freyd uses the example of two women on separate skiing trips to illustrate the notion of ignoring or becoming numb to pain. One woman breaks her leg while skiing with a friend and experiences such debilitating pain that she is unable to continue down the mountain. The friend leaves and returns with help so that she makes it down the mountain safely. The other woman also breaks her leg while skiing, but she is without a companion. She has no choice but to hobble downward to receive the medical attention she needs to survive. The first woman feels the intense physical pain, which inhibits her from further damaging her leg. The second is able to spontaneously block the pain. The difference between the two women is that, in the second case, survival is on the line. Although the second woman is not immune to leg pain, and in fact is likely to have worse pain in the future as a result of her trip down the mountain, her blockage of the pain is an adaptive response as long as she is alone and needs to move in order to save her life.

The same type of selective numbing is relevant to the case of domestic violence. In most instances, when someone is being attacked or degraded by another person, it is adaptive to flee from the situation to avoid continued assault. In other cases, it is adaptive to fight back. If a stranger verbally assaults a woman while she is walking down the street, for example, she might feel an instinct to run and likely act on that instinct, fearing a physical confrontation. If the stranger grabbed the woman, she would probably resist, possibly with violence, to

protect her safety. However, when someone is being assaulted by a partner in whom they may be deeply invested and upon whose support they
depend, the instinct to run or fight is thwarted because it is *not* to that
person's advantage to behave in the normal way. This is particularly true
in the case of intimate terrorism, a type of domestic violence characterized by one partner exhibiting behavior that is both violent and controlling. In this type of situation, men perpetrate the violence and their
female partners respond nonviolently more than 90 percent of the time.
Apart from the physical risks, running away or fighting can be seen as
threatening a relationship that the person feels is crucial to protect. In
other words, it is sometimes not a good idea for the victim to confront
the abuser or to leave the abusive situation right away. Sometimes survival depends—or seems to depend—on staying with the abuser. In a
relationship characterized by coercive control and violence, the victim
risks enduring an escalation of abuse, the loss of her partner's financial
support for herself and her children, and a host of additional challenges
to survival if she fights back or threatens to leave.

By adaptive, we do not mean to imply that it is necessarily healthful
to stay in a dangerous environment. Rather, we mean that it is a natural, survival-promoting response to act in ways that maintain the relationship under certain circumstances. To adapt means to make fit (as
for a specific or new use or situation) often by modification.[3] Much like
a chameleon adapts by turning green to become less visible to preda-
tors when walking along a leaf, a victim of domestic violence may
adapt by withdrawing and distancing herself from pain when she
depends upon the perpetrator for survival in some way. The next section illustrates some of the ways in which becoming blind to the abuse
may allow the victim to survive in her difficult situation.

MAINTAINING IMPORTANT RELATIONSHIPS

*I was married to "X" for 23 years. The assaults, the rape, started before we were
married. The worst assault was in 1999. After the assault, after he was in jail for
trying to kill me, my pastor at the time said I needed to make a whole account of
what happened that night and mail it to myself. I followed his advice and did it
and then I had never opened it. A few years ago, I read it again. And it is amazing
to me how much reality that you can block out. Because I literally went in the bathroom and almost vomited after I read my own account of what had happened that
night. (Becky)*

Becky said that she returned to her relationship with the perpetrator
even after an assault that thinking about years later made her feel sick
to her stomach. As long as her husband and triplet sons were all still
living together, she was able to block out the abuse to keep her family
intact. It was only after her husband had already divided the family by

moving one of their sons out of the house that Becky was able to recognize the severity of the abuse and finally leave him.

According to betrayal trauma theory, ignoring a traumatic event is
more adaptive when the event is social in nature. Of course, natural
disasters like hurricanes and terrible accidents can be traumatic without the presence or influence of another human being. If a man's car
swerves out of control while he is driving at night and hits a tree, and
he is badly injured as a result, he may respond by having vivid nightmares of his car veering out of control. His heart rate may quicken
when he drives a car, or he may avoid driving altogether or avoid
driving at night. He may fear that he will die earlier than he expected
and grapple with the realization that terrible things can happen at any
time. Such difficulties are typical of posttraumatic or acute stress
responses, which may result from an event evoking intense fear and
horror. The victim may attempt to maintain distance from thoughts of
the accident by avoiding driving, but he is unlikely to completely forget that the accident happened. In this case, it is probably best if he
addresses the physical and psychological wounds, regains confidence
in his driving, and moves on with his life. By facing the trauma, he
avoids the impairment associated with the avoidance of driving, and
he also opens the door to preventing the development of full-blown
posttraumatic stress disorder (PTSD) related to the accident, or treating
these symptoms if they do develop. In this case, it is adaptive for him
to recognize the event rather than ignore it.

The adaptive nature of facing the trauma changes if we assume the
car accident occurred under different circumstances. In the alternative
scenario, the same man is riding as a passenger in the same car, but
now his best friend is behind the wheel. The friend is driving a bit
erratically, perhaps because he has been drinking. The passenger
becomes alarmed and pleads with his friend to pull the car over and
let him drive. Instead, the driver accelerates. The car swerves out of
control and hits the tree. Both passenger and driver sustain serious
injuries. Now, however, in addition to possibly facing intrusive
thoughts of the accident and anxiety about driving, the man also must
choose between forgiving his friend for betraying his trust or confronting him and possibly losing the friendship. If the friendship is really
important to him, he may overlook aspects of the betrayal in order to
protect the relationship. He also may ignore the betrayal because he
cannot tolerate the sense of loss that the collapse of the friendship elic-
its in him. Although it may be adaptive for him to ignore the betrayal
from the perspective of avoiding loss and maintaining a relationship,
doing so also increases the likelihood that he will be hurt by his friend
again in the future.

Both the car accident scenario that involves betrayal and the one that
does not are single, one-time events. Now imagine the man as a little

boy living with his mother. She is generally loving and caring toward her son but becomes very angry and overreacts if he misbehaves, calling him names and sending him to bed without dinner if he spills his juice at lunch. Occasionally, she is violent, throwing dishes or the remote control at him and sometimes causing injury. The little boy cannot survive without the relationship with his mother. He is aware of the fact, if only subconsciously, that he needs her love and protection to survive. If he responds to her behavior toward him with withdrawal or confrontation he is likely to push his mother away and perhaps invite more abuse. It is thus adaptive for him to ignore or minimize the violence and be the good little boy to whom his mother usually responds with care. By being good—by ignoring the betrayal and staying connected with his mother—the little boy increases the chances that she will provide him with food, shelter, and love. It is adaptive for the boy to ignore the betrayal, even though his betrayal blindness may later result in psychological and physical consequences associated with enduring ongoing abuse.

DOMESTIC VIOLENCE AND BETRAYAL TRAUMA THEORY: WHY DOESN'T SHE LEAVE?

In the case of domestic violence, the victims usually do not enter into relationships utterly dependent on perpetrators for survival, as the little boy does with his mother. Victims may or may not become dependent on perpetrators over time. Additionally, these dependencies may be mediated by a range of social factors, such as a victim's access to an independent income or a support system that may reinforce any emotional attachment they feel. The closer the relationship with the perpetrator, and the more dependent the victim is on this perpetrator or on the relationship, the more adaptive it is to ignore or become blind to the abuse and betrayal. Over time, as relationship dynamics change, this adaptation can become more or less beneficial. She may be able to find ways to earn income, for instance, or to rebuild a support system among friends and family members. With these empowering shifts in place, she may be better able to tolerate the reality of the betrayal and use the memory to catalyze movement away from the abuse.

Most women do eventually leave abusive relationships, often many times before the final break. Thus, leaving is best thought about as a process rather than as a single decision and action. As mentioned previously, Tanya left eight times before finally leaving for good. Each time she left, she accumulated new coping skills that she could then draw upon in the future. Leaving also can be a bargaining chip that sends the message that the perpetrator must cease his violence or change other behaviors associated with violence (such as drinking) or the relationship will end. Gathering confidence, enduring and managing the violence, negotiating around control tactics, and acknowledging the abuse to herself and others—each step takes an enormous amount of strength and courage. The question "Why doesn't she leave him?" overlooks the staggering energy and resilience required simply to endure and acknowledge an abusive situation.

Tanya returned to her partner each time because she wasn't ready to make a final break. Whether this was because she hoped things would work out or because she feared she could not make it financially on her own, she describes being in denial during this period about the severity of the abuse. As we've argued, denial is adaptive in the face of a partner's betrayal because, in minimizing the risk present, it allows a victim to protect herself against an otherwise intolerable level of fear and threat. She becomes blind to a potentially devastating situation so that she can survive it until she is ready to leave.

DEPENDENCE THROUGH COERCIVE CONTROL

The perpetrator of domestic violence can manipulate his partner through patterns of coercive control as well with threats or violence. He may take away her power over finances, cut off her communication with loved ones, threaten her with retaining custody of the children, shut off access to other resources such as a car, a phone, or vital medication, and control her access to basic needs. In such instances, if she leaves the relationship, she will have nothing. If she stays, her life will be filled with physical and emotional pain and fear; but she perceives that not all will be lost. Financial control can be particularly devastating.

> It just got more controlling. Cars couldn't be in both of our names: everything was just totally in his name. Checkbooks, savings accounts, home, you get $10 a week allowance.... What can you do? There you are with little kids, no vehicle. No money to go buy a car, no credit to go buy a car. What do you do? You go back. I went back. (Julie)

Because the victim's dependence in this instance is rooted in enforced structural inequalities in the relationship, there are serious material constraints on her capacity to leave. Leaving requires that the victim have enough money for attorney's fees, for instance, to be able to support permanent housing, have access to transportation and possibly to child care, and have sufficient financial resources to meet daily living expenses for herself and the children. If her socioeconomic status is affluent or middle class with her abusive partner, she may have to adjust to living in poverty if she leaves. If she has been working at home, she may be unable to meet the most basic needs without the financial assistance of her abuser. In fact, a woman's employment status and income are the strongest factors determining whether she decides to leave the relationship.

But the house was in X's name. So the police officers wouldn't let me go in and get Brittany. Even though we're married, I'm not on the house. So I had to leave her behind. It was horrible, horrible. I had to leave my daughter behind. (Julie)

In addition to taking their partner's money or keeping them uninformed about finances, perpetrators of domestic violence may establish control through a range of constraints. They may lock their partner into or out of the house and prevent her from accessing medication, limit her access to her children, and destroy her most valued possessions. Or they may make access to friends, family members, or vital resources contingent on meeting a personal or sexual need, or dole out "favors" (the right to go out with a longtime friend, for example) in exchange for "being a good girl." Perpetrators often use child custody battles as a means of luring their partners back to the relationship (see the chapter by Stark in volume 2). The perpetrator also can threaten his victim with the loss of income or property that is rightfully hers. Unable to afford the legal fees and denied support from her partner, she returns to the relationship. Through his actions, she learns just how dependent she is on him to meet her needs. He may follow her wherever she goes, have someone else report on her whereabouts, or prevent her from going to work or school by demanding she sit still and listen to him lecture when it is time for her to go. Tanya explains the extent to which perpetrators go to exert control:

He used to cut my clothes up and set them on fire. Or take the keys so I couldn't go anywhere. He thought I was going to leave while he was in the tub. And I used to have to go sit on the toilet and wait while he was taking a bath, and I'd say, "Well, this is a waste of my time." . . . I have respiratory problems from getting hit in the face so much. (Tanya)

Coercive control destroys self-esteem and leaves the victim feeling helpless so that leaving the relationship becomes even less tenable. Tanya's partner attempted to make her feel as though she was unable to use a car to get herself from one place to another, that she had no control over her own clothing, and that she was not worthy of enough respect to decide when to go into which room of the house. Fortunately, Tanya recognized that his tactics were "a waste of [her] time," but not all victims of domestic violence are able to maintain this sense of self-worth in the face of severe manipulation.

I wasn't ever allowed to talk on the phone with my friends. If he'd find out about it, there would be a big fight. It'd be huge. And the consequences of that was not worth making that phone call. (Julie)

Communication is a powerful method of gathering the resources that eventually support leaving the relationship. It is a common area of interception by the abuser. Perpetrators frequently prohibit a victim's phone calls, rip out the phone, severely limit the time she can spend on the phone as well as whom she can call, monitor or listen in on calls, listen to the answering machine, hide her cell phone, and review the phone bills for signs she is calling people not on the approved list. He also may subject her to cyberstalking, tracking her Internet use, reading e-mail, and forcing her to check in and check out or answer her call, no matter what is happening, within a set time frame. He may steal her passwords, or put embarrassing information or photos on her MySpace site. The effect of controlling a victim's access to information or communication is that her partner becomes the major source of her connection to the outside world and even of how she understands the abuse. He is in a position to tell her that nobody will ever love her like he does, that she deserves to be hit, and that no one will believe her if she talks to them about the abuse. She internalizes these messages because she has nobody else to listen to, and so has no means of disproving his statements.

> Why did I stay? Fear and insecurity. I had nowhere to go. I had no money to just go buy my own house or get another apartment. They beat you down to the point where you believe what they tell you. "You can't make it. You're fat. You're ugly. You're never going to be anything." You start believing it. (Kris)

CULTURAL PERSPECTIVES

Cultural factors often influence patterns of coercive control in abusive relationships and the reasons it may be adaptive for the victim to ignore the betrayal.

> I think there are more cases with the Hispanics. Hispanics, they feel more macho. They feel if they marry, the woman is their property. (Marina)

This sense of machismo may depend on acculturation status and likely varies between relationships. Moreover, as Hispanic women are increasingly demanding a more equitable distribution of household responsibilities, the traditional Hispanic sentiment that a woman's place is in the home is shifting. Still, disagreements over women's proper role remain a frequent stimulus to violence in Hispanic relationships. Verbal and physical violence are not typically seen as acceptable means of conflict resolution in the Hispanic community, but the issue of sexual equality often triggers the abuse when it does occur.

A woman's immigration status is often a target of a perpetrator trying to coerce her into staying in the relationship. For instance, he may tell her, "You will be deported if you call the police." This threat has a realistic basis for illegal immigrants and those who need to remain married to the perpetrator to retain their citizenship. Although the Violence Against Women Act extends protections to immigrant women, this only applies to legal immigrants and only to couples who are married. Moreover, if she turns to the police for help, it is quite possible they will turn her over to immigration authorities if she is illegal. If the victim has children, deportation will pull the children out of school and into an unknown future. Again, therefore, their objective circumstances make it adaptive for victims with a tenuous immigrant status to become numb to the pain of the abuse while establishing a plan to deal with the threat of deportation.

People who are members of oppressed groups in terms of ethnicity, race, sexual orientation, socioeconomic status, or gender identity face additional challenges when deciding whether or not to leave an abusive partner. For example, a victim who is a member of a minority group (particularly a group with a shared visible characteristic like skin color) is often burdened with the expectation that she speak and act on behalf of her entire group. As a result, if she calls the police in response to abuse by a partner who is a member of the same minority group, she may feel that she is putting her entire group on trial. If the victim is being abused by a nonminority partner, she may be justified in her concern that nobody will listen to her if she attempts to leave the relationship and seek help. In either case, societal prejudice and fear of betraying other members of her cultural group compound the already daunting consequences associated with leaving an abusive relationship. Until she is able to confront the enormous challenge of this situation, she saves herself by numbing to the abuse.

People who speak little or no English are afforded little power in abusive relationships, especially if their abusive partners are English speaking. Additionally, those who do not speak English often have limited access to support groups, including shelters. An abused woman who decides to phone the police may have to ask her child or a neighbor to interpret the call for her, exposing her son or daughter to all the details of the abuse. If the perpetrator has isolated her from her friends and family, there may simply be no one for her to talk to in her own language.

> *I never spoke any English, because in California, everybody spoke Spanish. When I went to the doctor, at the doctor they spoke Spanish. So I didn't speak any English, but he did. I moved out. But all the time he came around with the same story: "I'm going to change, give me another chance." And I came back all the time. (Marina)*

Marina kept returning to an abusive situation because she depended on her partner for survival. Her inability to speak English made it very difficult for her to find a job. She depended on her partner for financial support from the beginning of their marriage. She moved out for one month to get away from the abuse, but when all of her belongings were stolen after an earthquake she moved back in with him so that she and her children would have enough money to survive. With no resources of her own, and a language barrier to obtaining resources, staying in an abusive relationship seemed to be Marina's best option at the time.

Like members of racial and ethnic minority groups, gay, lesbian, bisexual, and transgendered people face additional obstacles when seeking help. A lesbian woman who is abused may hesitate to move into a shelter for fear that her partner will move into the same shelter, posing as a victim. For lesbians, the perpetrator may warn the victim that there is nothing stopping her from following her wherever she goes, even if she attempts to flee to a shelter. For gay men, the abuser can manipulate his partner by telling him that "nobody will listen to a fag" if he tries to get help. Sadly, in both cases there may be some truth behind the abuser's threats. "Outing" a gay, lesbian, or transgendered partner at work or with family members who may not know about a victim's sexual identification is also a common means of control. Both lesbians and gay men who are abused may decide to overlook the violence because acknowledging it may mean facing additional prejudice or hostility from a society already nervous about sexual minorities.

For people who are members of a minority cultural group, oppression by the dominant cultural group (e.g., whites, heterosexuals, or English-speaking people) is interwoven with all aspects of domestic violence. In the African American community, for example, hopelessness fueled by negative stereotypes, marginalization, and decreased opportunities contributes to daily microtraumas that may, over time, trigger domestic violence (as well as other types of violent behavior). Exposure to ongoing homophobia sometimes leads to the displacement of fear and anger onto the partner, thus resulting in violent behavior. Although the victim is oppressed by his partner, he also needs his support in the daily struggle against oppression. He can ignore the violence and hold on to his one ally against oppression, or he can leave and face oppression alone. The victim may also deny the abuse because it seems so "understandable" given the oppressive circumstances to which a perpetrator has been subjected. Here, as elsewhere, preserving the relationship means becoming blind to his partner's betrayal.

BETRAYAL WITHIN THE COMMUNITY

Within all intimate relationships, each partner is affected not only by the other but also by the larger community context in which abuse occurs. Relationships involving domestic violence are no exception to this rule. It seems obvious that violence in intimate relationships betrays the trust and expectations in these relationships. But trust and betrayal also come into play in the larger world in which women participate and help to construct: their neighborhoods, schools, workplaces, and places of worship. It is important to understand how cultural and socioeconomic factors influence the choices women make about whom to talk with about the abuse in these settings, how these social settings become part of an intimate sphere of influence, and whether and how they bridge the gap between the abuse in the relationship and the institutions expected to provide health, protection, or other forms of help.

> *With the African American women, you don't go and tell anybody. You don't put your man in jail for stuff like that. Your family handles it. You deal with it within the family. That's just something you don't talk about. (Tanya M.)*

People trust the institutions that surround them to perform the social functions for which they are created. For example, religious institutions often provide not only spiritual strength but also a nurturing faith-based community. However, when an institution such as a church makes value judgments based on relationships, it can betray the faith placed in that institution. For women in situations of domestic violence who also are members of religious communities that place a high value on marriage and stigmatize divorce, there is a disconnect between what they need from a religious institution and what it provides. This lack of support for a woman in a domestic violence situation is a betrayal of the promise that was made by the church to that woman: to support her in part by providing refuge from life's difficulties. Similar disconnects and betrayals can occur when obvious signs of abuse are ignored by coworkers, by classmates, or in other social institutions.

INSTITUTIONAL BETRAYAL

There are also sociocultural systems in which people do not actively participate on an intimate and daily level but that impact their behaviors and worldviews. For a victim who works as a teacher at a public school, her workplace is a part of her intimate system. By selecting which colleagues to befriend and which instructional materials she will display in her classroom, for example, she helps to construct her world at the school. Whatever the situation at home, she has agency in this setting.

By contrast, when this same woman seeks assistance from the police, child protective services (CPS), or health care providers, she enters a world in which her agency cannot be taken for granted. She has no personal role with respect to decision making by police, CPS, or the hospital and so is particularly vulnerable to objectification or betrayal. These experiences then impact her life in intimate settings, like the family. Perpetrators often exploit these institutions to extend their control over victims. For instance, a perpetrator may threaten to call CPS and have the children taken away if the victim does not agree to his demands. When these institutions betray victims of domestic violence, the "secondary trauma" from this experience can amplify the feelings of helplessness and loss of control elicited by abuse.

Sometimes I rescinded the charges, when [he and his family] said they were going to call DHS to have my kids taken. They told me if I didn't agree they were going to call me in to DHS. So I went up and signed affidavits to drop the charges. (Tanesha)

Betrayal in these situations may be more abstract than the betrayal by an intimate partner. But the violations of promises implied by their standing in the community—the promise to protect, or heal, or provide for children's welfare—are no less devastating than a partner's betrayal. Despite the enactment of mandatory arrest policies in most U.S. jurisdictions, police frequently fail to make an arrest, or subvert the intent of these policies by arresting both parties because a victim has defended herself.

I came home and my house is empty. The kids are gone. Bank accounts are cleaned out. He even took my religious belongings. My rosary, he took everything. I am standing there with the clothes on my back and what little was left that he could not take in the haste of leaving, wondering, "Where in the hell are my kids?" I just go into a panic, absolute panic. I call the police, and they're like, "Huh, they're his kids too." (Ronnie)

Responses like this, whether rooted in bias, a lack of training, or pre-conceptions about the nature of domestic violence, become part of the decision-making process, including a victim's decisions not to report abuse or to remain with an abusive partner.

If a perpetrator is arrested, victims must then confront the legal system, another site where betrayal is commonplace. In criminal cases, or if victims pursue an order of protection, they are faced with dividing their energy between recovering from abuse and fighting for their rights within the legal bureaucracy. Although the general expectation is that the courts will mete out justice, this battle often begins with getting prosecutors to pursue cases of domestic violence. In family court, meanwhile, abuse victims are frequently forced to share custody with an abusive partner or actually have children removed because they "exposed" the children (by being beaten) to their partner's violence. Although there have been many reforms to the legal system in the area of domestic violence, the chance that this system will once again betray a victim of domestic violence remains high.

SOCIOCULTURAL BETRAYAL

In addition to intimate betrayal and institutional betrayal, victims of domestic violence also can be betrayed by societal attitudes and value systems. Myths about domestic violence are widespread. Because one pervasive myth is that domestic violence only occurs in poor, urban areas, for instance, there is a tendency to discredit white, middle-class victims of domestic violence when they come forward as victims, particularly in custodial proceedings. Another myth is that abuse cannot have been serious if a woman has not been injured, has not called the police, or has remained in an abusive relationship. As we've seen throughout this chapter, the significance of violence lies in its frequency and duration rather than in its severity. There are many reasons why women remain in abusive relationships other than the fact that the abuse is minor or has ended. These include the fact that leaving may be prevented by coercive control and that effecting a permanent separation often can be an extended and complicated process. Like the mistaken belief that domestic violence is primarily a problem for disadvantaged groups, myths about leaving often lead courts and other institutions to trivialize the experience of domestic violence victims. This minimization of their experiences makes it even more difficult for them to seek and obtain help, further contributing to their sense of betrayal.

Sociocultural betrayal is rooted in the tension between the values our society purports to embrace—life, liberty, and the pursuit of independence and personal responsibility—and the lived experiences of domestic violence victims. The United States places great emphasis on so-called family values. Although people have their own understanding of what valuing family means, the media and other institutions have created an ideal family to which everyone is expected to aspire. This socially constructed ideal family is most often able-bodied, white, and middle to upper class, and consists of a married man and woman and children. This ideal may pressure a victim of domestic violence to keep her family intact, despite ongoing abuse. In a better world, valuing the family would mean valuing well-functioning, healthy, mutually collaborative and respectful relationships whatever the composition or sexual identity of the parent(s).

There are additional ways in which this value on an ideal family betrays victims of domestic violence. First, it creates the illusion that there is a perfect family, and that this perfect family is singularly defined. If a victim of domestic violence does not have this perfect family, then any negative consequences that occur within her family can be blamed on her inability to achieve this goal. Second, when family values are emphasized, but then functional resources and support are not provided, attainment of the goal is unlikely. Struggling to achieve this perfect family, blamed for what it is not, lacking the resources to effect change, victims of domestic violence are once again betrayed—this time by a cultural value that appears to be innocuous, even wholesome.

I thought he loved me. I was young. 17. I was pregnant. I wanted that happy home, me and my daughter, my baby's daddy. Am I an optimistic person? Yes. Very. (Natasha)

DEVELOPING HELPFUL RESPONSES

Taken together, intimate, institutional, and cultural betrayals create an environment in which it can be difficult or impossible for domestic violence victims to acknowledge the level of violence in the home. As we've seen, these betrayals can define a victim's life course, creating a climate that makes betrayal blindness an adaptive response to persistent abuse. Against the risk of these betrayals, disclosing domestic violence is an act of bravery, a public acknowledgment that the victim's interpersonal life is not as society says it should be. When these courageous acts are discounted because of institutional betrayal, the psychological effects can be devastating.

Did I tell anyone? You don't tell anybody, because what does that say about you? I ended up going to the hospital from the stress. (Loretta)

It is important to remember that persons function not merely in intimate partnerships but also in a network that extends through myriad institutions and includes a host of cultural, religious, and societal beliefs. Responding helpfully to domestic violence situations requires taking all of these interacting systems into account.

At the most personal level, people turn first to family and friends for support, encouragement, and advice. To this extent, family members and friends can be considered first responders to domestic violence. Because her subsequent actions are shaped by the response that a domestic violence victim gets when she discloses to family or friends, an appropriate response can give her the strength to remove herself from the situation and begin the process of change required to heal.

Appropriate responses cannot be scripted, as they will change based on the cultural and personal situations of those involved. However, it is possible to set out some general recommendations.

LISTENING

Most importantly, the voices of domestic violence victims must be heard. Given the risks entailed in domestic violence relationships, it is natural to urge action or move to action ourselves without fully understanding the situation. But this approach can silence a victim who has yet to be heard. Domestic violence is complex and surrounded by conflicting thoughts and feelings. These can only be resolved if they are allowed to surface by giving a victim the freedom to explore the full range of her emotions and experiences. A critical component of this listening process is the capacity to respond nonjudgmentally. Cultural context is another critical aspect of this ability to listen well. This means working to put what is being said in the context of the social pressures felt by those within the subculture to which the victim belongs. Allowing victims to explore their conflicting feelings rather than imposing a societal expectation that she must leave gives her a better chance of regaining and maintaining her own sense of value and worth.

This may seem counterintuitive. One might think that if a victim knew that the situation were destructive, she would quickly exit. If she hasn't, it is because she does not understand the nature of the situation, and this misunderstanding should be corrected. In fact, telling women their situation is destructive or what they *should* do without fully understanding the context puts them in the same position they are put in by the perpetrator. It disempowers them in the same way by keeping them from defining their own course of action. The challenge is to support and respect the victim while also modeling a personal intolerance of abuse.

Domestic violence does not magically set victims apart from the rest of us. They remain colleagues, classmates, and fellow congregants at places of worship. Additionally, anyone in these settings can be victimized. This means that encouraging disclosure and help-seeking is everyone's responsibility, not merely the job of specialists. Something as simple as a flyer advertising services to victims of domestic violence placed on a church bulletin board may be encouragement enough for a victim to seek help. Additionally, it is in these larger social contexts that programs can be developed to teach people how to react appropriately to those who disclose information regarding domestic violence.

My friend, a police officer, made me go to the crisis center the first time. He was like, "Just go once. If you never go back, I won't say anything. But promise me you'll go once." ... My friend, he's proud of me for doing this. He thinks it's the bravest thing anybody could ever do. He's my biggest supporter. He really is. (Melissa)

ASKING

Just as people must not be afraid to listen, they must not be afraid to ask. Both interpersonally and institutionally, there must be an ongoing dialogue regarding domestic violence. By remaining silent, in particular when faced with direct evidence of a violent act, individuals align themselves with the perpetrators. This silence can be considered another betrayal of victims of domestic violence. For example, a large percentage of women who seek welfare assistance are victims of domestic violence. There are state and federal policies in place that encourage (and in some areas, require) social workers to ask whether those seeking welfare are victims of domestic violence. Despite these policies and mandates, recent research showed that only 9 percent of women seeking assistance were screened for domestic violence, and only 1 percent received effective screening that actually resulted in disclosure.[4]

Although changes in policy are critical, they are not sufficient to combat domestic violence. The myths surrounding domestic violence also must be addressed, requiring a change in social consciousness. Many of these myths reflect the gender roles and scripts that are part of a larger cultural context. For example, women are expected to have sex with their partners, and if they refuse they are not being good wives. In reality, more than one-third of women are victims of sexual coercion by husbands or intimate partners during their lifetimes. If the social script dictates that women be good wives to their husbands, and this script includes being available for intercourse at the husband's demand regardless of her own wishes, marital rape will continue to be denied as a form of domestic violence.

> I had been staying there because of the kids. But now, I had already lost my oldest son, and I was still married to the abuser. I don't know if there was just something about me that day. But let me tell you, I would have died that day before I was going to have sex with him. And that was it. I was done that day. (Becky)

An awareness of individual and cultural contexts can help increase knowledge of domestic violence. At the same time, the underlying value system that allows domestic violence to continue also must be addressed. Although redefining social values can pose a formidable challenge, consider how dramatically women's status already has changed since the time, less than a century ago, when women couldn't vote. Broadening our understanding of the family to emphasize respect for autonomy, equality, collaboration, and love would relieve considerable pressure on women to preserve their current family arrangements even in the face of violence.

Betrayal of a basic trust is one of the more profound harms persons can suffer. Victims of violence in intimate relationships are profoundly betrayed by someone they depend on. If they confront or withdraw from their perpetrator they risk losing the relationship and/or further abuse. Fully acknowledging the abuse may significantly risk their survival. It is not surprising, therefore, that many domestic violence victims adapt to or defend against these harms by denying or minimizing their abuse. Furthermore, as we've seen, institutional and cultural betrayal can build on intimate betrayal, compounding a perpetrator's attempts to entrap his partner. We have tried to bring the voices of those affected by domestic violence to bear on the problem of betrayal. When victims garner the strength, resources, and support, they may disclose what is happening to them and seek help. Whether they do this to friends and families, to co-workers, colleagues, or to helping professionals, there are two possible responses. One of these extends the betrayal initiated in the abusive relationship, implicitly supporting the perpetrator. The other reinforces the human connection between people and helps domestic violence victims make the transition from victim to survivor.

NOTES

1. Iowa Voices Project, "The Iowa Coalition against Domestic Violence," 2007, http://www.icadv.org/Iowa%20Voices%20Project.htm (last accessed February 1, 2008).

2. J. J. Freyd, "Betrayal Trauma: Traumatic Amnesia as an Adaptive Response to Childhood Abuse," *Ethics & Behavior* 4, no. 4 (1994): 307–29.

3. Merriam-Webster, *Merriam-Webster Online Dictionary*, 2008.

4. T. Lindhorst, M. Meyers, and E. Casey, "Screening for Domestic Violence in Public Welfare Offices: An Analysis of Case Manager and Client Interactions." *Violence against Women* 14, no. 1 (2008): 5–28.

Index

abuse advocates, 18–19, 19–20, 22–23, 66, 112. *See also* Women's Advocates

abusive relationship, 43, 44, 51, 52, 77, 173, 174, 186, 198, 199, 203, 206; African American, 156; entrapped, 17, 18, 93–110, 122–23, 190, 195–96; experience, 33–34; financial crisis, 82, 93, 120; mental effects of, 37–40; same-sex relationship (*see* lesbian relationships)

adaptive response, to domestic violence, 192–93; betrayal trauma theory, 190–92; ignoring pain, 192–93; maintaining relationship, 193–95

adolescent boys, sheltering policies, 57

advocacy, 53–54n7; of domestic violence, 111; employment opportunity, 23. *See also* abuse advocates; Women's Advocates

Advocacy for Women and Kids in Emergencies (AWAKE), 66–67

African American community, intimate violent relationships in, 151; activism, 157; Black male masculinity, 154–55; feminist theories, 153–56; incidence and prevalence, 151–52; institutionalized racism, 153–54, 155; physical health consequences, 152; popular culture interventions, 156–57; psychological consequences, 153; recommendations for improvements, 157–59; research and sharing ideas, 157; shelter programs for, 61–62; "Strong Black Women," 155–56

African American women, 74, 83

Aid to Families with Dependent Children (AFDC). *See* Temporary Assistance to Needy Families (TANF)

anti-rape movement, 16

Asha Family Services, Inc., 61–62

Asian American women, 74

Asian and Pacific Islander women, 147

Asian community, shelter programs for, 61

Asian Women's Shelter, 61

Assets for Independence Act of 1998 (AFIA), 87–88

Audenhove, Kristi Van, 31, 32

battered lesbians, 130

battered wife, 16

battered woman syndrome (BWS), 38, 180

battered women, 112; beyond shelter, 9–10; entrapped violent relationships, 122–23; involving in activities, 10–11; Native American, 62;

sexism, 11; shelters (*see* shelters);
South Asian, 61; Women House,
2, 5–6
battered women's movement:
coordinated community response
(CCR), 29; Decade of Change, 29;
diversities, 20; evolution of, 15, 16,
19–20, 21, 23, 29; fund-raising,
26–29; heterosexual, 143; involving
men in, 28; involving youth in,
28–29; openness, 31; organizational
diversity, 30; overall goal, 30; work
in progress, 31
battering, 11–12
being believed, 46, 47
Benson, Michael, 74
bereavement framework, 46
Bernice, biography excerpts of, 94–97
betrayal trauma perspective, on
domestic violence: betrayal of
trust, 186; betrayal trauma theory,
190–92; betrayal within community, 200–201; cultural perspective,
198–200; dependence through
coercive control, 196–98; helpful
responses, 204; ignoring pain,
192–93; impact on pregnancy and
children, 189–90; institutional
betrayal, 201–2; listening, 204–5;
maintaining relationship, 193–95;
physical and psychological scars,
185–86; physical impact, 187–89;
psychological impact, 190; reason
for staying, 195–96; seeking assistance, 205–6; sociocultural betrayal,
202–3; victims and survivors, 186
betrayal trauma theory, 190–92
Biden, Senator, 24
birth control sabotage, 96–97
Black church, 158
Black male masculinity, 154–55
Black women, 153, 155–56
Bradley/Angle House, 17
British Crime Survey (BCS), prevalence of domestic violence, 170
British women, 34
Brother to Brother, 28
Browning, Christopher, 81
Brush, Lisa, 83

Campbell, Jacquelyn, 126
Capital Area Response Effort (CARE),
68
Carter, Jimmy, 109
Casa Esperanza (House of Hope), 62
Centers for Disease Control and Prevention (CDC), 27, 28–29, 169
Chattel slavery, 154
Chicago Women Against Rape, 16
Child Protective Services, 59
child sexual abuse, 78
children, support and education
group, 65
Chiswick Women's Aid, 17
Christy-McMullin, K., 87–88
classroom programs, 27
Clinton, Bill, 83
"Coaching Boys Into Men," 26–27
coalitions, 13, 18, 21–23, 24, 26–31, 125
coercive control, 196–98; communication, 197–98; and intimate terrorism, 171–73; language barrier,
199–200; oppression, 200; societal
prejudice, 199; woman's immigration status, 198–99
cognitive landscapes, 82, 85, 86
collective efficacy, 81, 85
communities of color, domestic
violence programs, 61–62
community: characteristics, 115–16;
identity, 115; without work, 115–16
community-based services, 55–70,
147–48; family and social service
agencies in, 69; health care setting
programs, 66–67; home-based
advocacy programs, 65–66; non-
shelter-based, 65; shelter-based
(*see* shelter); universities in, 69
community context and crime, 79–83,
85
community intervention projects
(CIPs), 68–69
Comprehensive Employment and
Training Act (CETA), 18, 22, 56
confidentiality, 19, 141, 142, 147, 183
consciousness-raising group, 1–2, 5,
17, 23
coordinated community response
(CCR), 29

counseling, 54n9
counselor, 58, 141, 144–47
court services, 126
criminal justice system, 111, 112,
    125–27; programs located within,
    67–69; response to lesbian abuse,
    143–44
crisis line, 142
cultural factors, 198–200
cycle of violence, 136

dating violence, 27
Decade for Change conference, 29
decision to leave, 40–43; emotional
    aspects, 42; physical aspects, 41–42
deindustrialization, effects of, 115–16
DELTA, 27–28
dislocation, 133–34
dissociation, 190
divorce, 1
domestic violence, 15, 17, 111, 130;
    and criminal justice system,
    125–27; Family Violence Option
    (FVO), 124–25; and gendered
    dimension of work, 117–19, 121,
    122; and global political economy,
    113; ignorance about, 15–16; inter-
    vention strategies, 123–27; and
    market force, 114, 122–23; para-
    digm, 111–12; physical impact,
    187–89; pregnancy and children,
    impact on, 189–90; preventive
    measures, 27–28; programs (see
    individual entries); psychological
    impact, 190; public/private dichot-
    omy redux, 123–24; Trade Adjust-
    ment Assistance (TAA) programs,
    124–25; Workforce Investment Act
    (WIA) programs, 124–25
domestic violence movement, 21, 111,
    123–24
Domestic Violence Response Team
    (DVRT), 68
domestic violence shelter programs,
    56, 59, 61; and communities of
    color, 61–62; within criminal legal
    system, 67–69; services, 62–64;
    services to abusive partners' chil-
    dren, 64–65; support and education

group, 65; support group, 63; tran-
    sitional housing, 63–64; visitation
    centers, 64
Dove, Inc., 69
downward economic mobility, 86,
    115, 117, 121. See also economic
    entries; political economy
drugs use, 81
Duluth Visitation Center, 64

economic insecurity, 117; and male
    identity, 118; interventions, 121–22;
    socially constructed reactions,
    119–20
economic instability, effects of,
    115–16
economic uncertainty, consequences
    of, 117
Elizabeth Buffum Chace Center, 18
Else, Sue, 30
Emerge, 28
emergency housing, 2, 3, 4–5, 19, 22
emotional abuse, 35, 36, 37, 38
employment, and intimate partner
    violence, 82–85. See also work
empowerment, 6, 7, 9, 11, 14, 18, 25, 30

Fagan, Jeffrey, 116
family and friends support, 69, 119,
    127, 139–40
Family Violence Option (FVO), 84–85,
    124
Family Violence Prevention Fund, 156
fear and isolation, 36–37
feminists, 55
financial dependence, 82
Fineman, Martha, 127
first response team, 68. See also
    Capital Area Response Effort
Flitcraft, Anne, 17, 165
formal services, for support of
    same-sex relationship, 140–43
free services and complexities, 145

gender, cultural norms, 118–19
gendered dimension of work and
    domestic violence, 117–19, 121, 122
globalization, 114–15, 122
Gordon, Linda, 109–10

Harriet Tubman Shelter, 13
healing talk, 47
health care setting programs, 66–67
health system response, 163, 165–66;
    cost, 169; definitions of domestic
    violence, 167; English govern-
    ment's domestic violence strategy,
    167–68; harmful clinical responses,
    166–67; historical developments in
    research, 164; intimate terrorism
    and coercive control, 171–73; medi-
    cal response to abuse, 173–74;
    mental health and abused women,
    178–81; policies and protocols
    within institutions, 165; prevalence
    and impact, 170–71; screening,
    174–76; training, 176–78; Violence
    Against Women Act (VAWA),
    168–69
Herman, Judith, 35, 38, 180
heterosexism, 130, 135, 141
Hispanic ethnic group, 74
home-based advocacy programs,
    65–66
homicide, 40, 107, 117, 121, 126, 152
homophobia, 130, 131, 134–35, 141,
    200
hopelessness, 115, 117, 200
Hospital Crisis Intervention Project
    (HCIP), 67
hotlines, 2, 4, 17–18, 21, 24, 25, 29, 56,
    179
human need hierarchy, 38–40, 47, 48

INCITE! Women of Color against
    Violence, 157
individual development accounts
    (IDAs), 88
inequality at workplace, 121
Institute on Domestic Violence in the
    African American Community
    (IDVAAC), 157
institutional betrayal, 201–2
institutionalized racism, 153–54, 155
intimate partner violence (IPV), 28,
    73, 116, 126, 159. See also abusive
    relationships; domestic violence;
    and employment, 82–85; high rate
    of abuse, causes, 74–76; lifetime

abuse rate, 74; mental health
    problems, 77; physical health
    consequences, 152; physical health
    problems, 76–77; and poverty,
    77–79, 82–89; psychological health
    consequences, 153; race factors, 74;
    resiliency, 89; screening, 86; social
    class factors, 74–76; social relation-
    ships, 79–82; strategies for address-
    ing poverty and, 85–89; and
    substance abuse, 77–79
intimate terrorism, 171
Iowa Coalition Against Domestic
    Violence, 187
isolation, 43, 78–79, 133; and control,
    35–36; and fear, 36–37
"It's Your Business" campaign, 156,
    158

James, Susan, 80–81
Jane Doe, Inc., 28
joblessness, 125. See also
    unemployment
Johnson, Michael, 171–72
Journal of Marriage and the Family, 16

Klinefelter, Karen, 5, 13
Koop, Everett, 165

La Casa de las Madres, 17
Lac du Flambeau Domestic Abuse
    Program, 62
language barriers, 60–61
Latina community, shelter programs
    for, 62
Latina Domestic Violence Program of
    Congreso de Latinos Unidos, Inc.,
    62
Law Enforcement Assistance
    Administration (LEAA), 18
legal advocacy, 67
Legal Assistance office, 1–2
legal parity, 112
legal system, failure to respond to
    domestic violence, 111
lesbian activists, 21
lesbian relationships, violence in, 129,
    149n1; contexts, 131–33; counselors,
    144–47; dislocation, 133–34; family

and friends, 139–40; fighting back, 137–38; formal services, 140–43; homophobia, 134–35; innovative approaches, 147–48; intervention and support, 139–47; invisibility and isolation, 133; police and criminal justice system responses, 143–44; racism and poverty, 135–36; shifting power, 136–37

lesbians, shelter experience, 59

LGBTQ (lesbian, gay, bisexual, transgendered, and queer), 25, 132, 147, 148

lifetime of violence, 135–36

Lindsay Burke Act, 27

listening, 4–5, 46, 204–5

Lloyd, Susan, 75

Lobel, Kerry, 130

male dominance, 6, 130. *See also* patriarchy

male-female relationships, 17, 20

male identity, 118, 120

male poverty, elimination of, 126

marital relationships, 16–17

Martin, Del, 18

Maslow, Abraham, 38, 39, 48–49; hierarchy of human need, 38–40, 47, 48

masochism, 17

Mattern, Grace, 19, 30

Medical Advocacy Project, 67

men, engaged in violence against women eradication, 28

Menard, Anne, 20

mental effects of abuse, 37–38, 77, 178–81

Mental Health Program Board, 5–6

Michigan State University (MSU), 69

Middle Way House, Inc., 64

Miller, Jody, 78, 79, 85

Minneapolis Domestic Abuse Project, 68

minority group, 21, 40–41, 86, 171, 199, 200

misogyny, 111

music, 157

mutual abuse, 138

mutual battering, 129

mutual violent control, 171

National Coalition Against Domestic Violence (NCADV), 21–22, 23

National Crime Victimization Survey (NCVS), 74, 152

National Domestic Violence Hotline, 29

National Family Violence Survey (NFVS), 74

National Health Service (NHS), 169

National Network to End Domestic Violence (NNEDV), 22, 23, 26, 27, 28, 30

National Organization for Women (NOW), 18

National Survey of Families and Households (NSFH), 74

National Violence Against Women Survey (NVAWS), 74, 131

Native American women, 74

Native American community, shelter programs for, 62

negative counters, for women in same-sex relationships, 143–44

neighborhood, 60, 85, 113, 116, 126, 156; decline of, 115; disadvantaged, 74, 75, 86; and intimate partner violence, 79–83, 85

nonjudgmental approach, 46, 47

nonshelter-based community services, 65

occupational death, 121

Office of Justice Programs, 152

Olivia, biography excerpts of, 97–102

patriarchy, 8, 111, 112, 113, 114, 130, 133

peer support, 46, 47

perpetrators, 17

personality change process, 33–34; control and isolation, 35–36; coping ability, 46–49; fear and isolation, 36–37; focus group, 34; getting out of abusive relationship, 40–43; hierarchy of human need, 38–40; insight into women's need, 49–52; reception phase in recovery, 43–44; recognition in recovery, 44–45; reinvestment in recovery, 45–46; understanding mental effects of abuse, 37–40

Personal Responsibility and Work
    Opportunity Reconciliation Act
    (PRWORA), 83–84
Philadelphia Women Against Rape,
    16
physical abuse, 187–89; gynecological
    problems, 189; serial abuse, 188
plant closing, effects of, 113–14, 115,
    120, 122, 123, 124, 126
police response, 9–10, 56, 68, 69, 79,
    85–86, 126, 143–44
political economy, 113, 121; and
    domestic violence, 113; in
    transition, 113–14
poor women, 73–76, 78, 81, 83–84, 93,
    109, 145. See also unemployment;
    poverty
posttraumatic stress disorder (PTSD),
    38, 77, 153, 164, 180, 194
poverty, 125, 135–36
poverty, and intimate partner
    violence, 74–76, 76–77, 82–85; biog-
    raphy excerpts, 94–106; disempo-
    werment, 106–7; low self-esteem,
    107–8; personal failures, 108;
    powerlessness, 107
power: and control, 137; differentials,
    in work place and home, 120–21;
    shifting of, 136–37
Prevention of Domestic Violence Act,
    68
proactive retaliation, 138
professionals, 11–14
Progressive community policing, 125
psychiatric problems, 37–38. See also
    mental effects of abuse
psychoeducation, 125–26
public service announcements (PSAs),
    156–57

Queer Asian Women's Shelter, 147

racism, 10, 21, 73, 112, 135–36, 141,
    153–54, 159; institutionalized
    racism, 153–54, 155, 160; and
    poverty, 135–36
Raghavan, Chitra, 81–82
Rainbow Retreat, 17
Raj, Anita, 83

Ramsey County Mental Health
    Board, 6
rape, 16, 76
Rapp, Rayna, 119
realignment, 48
refuge. See shelters
religion, role in IVP, 87
resilience, 15, 48, 89, 196
respect, 46–47
restorative justice models, 125
Rhode Island Coalition Against
    Domestic Violence (RICADV), 21,
    26
Rhode Island Council on Domestic
    Violence. See Rhode Island Coali-
    tion Against Domestic Violence
Rhode Island Rape Crisis Center, 16
Richie, Beth E., 148
Robert Wood Johnson Foundation, 29
Roberts, Albert, 31
Rosen, Daniel, 80
routine enquiry, 175, 177
Ryan, Susan, 2, 6, 7

safe houses. See shelters
safety, 5, 18, 19, 40, 46, 51, 52, 59, 60,
    67, 78, 88, 123, 147
same-sex relationship. See lesbian
    relationships
San Francisco–based Family Violence
    Prevention Fund, 26
Schechter, Susan, 16, 31
schools, public awareness programs
    in, 27
Scottish Crime Survey, prevalence of
    domestic violence, 170
security, 10, 25, 48; economic security,
    87, 117, 118; job security, 113, 119;
    mental security, 46, 48; physical
    security, 48
self-actualization, 48
self-development, 48
self-esteem, 40, 48, 63, 83, 107, 119,
    120, 197
self-medication hypothesis, 78. See also
    substance abuse
self-sufficiency, 114, 116, 118–19
self-worth, 40, 46, 48, 114, 115, 118,
    119, 197

services to abusive partners' children, 64–65

sexism, 10, 73, 87, 137. *See also* heterosexism

sexual abuse, 106. *See also* lesbian relationships, violence in

sexual assault, 131

shame, 109, 132, 139, 186, 187

shelters, 1–3, 15, 17–18, 55–56, 158; age criteria, 59–60; communities of color in, 60, 61–62; experience, 56–57; fundraising, 2, 5, 18, 22, 55–56; immigrant women, 60–61; language barriers, 60–61; maximum length of stay, 58; policies for adolescent boys, 57; programs (*see individual entries*); providing assistance, 58–59; racism in shelters, 21; rules, 57–58; safety and discrimination issues, 59

situational couple violence, 171–72

social capital, deterioration effects, 114–15, 116

social disorder, 79, 80–81

social reform, 1

social service agencies, contribution in domestic violence programs, 69

sociocultural betrayal, 202–3

Sojourner House, 18, 19

Stark, Evan, 17, 165, 172–73, 183

state intervention, 111–12

stigmatization, 93, 104, 109, 115

stories of battered women, 5, 11–12; listening, 4–5; sharing, 1, 3–4

"Strong Black Women," 155–56

substance abuse: illegal behavior, 78; intimate partner violence (IPV), 77–78; social isolation, 78–79

support and education group, 65

support group, 33, 63, 146

Tammy, biography excerpts of, 102–6

Temporary Assistance to Needy Families (TANF), 73, 83–84

therapists, and handling of lesbian relationships, 145–46

time to talk and be heard, 46, 47

Tjaden, P., 152

tolerance for violence/crime, 17, 26, 86

Trade Adjustment Assistance (TAA) programs, 124, 125

traditional beliefs, 7, 25, 118, 198

transitional housing, 63–64

UK National Screening Committee, 175

unemployment, 114–15, 122

unintended consequences for victims of abuse, 25, 58

United Way, 22

universities, contribution in domestic violence programs, 69

U.S. Preventive Task Force, 175–76

Vaughan, Sharon R., 1, 7

victim, 17; changing to survivor, 33; women as, 18

victim blaming, 12, 17, 180, 182

Violence Against Women Act (VAWA), 23–25, 56, 168–69

violent relationships, entrapment, 17, 18, 93–110, 122–23, 190, 195–96. *See also* abusive relationships; intimate partner violence

violent resistance, 171, 172, 180

visitation centers, 64

Volunteers in Service to America (VISTA), 1–3, 4, 18; connecting the diversities, 10–11; power problems, 6–8

vulnerability, 133, 134

waged labor, 114; power differentials in, 120–21; social construction of gender in, 117–19

Walker, Lenore, 136, 180

Welchans, S., 152

welfare, 73, 83, 87, 96, 107–8, 124

white ribbon campaign, 28

white women, 74

wifebeaters, 16

Wilson, William Julius, 115

Woman House, 2, 5–6, 9–10, 17. *See also* shelters; Women's Advocates

women, leaving violent relationships: economic dependence, 122; factors preventing, 121, 122

women abuse, 13

women of color, 20, 60, 112, 126, 142, 157

Women's Advocates: collective decision-making, 6, 7–8; experts, 11–14; history, 1–3; philosophy, 4–5; power problem, 6–8; professionals, 12; rules setting, 8–9. *See also* abuse advocates

Women's Aid Federation of England, 34

Women's Center and Shelter (WC&S) of Greater Pittsburgh, 64–65

Women's Center of Rhode Island, 18

women's liberation movement, 17

Women's Resource Center of Newport, 18

Women's Resource Center of Wood River, 18

Worcester Family Research Project (WFRP), 74; homeless women, 75–76; poor women, 75, 76

work: communities without, 115–16; dominant cultural norm, 114; gendered dimension and domestic violence, 117–19, 121, 122; loss of, 117; as social stability, 114–15; uncertainty in workplace, 114–17; violence at, 120–21

Workforce Investment Act (WIA) programs, 124

working women, 114, 118–19

youth, 28–29

YWCA, 18, 55, 64

About the Editors and Contributors

Evan Stark is a professor at the Rutgers School of Public Affairs and Administration, Rutgers University–Newark; the Department of Women and Gender Studies, Rutgers University-New Brunswick; and the University of Medicine and Dentistry School of Public Health, where he chairs the Department of Urban Health Administration. His most recent book is *Coercive Control: How Men Entrap Women in Personal Life* (Oxford University Press, 2007).

Eve S. Buzawa is a professor and the chairperson of the Department of Criminal Justice at the University of Massachusetts–Lowell. She is the co-author of the best-selling *Domestic Violence: The Criminal Justice Response* (Sage, 2003) among other works.

Hilary Abrahams is an honorary research fellow in the Violence Against Women Research Group at the University of Bristol, UK. She has worked extensively on support needs and service provision for families for whom domestic violence is an issue.

Jocelyn Barton is a doctoral student in clinical psychology at the University of Oregon. Her research interests include investigating the efficacy of therapeutic interventions for trauma survivors using both behavioral and neurobiological measures.

Deborah DeBare is the executive director of the Rhode Island Coalition Against Domestic Violence in Warwick, Rhode Island. She has worked in the domestic violence movement since 1982, when she started as a volunteer advocate. She has served on the board of directors of the

National Network to End Domestic Violence and the Rhode Island attorney general's Task Force on Domestic Violence.

Jennifer J. Freyd, PhD, is a professor of psychology at the University of Oregon. The author of numerous scholarly articles, Freyd is also the author of the award-winning Harvard University Press book *Betrayal Trauma: The Logic of Forgetting Childhood Abuse*. Freyd is a fellow of the American Psychological Association, the American Psychological Society, and the American Association for the Advancement of Science.

Tameka L. Gillum, PhD, is an assistant professor in the School of Public Health and Health Sciences at the University of Massachusetts–Amherst. Dr. Gillum's research interests are in exploring and addressing intimate partner violence (IPV) within racial-ethnic minority and sexual minority populations, the development and evaluation of culturally specific prevention and intervention efforts, health clinic–based IPV interventions, and the intersection between HIV and IPV.

Katherine E. Morrison is an associate professor of health education at Curry College in Milton, Massachusetts, with a PhD in public health from the University of South Carolina.

Melissa Platt, MA, is a doctoral student in clinical psychology at the University of Oregon. Her research interests include the role of shame and cognitive distortions in adjustment following traumatic events, as well as sociocultural issues in trauma disclosure. Platt obtained her master's degree in counseling psychology from Boston College.

Jody Raphael serves as senior research fellow at the Schiller DuCanto & Fleck Family Law Center at DePaul College of Law in Chicago. The author of numerous research reports about violence against women and women in prostitution, she recently completed her three-volume trilogy about poverty and violence published by Northeastern University Press.

Claire M. Renzetti is a professor of sociology at the University of Dayton. She is editor of the international, interdisciplinary journal *Violence against Women*. She has authored or edited 16 books as well as numerous book chapters and articles in professional journals. Her current research focuses on the violent victimization experiences of economically marginalized women living in public housing developments.

Janice Ristock is professor of women's and gender studies and associate dean (research), Faculty of Arts, University of Manitoba. She has written extensively about feminist, community-based research and about violence in lesbian and same-sex relationships, including an award-winning book, *No More Secrets: Violence in Lesbian Relationships* (Routledge, 2002).

Cris M. Sullivan, PhD, is a professor of ecological/community psychology at Michigan State University. Her areas of research expertise include developing and evaluating community interventions for battered women and their children, improving the community response to violence against women, and evaluating victim service programs.

Sharon Rice Vaughan is a founder of Women's Advocates, 1972, St. Paul, Minnesota, one of the first shelters for battered women and their children in the United States. She has held leadership positions in the National Coalition Against Domestic Violence and the Minnesota Coalition for Battered Women, and produced an award-winning radio series *Breaking the Silence: Voices on Battered Women* (1987). She is an associate professor of human services at Metropolitan State University, St. Paul, Minnesota.

Deborah M. Weissman is the Reef Ivey II Distinguished Professor of Law and director of clinical programs at the University of North Carolina, School of Law. Her current teaching interests include immigration, human rights, and gender violence. For the past 10 years she has been engaged in comparative analyses of law-related responses to gender violence and its political economic determinants in Cuba, Mexico, and the United States.

Emma Williamson is a research fellow in gender-based violence at the University of Bristol, Center for Policy Studies, where she works on a range of projects evaluating services to victims and perpetrators. She previously worked as a researcher with the Centre for Ethics in Medicine and as the domestic violence information and membership manager for Women's Aid, the National Domestic Violence charity.